CREATING GRAPHICS FOR LEARNING AND PERFORMANCE

Lessons in Visual Literacy

Linda L. Lohr

University of Northern Colorado

Upper Saddle River, New Jersey
Columbus, Ohio

Library of Congress Cataloging in Publication Data

Lohr, Linda L.
    Creating graphics for learning and performance : lessons in visual literacy / Linda Lohr.
      p. cm.
    Includes bibliographical references and index.
    ISBN 0-13-090712-X
     1. Visual literacy. 2. Visual learning. 3. Visual communication—Technique. 4. Graphic
arts—Study and teaching. I. Title

    LB1068 .L65 2003
    371.33'5—dc21

                         2002070971

Vice President and Publisher: Jeffery W. Johnston
Executive Editor: Debra A. Stollenwerk
Editorial Assistant: Mary Morrill
Production Editor: JoEllen Gohr
Production Coordination: Carlisle Publishers Services
Design Coordinator: Diane C. Lorenzo
Cover Designer: Thomas Borah
Production Manager: Pamela Bennett
Director of Marketing: Ann Castel Davis
Marketing Manager: Krista Groshong
Marketing Coordinator: Tyra Cooper

This book was set in Garamond by Carlisle Communications, Ltd. It was printed and bound by Courier, Kendallville. The cover was printed by Phoenix Color Corp.

Pearson Education Ltd.
Pearson Education Australia Pty. Limited
Pearson Education Singapore Pte. Ltd.
Pearson Education North Asia Ltd.
Pearson Education Canada, Ltd.
Pearson Educación de Mexico, S.A. de C.V.
Pearson Education—Japan
Pearson Education Malaysia Pte. Ltd.
Pearson Education, *Upper Saddle River, New Jersey*

10 9 8 7 6 5 4
ISBN 0-13-090712-X

DEDICATION

To Gary and Kelly

PREFACE

I wrote this book to help people create effective visuals—visuals that are clear, that communicate well, and that help people learn and/or perform their jobs better. As both an instructional design teacher and a practitioner in the field, I have encountered numerous examples of "bad" visual design. I have also talked with many professionals in a number of arenas (teachers, computer programmers, graphic artists, instructional designers). These people have extensive knowledge of their discipline, but they either lack knowledge or skill in visual design or think these principles are too complicated and time consuming to integrate into their daily practices. These professionals have voiced concerns like these:

- "When it comes to design, I just start grabbing any book I can, but I don't really know what I'm looking for."
- "There is an abundance of advice out there; it's hard to know which advice to pay attention to or where to begin."
- "I know something such as contrast is a good thing, and I'm supposed to teach contrast, but I don't even know what good contrast is. Is there enough … too little?"
- "There seems to be this giant invisible step between analysis and creating something visual."

These comments aren't too surprising when one considers that most people receive years of training in verbal communication but receive almost no assistance in the art and science of communicating visually. Technology makes creating visuals easier than ever, yet mastering a tool is not the same thing as using that tool wisely. Teachers, students, and practitioners everywhere need a resource that clearly and quickly explains why limiting the number of fonts is important, why using all capital letters in copy is not desirable, why it is important to go easy on the "bells and whistles," and how to make charts and graphs understandable.

This book helps people create instructional visuals without overwhelming them with seemingly endless rules and principles. Rather than giving a plethora of design advice, this text focuses on just three cognitively based principles of design (figure/ground, hierarchy, and gestalt) and a process for creating visuals based upon these principles. Underlying these three principles is information processing theory and the idea that effective visuals should support the cognitive processes of learners.

COVERAGE

In this book, a tools, actions, and perceptions framework is used. **Tools** are the basic elements of design and include type, shape, color, depth, and space. The tools chapters cover research on typography; descriptions of different typefaces; the difference between a type family and a font; how to use different shapes to unify, separate, and chunk information; how to use color effectively; how to put research on color to work; and how to use texture, depth, and space to focus attention.

Actions are the manipulations made to type, shape, color, depth, and space. By manipulating contrast, alignment, repetition, and proximity, designers learn to make an image more aesthetically pleasing and more instructionally efficient as well.

Learner **perceptions** are what the visual designer wants to influence by using tools and actions. The three chapters that cover perceptions are the heart and soul of this book. In the figure/ground, hierarchy, and gestalt chapters (chapters 8, 9, and 10) the reader learns how to work with tools and actions to manipulate how the learner will "see" or perceive instructional information. These chapters integrate the information about tools and actions and cover, among other things, research-based rules for tables and charts, strategies for working with symmetrical and asymmetrical balance, and principles for instructional interface design.

In the last section of the text, an **analyze, create, and evaluate (ACE)** process, presented in the context of traditional and nontraditional instructional design models, explains how visuals are imagined, created, and tested for usability. This chapter covers synectic and other strategies for visual design, helpful advice (such as the diamond approach to design), and basic rules for usability testing. The final chapter, which covers resources, provides a quick guide to the tools of graphic design, including hardware, software, books, and Web resources.

Features

Throughout the text a delicate but user-friendly balance between theory and practice has been maintained. To afford the reader the best opportunity to learn theory and practice, the book has been set up to teach the knowledge and skills from both a collaborative and a constructivist orientation. From the first chapter on, readers are prompted to involve themselves in a series of visual design situations that can best be solved by applying the knowledge and skills learned as they progress through the book. First, readers experiment with such tools as type, shape, color, depth, and space. Once they have learned to integrate these tools into their design practices, they will next learn how to apply actions of contrast, alignment, repetition, and proximity. In the final chapters readers are asked to experiment with combining tools and actions to facilitate cognitive processes by making optimal use of figure/ground, hierarchy, and gestalt.

Format

The book has two structures, macro and micro. The macro structure uses the tools, actions, and perceptions organization with the intent of encouraging readers to experiment and gain confidence with type, shape, and color—before addressing the bigger challenge of using design to influence perception.

The micro, or chapter, structure uses the following sequence:

- **Notes about the opening visual**, a section in which the reader learns what the artist was thinking while he or she created the chapter opening design.
- **Focus questions.**
- **Key terms.**

- **Introductory case study,** in which one of four book characters is involved in a real-life chapter-related project.
- **Numerous visual examples.**
- **Web activity,** in which the text breaks in the middle of the chapter to allow the reader some hands-on practice with a visual problem.
- **Summary.**
- **For more challenge** activities on the Web with many examples.
- **Questions for distance learning** environments.

The text has been designed with both distance education and face-to-face learning environments in mind. Readers will find that both the layout of the book and the practices contained within implement well what the book preaches. Each chapter is filled with numerous graphics, easy-to-understand writing, and many hands-on activities. The book is also augmented with an extensive website where readers can view additional and frequently updated information and see other visual solutions to the various chapter activities. Given the nature and format of the assignments, teachers and students alike can participate in the learning process.

Ancillary Materials Available with This Text

An extensive website at **http://www.coe.unco.edu/LindaLohr** complements the textbook. This website includes the following for Chapters 1–10:

- A **Web Activity section** that presents a visual problem for readers to solve. Reader solutions to the visual problem are shared. Readers are encouraged to submit their own solutions to this website to provide additional examples.
- A **More Info section** that includes extra information about the chapter topic and "how to" steps for using software.
- A **Challenge section** that includes two or more hands-on activities that allow readers to practice their visual skills. Readers can see the solutions of other readers and submit their own solutions.
- A **Discussion section** that poses two or more thought-provoking questions that can be used for class or Web-based dialogue.
- A **Links section** that allows the reader to jump to related websites.

ACKNOWLEDGMENTS

I'd like to thank the many people involved in producing this book, especially Debra Stollenwerk and JoEllen Gohr for always being encouraging, upbeat, and very responsive. I also thank the reviewers for their very thoughtful and professional advice: Gayle V. Davidson-Shivers, University of South Alabama; Leticia Ekhaml, State University of West Georgia; Gary Ellerman, Radford University; Alfred P. Large, Indiana University; Sara McNeil, University of Houston; and Don Stepich, Northeastern Illinois University.

A special thanks to the many students at the University of Northern Colorado (Krista Brackhage, Cyndie Conn, Kristen Draper, Sue Fody, Christine Gaudinsky, James Hock, Manisha Javeri, Don Klumker, Peilyn Liu, Kay Lowell, Nate Lowell, Chris Mahoney, Cassie McClure, Clark Parsons, Amy Peterson, Stephanie Piersma, Sally Reid, Jeff Reynolds, Carrie Sanzone, Stephanie Roberts, Ouna Taiwei, Mark Trimble) who provided feedback on the text and graphics and supplied some graphics of their own. A special thanks to Erin Hunt, one of the best instructional artists I know, for providing many of the illustrations on the website and in the text.

I appreciated the help I received from Jackie Dobrovolny and her students at the University of Colorado, Denver, for usability testing the book and providing valuable feedback.

Underlying the idea was the inspiration, and for that I'd like to thank Elizabeth Boling for her outstanding website; Carol Eikleberry for her friendship, encouragement, and brilliant ideas on creativity; Bill Hinson for his life-changing typography class; Diane Horgan for helping me see the connection between cognitive psychology and instructional visuals; and Gary Morrison and Steve Ross for their scientific approach to instructional design. Finally, I'd like to thank Bea Doyle, Bill and Lois Eikleberry, and Gary and Kelly Lohr.

CONTENTS

PART II   SHAPING INSTRUCTION TO FACILITATE LEARNING   61

Chapter 4   From Type to Typography   63

Chapter 5   Shape Tools   103

Chapter 6   Color, Depth, and Space   131

Chapter 10 Gestalt Perceptions   241

PART III   PUTTING IT ALL TOGETHER   281

Chapter 11 ACE It! Analyze, Create, Evaluate   283

Chapter 12 Resources   305

PART I

Introduction

CHAPTER 1

Visual Literacy for Educators and Trainers

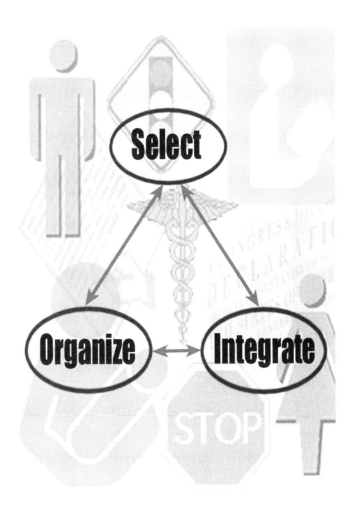

"Visual literacy is defined as the ability to understand and use images, including the ability to think, learn, and express oneself in terms of images."

Roberts Braden

NOTES ABOUT THE OPENING VISUAL

The first visual you see in each chapter relates to a central idea or theme within the chapter. On the previous page the opening visual shows symbols and the words *Select, Organize,* and *Integrate.* This combination of symbols and words is what this book is all about—all in all a fitting display for the introductory chapter of the book.

I chose this image (created by Kay Lowell) because I want to stress at the outset the importance of words. Just because the book is about visuals doesn't mean that words aren't important. Words are often the quickest way to communicate. You'll learn how to make words a powerful visual element in Chapter 4, From Type to Typography.

Simple shapes are powerful tools for communication, too. Notice the triangle and the rectangle in Kay's visual. The triangle is often used to show three aspects of something. In this example the three aspects are *Select, Organize,* and *Integrate*—all things the learner's mind is at work doing when looking at an image. (Chapter 2, Visuals and Learning, tells you more.) The rectangle is the overall background shape. By placing all of the images into an easily perceived space, Kay makes the image easier to think about. You'll learn why in Chapter 5, Shape.

FOCUS QUESTIONS

- What is visual literacy, and why is it challenging?
- Why are visual design skills important for educators, trainers, and others?
- Do you need to be computer literate to be visually literate?

KEY TERMS

EYE CANDY   flashy graphics that look good or catchy but have minimal instructional value; also called *flash*

HUMAN FACTORS   a discipline that studies people's relationship to machines (among other things)

INSTRUCTIONAL DESIGNER   a professional who analyzes instructional problems and their solutions and creates, implements, and tests appropriate interventions

LEARNER-FRIENDLY   a description of design that focuses on making instruction effective, efficient, and appealing to the learner

TECHNOCENTRIC   a description of design that is driven by technical rather than functional features

USABILITY   how effective, efficient, or appealing something is

INTRODUCTION

You are about to experience interactive hamburgers, a story about a bad design idea. I'm sharing this story because it shows you how visual displays can confuse people and also how the goal of technology should be to make people's lives easier, not harder. These are important things to think about as you read this book.

The story begins one evening after a tiring day at work. I took my nieces to a local mall to do some shopping. We were hungry so we headed toward Hamburger World in the food court—partly because there weren't any people waiting in line. When we arrived, the clerk motioned toward a computer display (see Figure 1-1) and asked me to enter our order. I floundered a bit until the clerk informed me that I needed to make selections by pressing

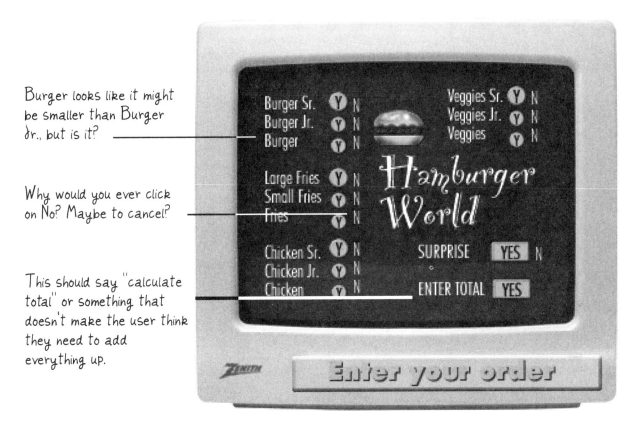

Burger looks like it might be smaller than Burger Jr., but is it? ———

Why would you ever click on No? Maybe to cancel? ———

This should say "calculate total" or something that doesn't make the user think they need to add everything up.

FIGURE 1-1   "Customer service" at Hamburger World

on the computer screen (I had been looking for a mouse). When the order arrived, I discovered I'd ordered four hamburgers (I wanted three) and a surprise (a plastic toy), which truly was a surprise.

You may think I made this up, but I assure you I didn't. What is the problem, other than momentary embarrassment? And how does this relate to education and training?

I see two problems. One, why is Hamburger World asking customers to place their own orders? Managers of this fast-food chain must be pretty enamored with technology to think that the unfriendly order entry screen is a sign of customer service, especially when the counter person isn't even busy taking orders from anybody else.

Two, the visual design of the screen is too confusing. Is Burger smaller than Burger Jr., or is it a medium sized burger? Why were the words "Enter total" used for a button that calculates the total? Presumably the Y and N are used for Yes and No, but why would anybody select No? If No is used to allow the user to back out of a decision, wouldn't the word *cancel* be more accurate? Notice how there isn't much space between choices, making it hard to select something without selecting something else as well. General design principles of contrast, alignment, repetition, and proximity (you'll learn about these in Chapter 7) could have made this computer screen much more usable, but they were for the most part ignored.

How does this story relate to education and training? Similar events take place in training and education environments; they just look a little different. Have you ever tried to take part in a computer-based lesson, maybe on the Web, where you couldn't even access instructional content because a lengthy animation locked up your computer? Or have you ever misunderstood an overhead or electronic slide presentation because the graphics or colors got in the way, and didn't make sense? Perhaps some of the computer-based training you've used has been difficult to follow because the user interface is confusing or paper-based documentation is full of images that hardly seem related to the text. The list goes on.

Now that computers make the development of instructional products easier, more people are creating their own instruction and the visuals to go with it. Even more people are wondering how to do this. As you read this, you will become familiar with the stories of four characters who are looking for ways to make their training or instruction more visual:

- Sylvia, an instructional designer and trainer
- Zack, a computer programmer/artist
- Latisha, a community college instructor and technical writing contractor
- Antonio, a sixth grade teacher

Sylvia, the instructional designer/trainer, works for clients who demand that her instruction is not only excellent, but looks exciting and contemporary. Sylvia creates all types of training materials and environments: print-based instruction, computer and Web-based training, electronic presentations, job aids, and traditional overhead transparencies.

Zack, the computer programmer/graphic artist who works with Sylvia, is frequently in conflict between trying to express himself, test graphics applications, create understandable navigation systems, and make Sylvia and others happy with his work. Zack programs computer and Web-based training and creates the instructional graphics and interfaces.

Latisha, the community college instructor and part-time technical writing contractor, creates classroom overheads, electronic slide presentations, class handouts, and print and computer-based documentation. She would like to be able to create graphics that enhance her technical writing contract work. Since Latisha is about to teach an online course, she is interested in knowing how to design materials for the Web as well.

Antonio, the sixth grade teacher, wants to create highly visual self-paced instruction for his science classes. He also creates bulletin boards, student worksheets, and overhead transparencies.

IS THIS BOOK FOR YOU?

Since you are browsing through this book, I assume you are somewhat like Sylvia, Zack, Latisha, or Antonio and hope that you will relate to one or more of the visual tasks they handle. You want to know more about how to create visuals specifically for learning and performance environments. My guess is that you represent any number of professions. Perhaps you are:

- an education or instructional design major in college
- a K–12 teacher, corporate trainer, or manager
- an **instructional designer** who creates and develops computer-based training, Web-based training, or distance learning environments
- a technical writer who wants to compose instructional visuals to enhance your writing
- a graphic artist who wants to know more about the special requirements of educational graphics
- a computer scientist or Web designer who creates icons and interfaces for software

It is possible you do all of these tasks: train, develop instruction, create graphics, program computers, design interfaces, and write. Whatever you do, whether you are a college student, a professional who designs training for others, or a manager who manages the process of design, you will find this book filled with information and inspiration on creating visuals that help people learn and perform.

WHY DO YOU NEED *VISUAL* COMMUNICATION SKILLS?

While you might think that people who study education and cognition—educators, trainers, and even instructional designers—would be knowledgeable about creating effective visuals, many are not. Although these professionals are often gifted at verbal forms of com-

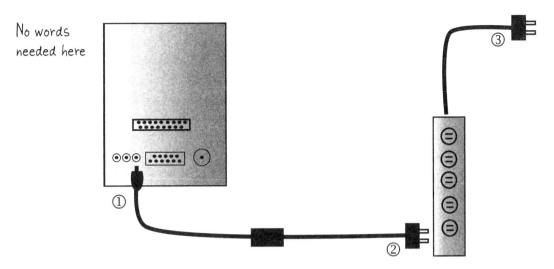

No words
needed here

FIGURE 1-2 Instructions without words

Compare the
underlying shapes.

SHI   STOP

FIGURE 1-3 Power of visuals to instruct

munication that make information memorable and useful, these same people are not as comfortable with nonverbal formats, such as visuals. Many are aware of their design limitations and want to improve their visual literacy skills but lack confidence in their ability. At a recent conference, a member of a work session expressed her dilemma this way: "I'm not an artistic person, so even though I know that something like contrast is a good thing, I'm not really sure what good contrast is. Does something have the right amount of contrast, or does it need more or less contrast?" Several people in this workshop nodded their heads in agreement. Another person summarized frustration: "I'm supposed to teach visual literacy, yet I'm not really visually literate myself." Using visuals to communicate is simply not a natural skill for most people.

Feeling visually illiterate may not have mattered much in the past. Our world, however, is increasingly information oriented. To be effective as well as competitive requires skill in presenting and communicating, verbally and visually, since visuals can condense vast amounts of information into formats that are easy to understand.

Among other things, the effective use of visuals can help people:

- **perform procedures** with or without words, as seen in Figure 1-2.
- **learn vocabulary** as depicted in Figures 1-3 through 1-5. Figure 1-3 shows how Japanese Kanji (pictographs) is learned by placing the Kanji symbol next to an image that helps you understand the symbol's meaning (Rowley, 1992). Krista Brakhage designed Figures 1-4 and 1-5 to teach the words *circumnavigate* and *retrospect* to her high school students,

Although he tried, Christopher Columbus never managed to circumnavigate the earth.

verb, to sail around (the earth, Australia, etc.)

Now create your own vocabulary illustration for one of the following words: circumference, circumambulated, circumscription, circumvent. Also write a sentence that demonstrates the meaning of the word you choose.

FIGURE 1–4 Visualizing 'circumnavigate'
Source: Created by Krista Brakhage. Used with permission.

The retrospective museum exhibit displayed artifacts describing the Civil Rights movement in the 1960s.

adj., looking back on past experiences or events

Now create your own vocabulary illustration for one of the following words: retrograde, retroactive, retrogress, retrorocket. Also write a sentence thatdemonstrates the meaning of the word you choose.

FIGURE 1–5 Visualizing 'retrospective'
Source: Created by Krista Brakhage. Used with permission.

1854
Section of Snow's Cholera Map

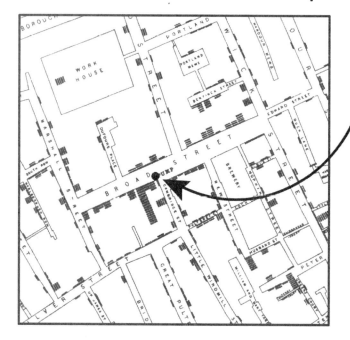

Key

▤ Deaths from Cholera
● Water pump well

Notice how the death symbols cluster around the water well.

FIGURE 1–6 Organizing data using visuals

■ **organize data to solve problems**, as depicted in statistical charts that summarize data, making trends easier to see and decisions easier to make. Edward Tufte (1997) shares an excellent example in his book *Visual Explanations*. Tufte describes how in 1854 John Snow effectively used a map with symbols to communicate that a polluted water well was causing a cholera epidemic (see Figure 1-6). If you look at Snow's map, you see a cluster of death symbols around the water pump. Because the death symbols were not as thickly represented in any other part of the map, Snow was able

This is my oversimplification of the data and charts presented during the Challenger incident. The point Tufte makes in his book Visual Explanations, (1997) is that the data were present (as in the chart on the left) but weren't presented effectively. Tufte recommends showing all of the data and how they are related to each other. The chart on the right shows a causal relationship between temperature and O-ring damage and more effectively communicates the need to delay a launch when temperatures are low.

The type of data that was presented

The type of data that SHOULD have been presented

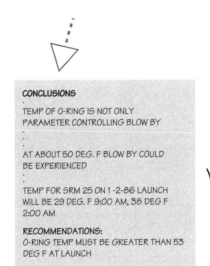

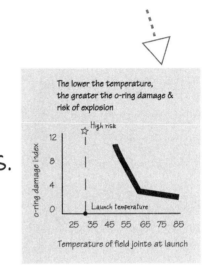

FIGURE 1–7   The cost of poor presentation

Source: Adapted from Tufte, E. R. (1997). Visual Explanations, Images and Quantities, Evidence and Narrative. Cheshire, CT: Graphic Press, pp. 39–53.

Most people understand these symbols

FIGURE 1–8   Easily recognized Symbols for Red Cross, bus and no smoking

to visually communicate that water from that well was causing the cholera. When the health officials shut down the well, the epidemic stopped.

Tufte also describes the Challenger tragedy from a unique and visual perspective. Seven astronauts died because two rubber O-rings in the Challenger spacecraft leaked. This tragedy might have been prevented had the decision makers understood the causal link between low temperatures and O-ring damage. The day before the launch, rockct engineers created 13 charts to convince NASA to cancel the launch. The charts contained convincing data, but unlike Snow's life-saving map, failed to *communicate* this information. Needed was a display showing a causal effect between low temperatures and O-ring damage similar to the causal effect that Snow was able to show between the water well and death from cholera.

Tufte's book *Visual Explanations* shows examples of the communication that took place the night before the Challenger explosion. Tragically, most of the charts did not make it easy to see any kind of relationship between low temperatures and O-ring damage. Figure 1–7 is my quick sketch of how Tufte presented the information design problems in his book. To experience the powerful impact of the original charts and redesigns by Tufte, see pages 38–50 of *Visual Explanations*.

■ **communicate across cultures** (see Figure 1–8). Most people recognize the symbols for the Red Cross, a bus, and no smoking. The image on the first page of this chapter shows other symbols that communicate to people everywhere, regardless of language.

In the next chapter you will learn more about several identified functions of visuals; you've just been exposed to some of them. How you create and use these types of visuals effectively depends on your level of visual literacy. Braden (1996) defines *visual literacy* as "the ability to understand and use images, including the ability to think, learn, and express oneself in terms of images." This book helps you think and express your message in images.

WITH ALL THE TECHNOLOGY, WHY THE CHALLENGE?

Because new software for electronic presentations, newsletters, Web pages, and computer-based education are more accessible, it would seem that creating visuals for learning would be easier than ever. After all, even simple word processing programs now feature graphic tools for creating shapes, changing colors, experimenting with visual layouts, and importing clip art or photographs.

The challenge, however, is using these tools effectively. Knowing how to use a tool technically is not the same thing as knowing how to use the tool for instructional purposes. Technical skills and design skills are two completely different things. Most people can easily master the technical skills, but fewer people know how to use the tools effectively. In all likelihood there are more bad than good designs today simply because more people are creating visuals without a good background in design. Their design skills are developed mostly from using a tool, without considering the learner or user. Therefore, many visual designs have a technocentric quality. The following section describes types of thinking and an overwhelming number of principles that get in the way of learning visual design.

Technocentric Thinking

Technocentric means the technology drives the design. Usually this is *not* a good thing. The Hamburger World incident is a perfect example of a technology-driven product that was not designed well from either a practical or a visual perspective. **Learner-friendly** means the instruction drives the design. That *is* a good thing. The designer's focus is more on the instruction than on using the tool to create the instruction. Take a look at the two computer-based training menus in Figures 1–9a and 1–9b. Which one do you think is more learner-friendly?

Most people would say Figure 1–9b is learner friendly, and Figure 1–9a is technocentric. The menu options on Figure 1–9a look like computer input fields, not lessons. Is the learner supposed to type something in? When learners worked with Figure 1–9a, they did not know what the box was. They thought they were looking at a software program, not the training for the software program. Notice the tabs at the top of Figure 1–9a, which look just like tabs for computer software. The lesson titles, such *as 2709 Searching for text*, are confusing. What are those numbers for? (It turns out that the numbers were a computer address that had meaning only for the developer.)

When the design of the interface was changed from Figure 1–9a to Figure 1–9b, the learners were happier. They knew that they were looking at training when they saw the Figure 1–9b screen. The words "Learn" and "How To" helped them immediately understand that listed items were lessons. The lesson time estimates were also more motivating. Most of the learners could take the time to go through a 15-minute lesson and could eventually finish the entire lesson over a period of time. Few learners wanted to start a two-hour lesson as was indicated on the CD (see Figure 1–9a).

Would you say that Figure 1–10 is technocentric or learner-friendly? This computer-based training menu may be aesthetically appealing, but it confused most of the people asked to use it. These learners did not know where to click to go to the lessons. Nor could they identify the instructional topic.

Examples of technocentric designs are commonplace. I see technocentric work every day in lessons from beginning instructional designers who create instructional units that

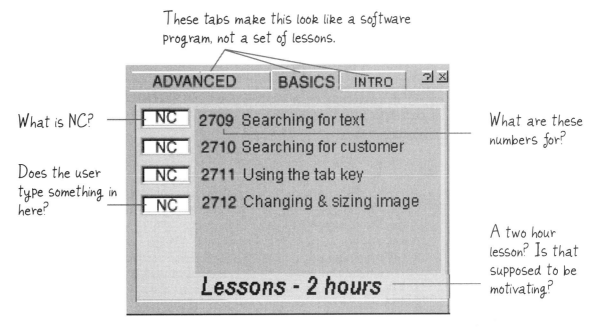

FIGURE 1–9a   Training menu, version 1

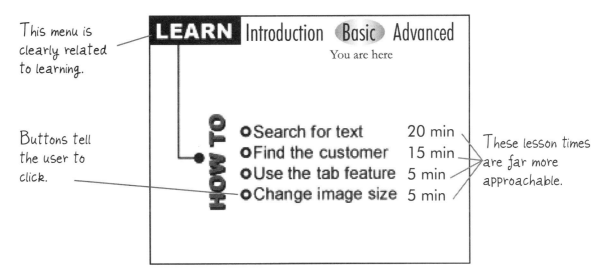

FIGURE 1–9b   Training menu, version 2

employ inconsistent grid systems, too many boxes and drop shadows, multiple font sizes and types, and numerous colors and color schemes. When students "play" with too many features of the technology, they mark themselves as a novice.

Figure 1-11a shows an electronic slide presentation in two extremes; the top example shows too much embellishment and the bottom doesn't show enough. Notice in the top row how too much variation between screens results in an inconsistent look. The graphics have limited meaning and the layout isn't aligned. The learner watching this presentation is likely to have lapses in memory when he or she moves from one screen to the next simply because there isn't a consistent placement of text or graphics. The learner may wonder, "What am I looking at now? Is this an example of a concept on the previous screen? Or is it a completely new thought?" You will learn why consistency is crucial in Chapter 7, when

This computer-based training menu has nice typographic design but learners did not know what to do with it. Learners were supposed to click on Introduction.

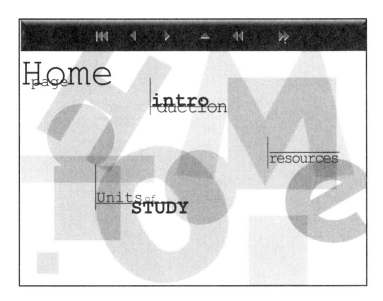

FIGURE 1-10   Training menu, version 3

Notice how the graphic elements are in different places

■ Too much embellishment

■ Inconsistent

■ Too little embellishment

■ Boring consistency

Notice how the text looks similar from slide to slide

FIGURE 1-11a   Slide presentation, versions 1 and 2

you learn about the importance of repetition. Figure 1-11b is an example of a slide presentation with about the right amount of embellishment. Notice how text and graphics are more consistently displayed from screen to screen, but there is enough variation in size and placement to keep the slides interesting.

The Blind Belief That a Picture Is Always Worth 1,000 Words

Aside from a tendency toward technocentrism, there seems to be a widespread belief that *all* pictures are valuable. The cliché "A picture is worth a 1,000 words" makes sense some of the time, as in the case of the Snow cholera map, but just because something is visually composed does not necessarily mean it is easy to understand. Too often poorly designed in-

■ Embellished

■ Consistent

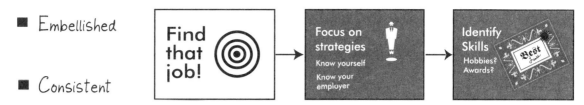

There is consistency in the layout here but not so much that the slides become predictable and boring.

FIGURE 1–11b   Slide presentation, version 3

structional materials impede rather than facilitate instruction or performance. We can all relate to the poorly designed instructional manuals that accompany children's toys, appliances, and other new products. For example, look at the instructions to place the image face down on a scanner in Figure 1–12a. This image isn't really worth 1,000 words because the arrow does not quite communicate what to do. Does that swirl in the arrow mean that the user is supposed to rotate the page and turn it somehow? The words "turn scannable image face down" and the image of a sheet of paper with the words facing down in Figure 1–12b do a better job of communicating the task.

Another example from the technical world is the computer-training disk that arrives with a new software product (see the left side of Figure 1–13). Most users don't know what the disk is. For one thing, they don't know what CBT stands for (computer-based training), and consequently they don't use the training. A redesign of the disk (see the right side of Figure 1–13) makes the training more successful. Notice how the disk's purpose is clearer in this redesign since the words "Training Disk" are the largest, most noticeable words on the disk.

A Plethora of Design Guidelines, Many That Overlap and Contradict

You've learned that technocentric design and a falsely optimistic faith in the instructional power of visuals aren't the way to proceed. Where, then, do you begin to learn, and where do you turn for advice to avoid the problems mentioned so far? While it might seem that good design information is scarce, the truth is that the opposite is true. There are almost too many design recommendations. As expressed by a student recently, "There's this plethora of advice and design guidelines. Which ones should I go with and where do I begin?"

To illustrate this point, Table 1-1 lists the terms used to guide design from disciplines of human factors, graphic design, and instructional message design. These are classified into two categories: terms that relate to making a product or a visual easier to understand (the efficiency column) and terms that relate to making a product more visually or aesthetically attractive (the appeal column). Which do you follow? If you are working on a computer program, do you follow the suggestions of human factors experts, or do you follow graphic designers? When should you follow the advice from instructional message designers? Since visual design for learning involves many of the variables listed in Table 1-1, creating visuals for learning can get pretty complicated. We are, however, going to simplify the process considerably.

How Does This Book Help?

Rather than trying to teach all of the critical principles, this book will make the whole process of creating visuals for learning and performance easier by focusing on just three learner-driven principles of design (figure/ground, hierarchy, and gestalt). Since these three

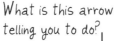

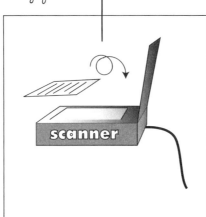

This instruction uses only graphics.

FIGURE 1-12a Scanner instruction, version 1

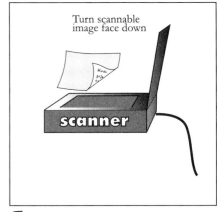

This instruction uses words and graphics.

FIGURE 1-12b Scanner instruction, version 2

principles are based on human perception, they have a learning focus that other design principles do not emphasize. Using these three principles to guide your design will help you create better electronic presentations, instructional handouts, job aids, performance support tools, computer and Web-based training, and paper-based training like those in Figure 1-14. We are not going to cover these principles just yet. If you are interested though, you can skip ahead to Chapters 8, 9, and 10 to learn more.

Figure/ground, hierarchy, and gestalt principles are represented across a variety of disciplines, using different names, but they mean essentially the same thing. These three perception principles help you create instruction based upon what the learner is likely to perceive. I noticed that graphic arts books, information design books, and instructional message design books stressed these, and I observed these principles time and again in the work of others. You will experience too that once you understand these principles, you'll start to recognize their power everywhere. As a result, you'll find it easier to create instruction that is based on the learner and that the learner is more likely to perceive in a way you intended.

HOW HANDS ON DO YOU NEED TO BE?

When confronted with the task of creating instructional visuals, you may decide to leave the task up to graphic artists. Most teachers and instructional designers are too busy to deal with the more visual and aesthetic side of instruction. Hiring a graphic artist is a good way to go if the graphic artist you hire is focused on the learner instead of self-expression.

Unfortunately, this is often not the case because many graphic artists do not have a learner-centered approach. This problem can also be compounded by other decision makers who like the artist's work, even if the work doesn't facilitate the instruction or even detracts from it. A further complication is the need to market, sell, or motivate. To some extent, the public demands **eye candy** and **flash**, terms that describe visually embellished materials.

This demand is in part due to the exceedingly high standards people apply to multimedia. They compare everything to what they see on television or at the movies. In many training products, learners complain when a page isn't catchy or visually embellished (Lohr, 1999). This presents real problems to instructional designers who rightly want the instruc-

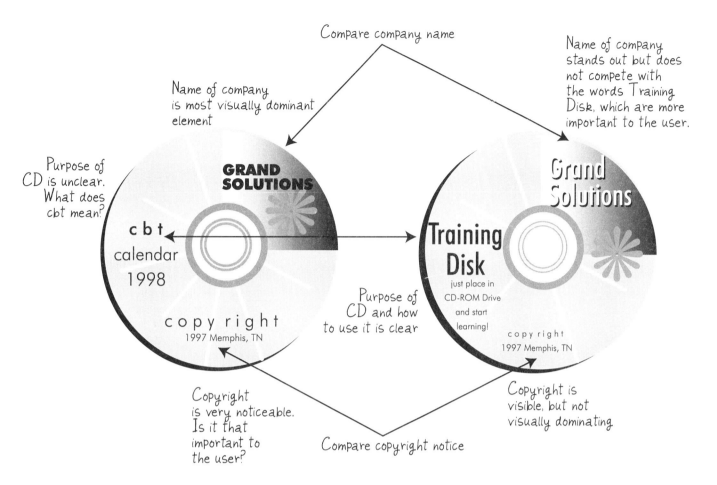

FIGURE 1–13   Training label, version 1 (left side) and version 2 (right side)

tional content to be the emphasis. Although it is difficult to compete with the million dollar budgets of the television and movie industry, the instructional designer must consider the possibility that the audience will reject instruction, or be less enthusiastic about its merits, simply based on its appearance.

You can take several approaches to deal with this issue:

- leave everything up to a graphic artist
- learn to be a better graphic artist yourself
- take the middle road and learn enough to communicate better with those who will be creating your graphics

Managers of instructional products are likely to take the first approach and leave everything up to a graphic artist. If this is you, this book will help you understand the goals of instructional visuals and hire people who can get the job done correctly.

The second approach, learning to be a better graphic artist, is likely to be taken by those who do not have the budget to outsource the work or by those who simply want to learn the skills. If this is you, this book has many tips, techniques, and practice exercises to get you started.

The third approach is to become a better designer with the goal of communicating more effectively with those who are artists. Many instructional designers choose this approach since it allows them to take a strong role in the conceptual design of information. The closer the designer can come to the visual goal, the easier it is to communicate with the artist about what is needed to keep things instructionally optimal.

TABLE 1–1 *Design Terminology*

Discipline	Efficiency Ways to make a visual or product easier to understand and use	Appeal Ways to make a visual or product attractive and motivating
Human Factors	*Galitz, 1997* Compatibility, clarity, recovery, responsiveness, consistency, configurability, efficiency, and forgiveness	*Galitz, 1997* Aesthetic appeal
	Nielsen, 1993 Minimization of user memory load, consistency, feedback, clearly marked exits, shortcuts, good error messages, prevention of errors, help, and documentation	*Nielsen, 1993* Simple and natural dialogue (using words that are immediately familiar)
Graphic Arts	*Mullet and Sano (1995)* Simplicity (achieved through unity, refinement, and fitness)	*Mullet and Sano (1995)* Elegance (achieved through unity, refinement, and fitness), scale contrast and proportion (achieved through clarity, harmony, activity, and restraint)
		Williams (1994) Contrast, alignment, repetition, and proximity
Instructional Message Design	*Schwier and Misanchuk (1993)* Simplicity, consistency, clarity, time, and minimal memory load	*Schwier and Misanchuk (1993)* Aesthetic considerations (balance, harmony, unity), and white space
	Reilly and Roach (1986) Sequence and emphasis	*Reilly and Roach (1986)* Proportion and balance
	Hartley (1985) Repetition, outlining, and spacing	*Hartley (1985)* Reward, novelty, and sensory experiences

Some of these words mean roughly the same thing.

This book will help you in whatever approach to learning design you take as long as you have a strong interest in the learner. Rather than having a technocentric focus, you'll need to develop a learner-centered focus and understand what makes visuals instructionally effective.

Regardless of which approach you take, the three principles covered in this book all deal with learner perception and are an excellent way to approach design. Knowing how people process information and learn is the key to creating effective visuals for learning and performance. Thus, when you work with designs, you look at them with the learner in mind. You think about what learners notice first, what stands out to them, how they perceive the relationship of elements in an image and the overall gestalt. In this book, you'll see numerous examples of good, bad, and evolving design. As you read, you'll find yourself getting better at spotting good and bad designs. You'll be able to practice your developing skills as well. In the process you will become a better artist, or someone who knows how to talk effectively with an artist.

It is time to take a break from reading. Suppose you've been asked to create instructions for making a cup of hot chocolate for people with limited speaking skills. The instructions are: Heat one cup of milk until very warm (not boiling). Stir in 3 table-

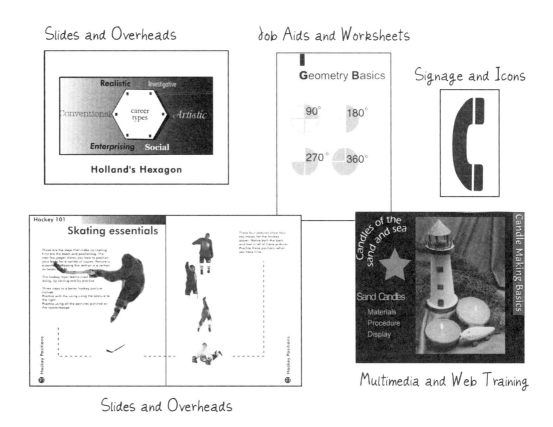

FIGURE 1-14   Examples of visual presentations

spoons of cocoa mix. Pour into a mug. Enjoy! Create a one-page recipe, and then visit the book website (Chapter 1 > Web activity) to compare your solution to those of others.

DO YOU NEED COMPUTER SKILLS?

Many of you will complete the preceding Web activity using a computer. You may ask, "Are computer skills absolutely necessary?" No, they aren't, because basic design sense does not involve using a computer. You can learn basic design information with traditional tools of the trade, such as pencils and pens, T-squares, and protractors. If you want to implement the information in this book, however, you will find that knowing how to use a computer will make the job easier. To do basic design work, you need to be able to experiment with type, shape, color, white space, and dimension. The computer allows you to work with all of these elements easily. You will most likely find that computer-generated examples are easier and more satisfactory to manipulate.

If you are unfamiliar with the computer, this book will introduce how to do some basic tasks. Parts of the book website describe basic functions performed by most software applications. These descriptions assume a rudimentary level of knowledge and are thus not overly detailed. If you are computer illiterate, see the resources in Chapter 12 for some useful introductory self-paced training that can help you get started (some of it is free on the Web).

How Do You Learn?

You learn by doing and reflecting using the mid-chapter Web activities and the Challenge activities at the end of each chapter. These activities have been tested by students who report the problems are not only educational but fun. What's more, you can compare your visual solutions to the work of others on the book website. You will be amazed at how many ways a visual problem can be solved.

If you feel some anxiety at this point—"I'm not ready for exercises yet," or "I don't know how to use a computer"—just take a few deep breaths! At some point you just have to jump in and get started. It feels risky, but one of the first steps to learning anything new is to take a risk. Most of your learning will come from doing anyway.

It is also good practice to create visual instructions whenever you can, just to get practice. Make advertisements, flyers, and simple things first. A designer who worked in a public library used every chance he had to create interesting posters, flyers (see Figure 1–15), or library signage just to keep learning. As you experiment, keep these important rules in mind: (1) don't be too hard on yourself when you make mistakes, (2) play a little, (3) get inspired, and (4) revise a lot (get used to doing things over and over).

Don't Be Too Hard on Yourself When You Make Mistakes

While the purpose of this book is to alleviate as many mistakes as possible, you still need to be open to learning from visuals that may not be as effective as you planned. In the world of art education, students are encouraged to make their first 100 mistakes as soon as possible to learn their first 100 lessons. Book knowledge helps, but to get really good you need to be doing design and watching how people react to your instruction. People's reactions teach you. Your "mistakes" teach you. Your analysis of what works and what does not work teaches you. Even though the overriding purpose of this book is to eliminate as much trial and error as possible on your journey to good design, you'll want to analyze carefully what works and doesn't work.

Play a Little

Have fun, especially for low-risk projects (projects that do not put your career at risk). While this book simplifies and explains why certain techniques are better than others, quite often designs "work" that theoretically shouldn't work. These designs are often more interesting and are more likely to happen if you are relaxed.

Get Inspired

People want to be original and come up with creative ideas, but they forget that the best work often comes from inspiration. Seeing other people work, or things another person does, can inspire you to create completely original work. Look at what professional graphic designers have done in books, magazines, brochures, flyers, and websites. Think too of how the French Impressionists had tremendous influence on each other's work. I was surprised to learn that talented art students often start by practicing with images created by someone else. By the time they are finished with their work, the image is completely different.

One student told me she learned the most from the previous paragraph while using this book. She summarized it as "It is OK to cheat a little." By that she meant, it is OK to use designs, clip art, and other things that would make her job easier.

A word of caution, though. Copyright laws make a distinction between illegal copying and inspiration. It is unlawful to represent any form of someone else's image or visual as your own. Inspiration is considered a suitable degree of departure from an original work.

I watched the artist of this poster paint many, many Xs until he painted one he liked.

FIGURE 1–15   Poster presentation
Source: Created by Bill Hinson. Used with permission.

What is considered suitable is open to legal interpretation, so my advice is to be sure to make your work really different than your inspiration piece. More on copyright is found in Chapter 5, Shape.

Revise a Lot

Get used to creating prototypes or quick copies of your work that you can get feedback on immediately. The prototyping process involves analyzing (planning) a design, creating it, and evaluating and changing the design (ACE)—over and over. Rarely will your work be good enough on its first draft. The ACE process will be described in Chapter 11, but there is no reason you cannot get started on it now. As we created the examples for this book, we often used what we originally thought were good examples as our "bad" examples. This is because even though we were using all the theory, things didn't quite go right when we showed our work to others. The prototyping process is what made our work acceptable.

The Challenge activities on the book website for each chapter are important to your learning. You can compose your solutions to these problems in a variety of ways. You can simply sketch the solution on unlined paper if you do not have skills using a computer. Or, you can use a word processing program that allows you to insert graphics and position text. If you know how to insert graphics and create text blocks, you can make professional looking images in a simple word processing program. The Chapter 4 website has a section on working with text blocks, and the Chapter 5 website has a section on inserting graphics. If you need a little help now with these tasks, you might visit Chapter 4 and 5 on the book's website.

Chapter 12, Resources, describes some of the more popular software tools available and tutorials to help you learn these packages. Students in my classes either sketch the images or use Microsoft Word, Microsoft PowerPoint, Adobe Illustrator, or Adobe PhotoShop. Most students use Adobe Illustrator or Adobe PhotoShop. Although these are advanced tools, they are worth the effort. A majority of students learn the basics adequately in a semester if they use the Adobe *Classroom in a Book* tutorial for Illustrator and PhotoShop or Linda Weinman's self-paced computer training (excellent!). See Chapter 12 for more information on these products.

One tip before you start: Try to minimize the use of clip art! By visual I do not mean that now is the time to add as many little graphics as you can. Think of the message and what you want to communicate. Do not be afraid of using words!

How Is This Book Organized?

This book is divided into three sections (see Figure 1-16 for chapter information.)

Section I   Introduction, describes the intended audience for this book, the general theories that support the book's approach, and the tools, actions, and perceptions (TAP) model.

Section II   Shaping Instruction to Facilitate Learning, is the heart and soul of the book. This section thoroughly describes the tools, actions, and perceptions (TAP) that you'll use or manipulate to create effective instruction.

Section III   Putting It All Together, shows you how to integrate all the chapters and describes the resources (software, hardware, and books) that you might want to have around to help you work more efficiently and effectively.

I suggest you read the book sequentially, at least the first three chapters. These chapters build upon each other, and if you skip a chapter, there is a possibility you might not understand what certain phrases or words mean later on.

Summary

Today's information-rich world increasingly requires visual literacy skills, defined as the ability to understand and use images, including the ability to think and express oneself in images. Teachers, trainers, and those who design instruction, manuals, and programs all depend in part on visuals to communicate. Using visuals effectively, however, is not a natural skill for many people. While tools for design are more accessible than ever, many people have too much of a tools or technocentric focus—that is, they let the features of a particular technology drive the design of their message, often to the detriment of their instruction.

Likewise, there is a popular opinion that any visual is worth 1,000 words; therefore, many images are created without the awareness that these images may or may not be understood, often depending on the skill of the designer.

While design advice abounds, from diverse fields such as graphic arts, information design, computer science, interface design, human factors, and message design, this plethora of rules often confuses people instead of helping them. This book reduces confusion by simplifying the number of relevant principles to three: figure/ground, hierarchy, and gestalt — all principles of human perception. By considering learner perception as the critical design element, this book takes a learner-centered rather than technocentric approach to design. Review Figure 1-16 for an overview of the coming chapters.

Part I Introduction

 Visual Literacy for Educators and Trainers provides an overview of why visual design skills are important to educators and trainers today.

 Visuals and Learning examines what research and theory tell us about learning from visuals. You'll learn about the "picture superiority effect" and how people perceive or "read" images.

 The Building Blocks: Tools, Actions, and Perceptions (TAP) presents a design process that explains the sequence of subsequent chapters.

Part II Shaping Instruction to Facilitate Learning

Tools

 Typography introduces the power of typography, the art and science of using the letter form to communicate.

 Shape introduces the strength of using circles, squares, lines, and common shapes to enhance learning.

 Color, Depth, and Space introduces the instructional implications of color, advancing and receding images, and the importance of white space.

Actions

 Actions covers how contrast, alignment, repetition, and proximity make visuals easier to understand **and** look better.

Perceptions

 Helping the Learner Select (Figure Ground) describes how the figure/ground principle works to improve learner access to information.

 Helping the Learner Organize (Hierarchy) describes how the hierarchy principle works to improve learner understanding of how content is organized.

 Helping the Learner Integrate (Gestalt) describes how the gestalt principle works to improve learner understanding of the "big picture."

FIGURE 1–16　Book organization

FOR MORE CHALLENGE

 Visit Chapter 1's *Challenge* section on the book's website. There you'll find several instructional problems that require your visual solutions. Compare your solutions to those of others.

DISCUSSION FOR DISTANCE LEARNING

 | Visit the book's website (Chapter 1 > Discussion) for discussion or chat questions.

REFERENCES

Braden, R. A. (1996). Visual literacy. In D. H. Jonassen (Ed.) *Handbook of research for educational communications and technology*. New York: Simon & Schuster.

Galitz, W. O. (1997). *The essential guide to user interface design: An introduction to GUI design principles and techniques*. New York: Wiley Computer Publishing.

Hartley, J. (1985). *Designing instructional text*. New York: Nichols.

Lohr, L. (1999). Development of a procedure for GUI design. In R. E. Griffin, W. J. Gibbs, & B. Wiegmann (Eds.), *Visual literacy in an information age: Selected readings from the Annual Conference of the International Visual Literacy Association*, Athens, Georgia, October 21-24, 225-233.

Martin, D. (1989). *Book design*. New York: Van Nostrand Reinhold.

Mullet, K., & Sano, D. (1995). *Designing visual interfaces: Communication oriented techniques*. Englewood Cliffs, NJ: Prentice Hall PTR.

Nielsen, J. (1993). *Usability engineering*. Boston: Academic Press.

Reilly, S. S., & Roach, J. W. (1986). Designing human/computer interfaces: A comparison of human factors and graphic arts principles. *Educational Technology, 26*(1), 38-40.

Rowley, M. (1992). *Kanji: pictographics: Over 1,000 Japanese Kanji and Mana mnemonics*. Berkeley, CA: Stone Bridge Press.

Schwier, R. A., & Misanchuk, E. R. (1993). *Interactive multimedia instruction*. Englewood Cliffs, NJ: Educational Technology Publications.

Tufte, E. R. (1997). *Visual explanations: Images and quantities, evidence and narrative*. Cheshire, CT: Graphics Press.

Williams, R. (1994). *The non-designer's design book: Design and typographic principles for the visual novice*. Berkeley, CA: Addison-Wesley.

CHAPTER *2*

Visuals and Learning

"Perceiving and thinking are indivisibly intertwined."

Rudolf Arnheim

NOTES ABOUT THE OPENING VISUAL

As in the Chapter 1 opening visual, I use words and symbols on the chapter cover to express how visuals and learning are related. You'll learn in this chapter that your mind has separate verbal and visual memory. Thus, the words on the cover image represent verbal memory, and symbols represent visual memory. I also made the chapter cover image fuzzy to communicate that the role of visuals in instruction is not crystal clear. Words are used as graphic elements too, and I chose to use them as such for five reasons.

The first reason I've employed words as visuals in the opening graphic is because words are often the easiest and clearest graphic tool you can use. Too much effort is spent trying to come up with clever metaphors and analogies when simple words do the job and are often easier to understand. I also used words because they make an image look good by providing texture, a topic you'll learn about later in Chapter 6. Texture refers to visual characteristics that give an object a tactile quality.

The second reason for using words or symbols as graphic elements in the opening visual is because they are easily accessible. I use the eye and the man symbols on the cover because they are part of the Webding font family on my computer, so they were easy for me to find and use. I don't have a lot of time, so if I can find a suitable image in a font family, then I use it. I encourage students to get to know the font families on their computer for this reason. They are great sources of well-designed images.

If you are unfamiliar with fonts, you'll learn more about them in Chapter 4. Since I'm mentioning them, I'll explain what they are briefly. Fonts are typefaces, like Arial and Times New Roman. There are thousands of typefaces, and each one makes the alphabet look different. When you use word processing and other desktop publishing programs, you have the option of changing the fonts you use.

The third reason I've used words and symbols as graphics is because the design of fonts is flawless in most cases. When I teach typography (the art and science of the letterform) one of the first assignments is to take a letter or a symbol and make it huge, around 300 or 400 points (see Figure 2–1). Then I ask students to study the perfection of the symbol or letter, or perhaps just part of the symbol or letter, such as the darkened section of Figure 2–1.

The fourth reason I used words and symbols as graphics is because they are copyright free, an important consideration for a busy person. You can use them without seeking permission from the typeface designer, something that could take time and cause considerable delay in your development.

The fifth and last reason I've used symbols and words in the opening visual is because the symbols I just so happened to choose have a circular shape, a shape I find pleasing to the eye. Circles tend to connect information too—a topic we'll cover more in Chapter 5. The eye symbol is a symmetrical shape; therefore, it is fairly easy to work with and to get visually "right." In other words, balance is easy to achieve with symmetrical symbols. Since the

FIGURE 2–1 The letterform in detail

Notice the simple beauty in the graceful strokes of this letter.

information symbol is enlarged to span the background, the shape gives that space harmony, connecting the words with the image. Later you'll see how we call this balance a form of gestalt, one of the three key perception principles covered in this book.

FOCUS QUESTIONS

- What is an instructional visual?
- Do visuals really help people learn?
- Is there a visual language?
- How are visuals used in educational and performance settings?
- How do information-processing theories explain learning from visuals?

KEY TERMS

INFORMATION PROCESSING THEORY   A theoretical perspective that focuses on the specific ways in which individuals mentally think about and "process" the information they receive. (Ormrod, 2000, p. G4)

WORKING MEMORY   A component of memory that holds and processes a limited amount of information; also known as short-term memory. The duration of information stored in working memory is believed to be approximately five to twenty seconds. (Ormrod, 2000, p. G9)

LONG-TERM MEMORY   The component of memory that holds knowledge and skills for a relatively long period of time. (Ormrod, 2000, G5).

SENSORY MEMORY   A component of memory that holds incoming information in an unanalyzed form for a very brief period of time (probably less than a second for visual input and two or three seconds for auditory input).

SELECTION   Attending to particular information for cognitive processing.

REHEARSAL   A cognitive process in which information is repeated over and over as a possible way of learning and remembering it (Ormrod, 2000, p. G8).

VISUAL MEMORY   information encoded pictorially, or in pictures.

VERBAL MEMORY   information encoded verbally, or in words.

FIGURE-GROUND PRINCIPLE   Perception principle describing the mind's tendency to see edges and in doing so to separate figure elements from ground elements.

ORGANIZATION   A cognitive process in which learners find connections (e.g. forming categories, identifying hierarchical relationships) among the various pieces of information they need to learn. (Ormrod, 2000, p. G5).

INTEGRATION   The simultaneous presentation of text and images to facilitate cognition.

HIERARCHY   The layering information into categories that have an order of importance.

GESTALT THEORY   Perception principle describing how the whole is greater than the sum of its parts.

INTRODUCTION

Sylvia, the instructional designer described in Chapter 1, is in charge of a multimedia-training project on customer service skills. She develops a project plan for her design team, which includes a storyboard with several interactive sections using video clip segments of customer calls, then delegates some of the work to her development team.

After a few days, one of Sylvia's designers shows her a prototype of the project along with a storyboard (see Figure 2-2). Sylvia is dismayed; too much information is presented on the computer screen, none of it synchronized. The animated graphics do not make sense

The nonsynchronized content bothers Sylvia.

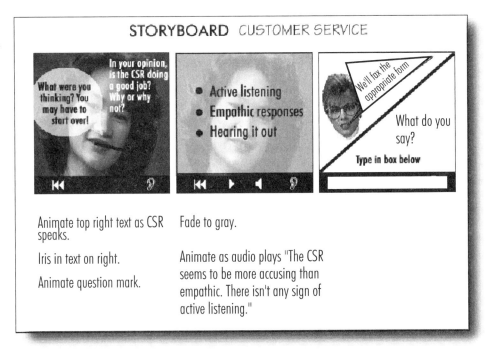

FIGURE 2–2   Customer service storyboard

and are out of sync with the narration. To make matters worse, her manager and her design team think the prototype is great. Sylvia guesses they are just responding to flashy animation and graphics rather than the instructional value of the material.

Fortunately, Sylvia knows of research on visual learning that addresses her concerns. She summarizes a number of research articles by Mayer (Mayer, 1993; Mayer, Steinhoff, Bower, & Mars, 1995; Moreno & Mayer, 2000) that show learning improves when text and graphics are presented in a synchronized, simultaneous manner rather than in the disjointed style of the prototype. She also shares Reiber's (1989) guidelines to use animation when the content warrants it, particularly when motion or direction are parts of the learning task. When asked to look at the prototype more directly from a learning and research perspective, Sylvia is able to convince the design team that the prototype could be improved.

Many people react to multimedia the way Sylvia's team did. They assume that because instruction is visual or flashy, or if multiple media is used, then the instruction is effective. As we discussed in Chapter 1, pictures are not always worth 1,000 words. Because visuals are expensive to produce, it is important to understand the theories and research related to visual learning. As Sylvia's situation demonstrates, it often helps to have a rationale for design decisions and critiques.

WHAT ARE VISUALS AND DO THEY INCREASE LEARNING?

Sylvia's team is correct, however, in thinking that visuals for the most part contribute to learning. Significant research shows that many individuals have better memory for images than for words (Anglin, Towers, & Levie; 1996; Braden, 1996.) The combination of words and visuals appears to help learning especially when the pictures are related to the textual information (Levie & Lentz, 1982.)

Before getting into the results of other visual research, let's start with a basic question: "What exactly is a visual?" A **visual** is typically thought of as a form of communication that is not verbal. Braden (1996) identifies five categories of visuals that have been studied by educational researchers:

■ semiotics and film/video conventions
■ signs, symbols, and icons
■ images and illustrations
■ multi-images
■ graphic representation

Semiotics and Film/Video Conventions

Braden describes the first category, semiotics and film/video conventions, as a field that views signs and film as languages to be "read" much in the same way words are read. If you've seen a movie that "spoke" to you, that you would have understood had there been no words at all, you may relate to the belief that visuals can serve a linguistic function. Although many experience this type of a visual "language," there isn't much research to support it. "The theoretical literature on semiotics and symbol systems is rich. The research to validate it, as yet, is not so rich" (Braden, 1996, p. 496.)

Signs, Symbols, and Icons

Braden's second category, signs, symbols, and icons, examines research that often overlaps with semiotics research. Though researchers dispute whether a symbol is a type of sign or signs are a type of symbol, these studies for the most part do not support the idea of signs, symbols, and icons as elements of a linguistic system.

Braden refers to a series of studies by Griffin (1994, 1995) that indicated that signs, symbols, and icons are often not interpreted the way the designer of the information containing them intended. In one study by Griffin, clip art symbols used in business presentations were often misunderstood (1994). In another study, people interpreted symbols rapidly and often incorrectly. Think for a minute about how difficult computer application icons can be to figure out. As I'm typing now, I'm looking at the icons on my word processing screen. There is one icon with a magnifying glass superimposed over an image of a piece of paper. Does this icon mean "magnify" or "zoom in"? As it turns out, it means "Print preview," which was not at all obvious to me.

Often cultural differences accounted for much of the variation in a symbol's meaning (Griffin, Pettersson, Semali, & Takakuwa, 1995). Braden concludes his review of signs, symbols, and icons by stating, "An international symbol system based on intuitive interpretation of symbol meanings may not be possible until the world shares a common culture" (p. 496).

Images and Illustrations

Braden's third category, images and illustrations, has been widely researched with many positive implications for the role that images and illustrations play in learning. Of the studies most widely cited is Levie and Lentz's (1982) research on the effects of illustrated text for learning. Based on 155 experimental comparisons, Levie and Lentz concluded:

■ Illustrations can help with understanding, remembering, and performing.
■ Information in both an illustration and in text is likely to facilitate learning.
■ Illustrations can act as effective substitutes and enhancers of words.
■ Illustrations can enhance enjoyment and other affective reactions.
■ Illustrations that simply *embellish* content (superficial adornment) do not enhance learner understanding.

- Learners may need to be prompted to interact effectively with complex illustrations or pictures (for example, learners may need to be instructed on how to read charts or tables).
- Learning is not influenced when information in the text is not in the illustration.
- Illustrations may help poor readers more than they help good readers.
- Illustrations are often more effective than learner-generated images.

Multi-images

Multi-images, Braden's fourth categorization, include multimedia images and how these are processed in memory. Are single images or multiple images (presented simultaneously or sequentially) better for memory? In the chapter's opening scenario, Sylvia was struggling with this issue. On one hand, cue summation theory supports a belief that the more stimuli or cues you are exposed to, the more you learn (Severin, 1967). On the other hand, cognitive load theory (Sweller & Chandler, 1994) addresses the concern that memory can handle only so much information before reaching capacity; at cognitive overload, learning eventually breaks down when the mind has too much to process. Research by Moreno and Mayer (2000), covered later in this chapter, supports the idea that the simultaneous presentation of images and text has a positive impact on memory, if designed in a way that maximizes learner selection, organization, and integration of information.

Graphic Representation

Graphic representation, Braden's fifth categorization, encompasses many of the other categories. *Graphics* are defined by Saunders (1994) as a prepared form of visual communication. Graphics can be symbols (pictographic or abstract), maps, graphs, diagrams, illustrations or rendered pictures (realistic to abstract), models, composite graphics (multi-images), and photographs (still or moving).

This book's connotation for the word *visual* is identical to Saunder's definition of *graphics*, with one exception. I've added typography (the art and science of the letterform) to the list. In general, typography takes place when a word or letter is presented in a particular way to form a message. For example, the word "tension" in Figure 2–3 looks like tension. In this case, both the words and the presentation are considered visuals. A section titled "Visual Language: Text as Visuals" is included in Braden's (1996) review of research on visual literacy, suggesting that others consider text to be a graphic or visual element. Misanchuk (1992) also considers text having a visual connotation since he describes design decisions about typeface selection and page layout as graphic design. If you read through the pages of this book, you will see many examples where text could be classified as a visual by these definitions.

FIGURE 2–3   Example of text as visual

HOW ARE VISUALS USED IN INSTRUCTION?

Now that you know what some of the research says, let's review how visuals are used to help people learn. Several researchers (Alesandrini, 1984; Duchastel & Waller, 1979; Levin, 1981; Levie & Lentz, 1982; Reiber, 1994) have classified the instructional value of illustrations into taxonomies or categories. In this book, we will review the classifications articulated by Reiber, Alesandrini, and Levin to illustrate some of these perspectives. While the classifications may differ, you'll see that many of their functions describe similar learning events or visual formats.

Reiber's Cognitive and Affective Classification

Reiber's classification is similar to a model of instruction whereby one uses graphics to gain attention and facilitate presentation and practice. Two overall types of graphics are identified: (1) graphics that serve an affective function and (2) graphics that serve a cognitive function. Think of an advertisement as an affective visual. For example, the advertisement might be for a movie on geography. This type of visual motivates people to see the movie. When the movie shows continents shifting locations and colliding with each other, these visuals serve more of a cognitive function since they instruct or inform. In general, affective visuals include those that are cosmetic and motivating. Cognitive visuals include graphics that are used for attention gaining, presentation, and practice.

Alesandrini's Representational, Analogical, and Arbitrary Classification

Alesandrini focuses on the degree of realism portrayed by the graphic and classifies graphics into three categories: (1) representational, (2) analogical, and (3) arbitrary. A representational graphic, such as a photograph, looks similar physically to the object to which it refers. (Alesandrini argues that a photograph can be considered a graphic because it can be manipulated.) An analogical graphic refers to similarity. As the name implies, this type of graphic uses analogy or metaphor to communicate. For example, an analogical graphic might be a visual comparing the flow of electricity through a wire to water flowing through a hose:

> Voltage is not unlike water pressure, amperage corresponds to rate of flow, switches are like faucets, resistance is like a kink in the hose. (Winn, 1993, p. 90)

An arbitrary graphic, on the other hand, is one that does not resemble an object but uses graphs, charts, diagrams, and the like to show the organization of an object or the relationship of an object to other objects.

Levin's Decoration, Representation, Organization, Interpretation, and Transformation Classification

Levin (1981) classified five instructional functions of graphics: (1) decoration, (2) representation, (3) organization, (4) interpretation, and (5) transformation. Like Reiber's classification scheme, Levin's functions imply more of an instructional strategies perspective. In other words, they help us think of what we hope to accomplish in the learner's mind. Levin's scheme, particularly the first four functions, is closely aligned with the approach of this book. Let's review these functions more closely.

Decorative

Decorative visuals typically do not have a strong association with the instructional content. Rather, these visuals help a learner enjoy instructional content because they make it attractive or interesting. In general, a decorative visual improves the appearance of instructional content. Figure 2–4 shows two decorative visuals. The right image is part of Sylvia's customer service multimedia training; the left image is the main menu of a typography lesson. Figure 2–5 is a typographic ornament that can be used to decorate instruction. In all of these visuals, there is no attempt to foster learning of academic content. In this text, decorative graphics are considered useful in initial stages of perception by motivating and gaining attention. In a study of sixth grade science textbooks by Mayer (1993), more than 85 percent of the illustrations fell into the decorative category. This is a discouraging statistic since out of all the types of instructional visuals, the decorative category has the least to do with learning. That scientific texts use mostly decorative visuals and relatively few representative, explanative, organizational, and transformational images is somewhat alarming.

Representative

Representational visuals carry the same information as the text, making the information more concrete. They help a learner visualize information. For example, Figure 2–6 accompanies

These are decorative. Their appearance has minimal instructional value

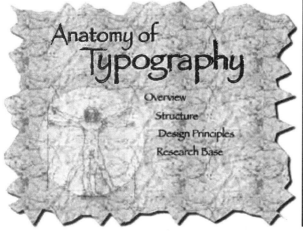

FIGURE 2–4 Decorative visuals

This ornamental typeface is used to make text passages more appealing.

FIGURE 2–5 Typographic ornament

This representational image makes it possible to see the camel's skeletal structure.

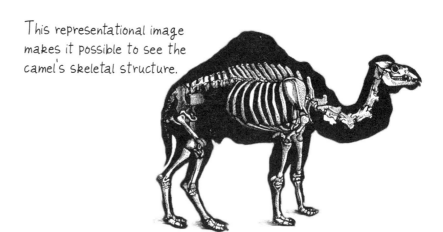

FIGURE 2–6 Representational visual

FIGURE 2–7 Representational visual with text

A computer interface is an organizational visual because it designates the consistent placement of information.

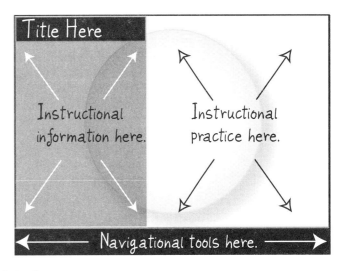

FIGURE 2-8   Organizational visual

A table of contents is also an organizational visual because it logically organizes the location of information within a book.

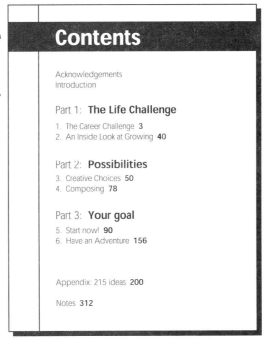

FIGURE 2-9   Organizational visual showing hierarchy of content

text describing a camel's skeletal structure. Figure 2-7 is used with text describing the difference between realistic, line, and icon images.

Organizational

Organizational visuals help learners understand the structure and hierarchy of information and help integrate information. A grid system for computer-based training (Figure 2-8) and a table of contents (Figure 2-9) are types of organizational visuals. Both of these figures show hierarchy and organization of content. Other types of organizational images are charts and graphs that help people see relationships between elements.

This interpretive visual helps explain supply and demand.

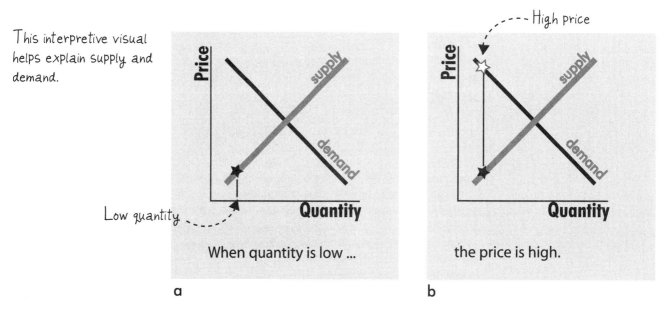

a   When quantity is low ...

b   the price is high.

High price

Low quantity

FIGURE 2-10   Interpretive visual

The blocks and circles help children make connections between numbers and quantity.

FIGURE 2-11   Interpretive visual to aid learning

Interpretive

Interpretive visuals help learners understand difficult and ambiguous content. In general, they help make information more comprehensible. Examples of interpretive visuals include models of systems and diagrams of processes. Figure 2–10 could be considered an interpretive chart because it is used to explain supply and demand relationships for economics. Figure 2–11 uses squares and circles to help children learn addition. In this text, interpretive graphics are those that challenge working memory and work the hardest to interact with long-term memory.

This is a transformational visual because its uniqueness helps transform or change your memory.

FIGURE 2-12 Transformational visual

The circles teach children how to use visual sections of a number to visualize values.

FIGURE 2-13
Transformational visual from early childhood education

Transformational

Transformational visuals make information more memorable. Visual mnemonics, such as showing a letter in a grocery cart to teach the Spanish word for letter, *carta* (Figure 2–12), are excellent examples of transformational visuals. Teaching numbers by showing counting points (Figure 2–13) is another example of a transformational visual. Transformational visuals are unconventional and difficult to find in traditional materials. Some believe that the learners, not the designers, gain the most from generating transformational visuals. Transformational visuals impact long-term memory because they rely on analogy, or previous experiences stored in memory, as devices to help people learn.

So what do all these categories mean to you? Aside from providing a richer understanding of how graphics might be used to improve instruction, the classification helps you answer the basic questions: What cognitive function do I want a visual to support? Do I need a visual to improve motivation? The learner's recognition of new content? The organization of information? The clarity of an explanation? Or the presentation of information in a new and highly memorable format?

It is time to take a break from reading. Suppose you've been asked to create a simple "takes dimes only" poster for a vending machine. Go ahead and create a poster, then visit the book website (Chapter 2 > Web activity) to compare your solution to those of others. Be sure to think about what type of cognitive activity you are trying to support.

WHAT IS THE THEORY BEHIND VISUALS?

As you've learned, a respectable body of research supports the use of visuals in learning. Behind that research are several theories that postulate what takes place in memory. I've selected three theories that I think will help you most in understanding what makes visuals effective. Atkinson and Shiffrin's (1968) information processing theory, Pavio's dual coding theory (1990), and the work of Mayer and his associates (Mayer et al., 1995). You'll find that the approaches suggested in this book go hand in hand with these three theories.

Information Processing Theory

A number of theories describe the transfer of information through memory (Atkinson & Shiffrin, 1968; Broadbent, 1984; Lockhart & Craik, 1994; Norman & Bobrow, 1975; Waugh & Norman, 1965). Atkinson and Shiffrin (1968) propose a model of memory based on two types of memory, short-term memory (including sensory and working memory) and long-term memory (see Table 2–1). The dual-store model of memory is commonly referred to as **information processing theory** (see Figure 2–14.) Short-term memory is limited, holding small quantities of information for a short time (seconds). A component of short-term

TABLE 2–1   *Capacity, Duration and Format of Long- and Short-Term Memory*

Memory store	Capacity	Duration	Format
Short-Term Memory			
Sensory Memory	Can hold an *unlimited* amount of information.	Seconds	Visual and auditory
Working Memory	Can hold a *very limited* amount of information.	Seconds	Visual and auditory
Long-Term Memory	Can hold an *unlimited* amount of information.	Indefinite, some think permanently	Visual, language, semantically (in a summarized or overall gist rather than detailed, word-for-word manner)

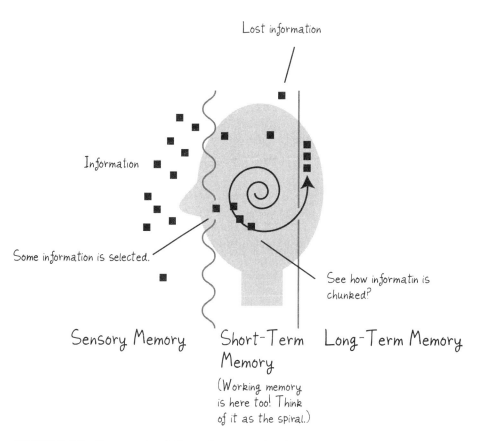

FIGURE 2–14   Components of information processing theory

memory is **working memory**, as a system that performs in an executive capacity by managing and manipulating information. **Long-term memory** is unlimited, capable of holding an infinite amount of data for an indefinitely long time.

The dual-store model of memory attributes learning to successful transfer of important information from one type of memory to the next. **Sensory memory** transfers some information to short-term memory; short-term memory transfers some information to long-term memory. Figure 2–14 represents this information flow by showing little black squares moving from one type of memory to the next. Notice how some of the information has not transferred between sensory, working, and long-term memory. When information is not transferred, it is considered lost or forgotten.

Working with Short-term Memory

Visual designers must understand sensory and working memory. Sensory memory holds an unlimited about of information, but just for a few seconds! Stop for a moment and think about everything that your sensory memory is taking in now. Try to hear sounds around you that you've been ignoring. You might hear a fan, the compressor in a refrigerator, the hum of a printer, the voices of neighbors, or any number of sounds. Because you've decided to pay attention to your environment, you are suddenly conscious of things you were unaware of just seconds before. Look back at this page now. Your sensory memory is taking in a lot of information just on the page; it sees individual letters, words, paper, your hand, the edges of your book. Much of what you sense you ignore because your sensory memory has a filter that directs your attention only to certain things. For example, you don't really pay attention to individual letters within a word; instead you attend to the word. **Selection**, or the process of attending to specific information and ignoring other information, is a key part of sensory memory.

The information that has been selected makes it to working memory, but it may not stay there since working memory is short term and does not have a large capacity.

Miller (1956) found that working memory holds anywhere from 5 to 9 units (7 plus or minus 2) of information. What comprises a unit can vary. For example, your short-term memory might have trouble with a number string like 120719411945. To help short-term memory, the numbers might be chunked: 1207 19 411 94 5. The telephone is a perfect example of chunking at work. Without chunking, a 10-digit telephone number is slightly past the limit of working memory capacity. When the telephone number is chunked into three groups (the area code, the first three numbers, and the last four numbers), it falls well below working memory capacity. Researchers believe, however, that the greater the number of items in a chunk, the fewer chunks that working memory can hold.

Chunking is only one way to help people work better with the limitation of working memory. In general, to keep information in working memory requires that the learner "do" something with that memory, either consciously or unconsciously. One type of "doing" is called **rehearsal**, or the process of repeating information. Repeating information can take place in a number of ways. For example, one might listen to information then repeat or elaborate on the information using any of these strategies: read the same information, look at a picture of the information, imagine the information, discuss the information with a friend, draw the information, organize the information into categories or a chart, or even act the information out. During each of the repetitive activities, the learner processes the information more thoroughly and theoretically should have more ways to keep the information alive in working memory long enough for it to transfer to long-term memory.

Working with Long-term Memory

Moving information from working memory to long-term memory is usually the biggest challenge! Rehearsal increases the chance that information remains in memory, but the best bet for getting information into long-term memory is by making the rehearsed information meaningful to the learner. Analogies have long been used to do just that. By comparing new information to something the learner already knows, the learner is more likely to understand the new information. Whenever you can make connections to things within your audience's experience, they are more likely to remember it.

Here's an example of a successful analogy from the computer science world that shows how a team of good designers used the previous experience concept to improve performance. Computers in the late 1970s were much harder for everyday people to use because they organized everything around directory structures (don't worry if you don't understand directory structure, not many people did — that was the problem.) To find a file in the "old" days required searching through a directory structure. If you wanted to pull up a file called CROOKSHANKS.doc, you'd have to give directions for the computer to go search in the correct subdirectory, which was often a subdirectory of other subdirectories. The command might look something like this:

DIR C:/POTTER/HOGWARTS/HERMIONE/CROOKSHANKS.doc

A team of smart human factors experts (people who study human relationships with the environment) decided most people related to filing systems better than directory structures. To find COOKSHANKS.doc using the file folder metaphor would require clicking on file folder icons that were embedded in each other. First you'd click on the POTTER file folder icon, then the HOGWARTS file folder, then the HERMIONE file folder, and finally on the CROOK-SHANKS.doc file. The idea of opening a file was much easier for people than the idea of traveling through a directory structure because most people had previous experience with files.

Your Job

As a designer your job is to design information for the three types of memory (sensory, short term, and long term.) You help people notice the important information (selection in sensory memory). You help people think about and work with information that has been selected (rehearsal in working memory). You help people associate new information to their previous experiences to make learning meaningful (working with long-term memory).

Here's a simple (admittedly contrived) example of how a designer might work with the three types of memory. Let's say it is vitally important you learn the numbers 120719411945 in the order they are presented.

To help your sensory memory select these numbers, the designer in charge of helping you learn these numbers would help you notice them, perhaps by surrounding the numbers with some space and by making the numbers bold.

120719411945

Now the designer wants to help you keep these numbers in working memory. The designer must find a way to help you "work" with these numbers. He or she could request that you write down these numbers repetitively until you have memorized them (a form of rehearsal); however, that is somewhat boring and easy to forget. Another strategy, as discussed in the previous file folder example, is to make the information meaningful. In order to make this meaningful the designer must think about what you might already know.

To help you move those numbers into long-term memory, the designer might suggest that you assign personal meaning to the numbers. For example you might look at the numbers and make up something like, "I lifted 120 pounds when I lived in area code 719. Now that I'm 41, I lift 194 pounds 5 times a week." Aside from making this information meaningful, notice too how you have also chunked it into five units of data (120, 719, 41, 194, 5). By grouping the 12-digit number into 5 chunks, you have made the numbers easier to remember.

Let's get back to making these numbers meaningful in other ways. Suppose the designer gives you the strategy, as opposed to having you make up the strategy, for remembering 120719411945. Since you probably know something about the dates of World War II and Pearl Harbor the designer might present the numbers to you this way:

Dates of U.S. involvement in World War II
12/07/1941–1945
12 07 1941 1945.

Memory is set up as a network with many paths leading to the same information. The more ways you think of information, the more "triggers" you'll have to recall that information later when you need it. Here the words "Wars", "WWII", and "Pearl Harbor" could all provide the appropriate path to the number 12071941945.

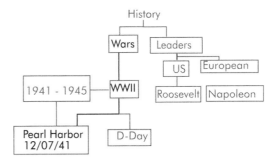

Schema

FIGURE 2-15   Schematic structure of long-term memory

Theoretically you'll remember this information because it has been linked to information you already know (if you did in fact know the dates of Pearl Harbor.) Long-term memory has a schematic structure, much like Figure 2–15. Because information is connected, it is traceable, allowing you to recall it later. Consider each part (node) of the schema as a potential trigger that could lead your memory down the required path. The more you think about information and hook it into previous knowledge, the more entry points you have for retrieval.

Although the examples I've provided are limited to factual information, information processing theory works with higher levels of learning like concepts, principles, procedures, and attitudes. Remember that learners are limited information processors, especially when it comes to short-term memory. People aren't computers that can store vast amounts of information. You need to facilitate the learner's: (1) attention to the most important information, and (2) ability to process information in a way that is meaningful. Many strategies to help you do this are shared in the pages ahead.

Pavio's Dual-Coding Theory

Pavio's dual-coding theory (1990) proposes that rather than just one sensory memory, one short-term memory, and long-term memory, as might be implied in information processing theory, there are actually separate memory systems for different types of information: one for verbal information and one for imaginal information. Pavio broadly defines verbal and imaginal memory. **Verbal memory** includes activity related to language systems (auditory and speech), while imaginal memory includes pictures, sounds, tastes, and nonverbal thoughts (imagination).

Verbal and imaginal memories are very different. Verbal information moves from sensory memory to verbal processors. Visual information moves from sensory memory to visual processors. Information in either processor can activate the information in the other processor. In other words, images can activate verbal information and vice versa. The power of images can be explained by the ability of concrete words (words that can easily be visualized, people, places, objects, tastes, touch, and smell) to stimulate nonverbal memory (images). Words that are abstract (emotions, ideas) are less likely to stimulate nonverbal memory and are less likely to be remembered, since the chance of learning is much greater when two, rather than one, memories are involved.

Take, for example, the concrete word "cat." The word alone will most likely trigger an image of a cat (see Figure 2–16). An abstract word like "distinct," however, is much less

FIGURE 2-16 Verbal vs. imaginal memory

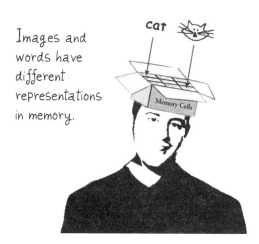

Images and words have different representations in memory.

likely to generate an image. Since some verbal representations are stored only in verbal memory, the theory argues for a "picture superiority effect" (Levie, 1987). Pavio's (1965) research, showing better memory for concrete rather than abstract word pairs, backs up this theory. Other research is similar. Shepard's (1967) study of college students who looked at 600 pictures (six seconds per picture) and 600 words found that 98 percent of the pictures, as contrasted with 88 percent of the words, were recalled later when paired with new images or words.

Mayer's Theory

Moreno & Mayer, 2000 have been interested in how visual and verbal memories interact. Mayer's theories suggests that visuals and words are most likely to facilitate learning when they are designed to help people select, organize, and integrate information in ways that are meaningful. You'll find that the processes of selection, organization, and integration are closely connected with information processing theory (see Figure 2-17). When you help the learner select, organize, and integrate, you are helping information move from sensory to working to long-term memory. As you read the following information, you may think it similar to what you've already read. It is! Where information processing theory focuses on the structure of memory, Mayer's theory focuses on facilitating memory.

Selection

As you've just read, the information processing model describes information moving through sensory memory into working memory in the early stages of learning. During this process, the mind acts as a filter. This selective perception is the mind's way of reducing information overload. What is interesting is that your mind is also selecting things of which you are unaware, and this has tremendous implications for design and the power you can exert as a designer.

Unconscious Selection

Though we tend to think of perception as highly influenced by past experiences, a certain degree of perception is predetermined. Research in artificial intelligence gives us insight into this type of predetermined perception. By programming computers to "see," scientists have studied how people "see" and have learned that features and boundaries of an image are detected first. Then the mind progressively fills the image until it represents "generalized cones" that are recognized (Marr, 1982).

FIGURE 2-17 Connections between information processing theory and Mayer's theory

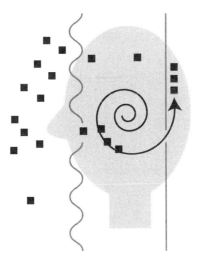

SELECTING   ORGANIZING   INTEGRATING
Sensory Memory   Short-Term   Long-Term Memory
                   Memory

If you were driving and saw in the far distance an octagonal outline at an intersection, what would you do? You'd probably prepare to stop without thinking about it much. Your mind would fill in the outline to be an octagonal shape, which by past association means "stop." Suppose that shape were filled with four letters such as "SLOW." What do you think you'd do if you saw this from a distance? Many people would stop anyway, not even noticing the word "SLOW."

Winn (1996) explains the implications of Marr's research:

> … perceptual organization strongly predisposes people to make one interpretation of what is seen rather than another. The net result is that, in spite of top-down influences that operate once attention is brought to bear, preattentive organization is a powerful determinant of what is actually understood in the perceived message. These include, but are not limited to, the relative placement, size, and dominance of objects in the visual field, and the way the eye is "led" over the image by various techniques of composition. The message designer cannot assume that people will see what they are told they are looking at, and cannot easily compensate for a poorly designed message with instructions on how it is to be perceived. (p. 56)

This is an important statement because it encapsulates the importance of understanding theory in order to create effective visual instruction. Basically Winn is saying learners are more likely to think about your visuals the way you want them to if you organize or present information in a way that the mind is predisposed to grasp.

Consider this example. We know from Marr's research, cited previously, that the mind seeks out the edges of an image; the mind is programmed or predisposed to do that. Although there may be many objects in any given image, the mind will seek out those objects that have the most distinct edges. As the mind fills in these edges, it begins to understand what the image is. This activity describes the **figure/ground principle**, which states that during perception the mind seeks to identify and separate figure and ground elements in an image. As a designer, you can manipulate an image so the edges are easier to detect since you know the mind is likely to be looking for edges. For example, if you want a particular shape to show up, you just make sure that the edges of the shape are distinct from everything else.

Conscious Selection

We've been exploring what takes place unconsciously and in sensory memory. Selection also takes place consciously. Meaningful learning begins when pictures and words move from sensory memory to working memory.

As you have already learned, working memory is limited in capacity, able to process seven plus or minus two units of information (Miller, 1956), or 10 to 20 seconds of information. During that time, the learner must select relevant information from visuals to store in visual memory, and relevant information from words and sentences to store in verbal memory. Mayer refers to this process as building mental representations. Learners essentially reconstruct what they see into their own representations. They do so in two ways—verbal and visual, in a process Mayer calls *organization*.

Organization

Organization takes place when information in verbal and visual memory is categorized and ordered by the learner to make more sense. Organization involves building representational connections in the information. For example, learners may try to structure the information sequentially, hierarchically, or according to past experiences. They might arrange things in a list or imagine parts of an image in a certain format. This process, rehearsal, is an important activity because the more learners think about or organize the information, the more likely they will remember it.

Integration

Integration takes place when related visual and verbal representations are held in working memory at the same time. You might show the learner a diagram of a person perspiring on the top floor of a building; in the same diagram you would depict a person on the bottom floor wearing a sweater. The words "warm air rises" would be displayed close to the two floors. This integration of visual and verbal information makes it more likely to transfer into long-term memory because it is more meaningful to the learner. Unlike short-term memory, long-term memory has an unlimited capacity for information.

Moreno and Mayer's (2000) research supports this interpretation of integration. In a series of experiments, they found that a verbal description of information during animation was better for learning than was a verbal description following the animation. In another experiment they found that the combination of animation and narration was better than the combination of animation and on-screen text. They suggest that narration was processed in a separate memory channel and didn't overload visual memory the way the on-screen text did. In another experiment music was added to an audio narration and compared to narration alone. The results of this experiment found that the addition of music impeded learning, suggesting that the auditory portion of verbal memory was overloaded.

Moreno and Mayer prescribe strategies to optimize the integration of visual and verbal memory. They suggest among other things: (1) presenting visual and verbal information simultaneously so that they can be processed at the same time, and (2) limiting the load placed on any one memory system by avoiding the need to split student attention between multiple sources of similar content. For example, you wouldn't repeat information in a narration by putting the same information in on-screen text for the learner to try to read simultaneously. This repetition would require too much memory.

How Do You Put It All Together?

It's time to put everything together and use this information to create instructional visuals. You've learned that people have both visual and verbal memory systems. You've also learned that the combination of text and visuals is a powerful learning strategy. Several theories explain why either visuals alone or the combination of visuals with verbal information make for effective learning strategies.

Stemming from the research related to these theories is Mayer's (Mayer et al., 1993) suggestion to design visuals so that they support cognitive processes of selection, organization, and integration. By using principles of design, you can, to some extent, help people do these things more easily. By making some things stand out more than others, you help people *select* information. By showing hierarchies and creating pathways through information, you help people *organize*. By repeating elements and themes (such as simultaneously showing pictures and related words), you help people see the big picture and *integrate* information.

I'd like to note here that this book's interpretation of integration is not the same as that of Moreno and Mayer. This book refers to integration in a broad sense, encompassing not only simultaneous presentations of text and graphics but a variety of methods that tap into a learner's previous experiences.

It is important to realize that a visual does not always warrant attention to all three of these processes. This is an important distinction to make since many visuals are used as support and performance tools, not as learning tools. When you are creating a support or performance tool, you do not need to design information for long-term learning. You just need to make it easy to understand and access.

For some situations you may want to design for selection, perhaps when you just want someone to notice something. This may be true for a decorative visual, a representative visual, or an organizational visual. For other situations you may choose to design for selection and organization because you want to present organized information to a person, as is the case for organizational visuals such as telephone numbers and recipes. In these situations the visuals support a performance task but do not teach anything so that it can be recalled later. For other situations you want to go all the way and design for selection, organization, and integration because you want the person to learn the information and be able to recall it later. Representation, transformation, and interpretation visuals may require attention to all three of these processes. For example, Mayer's work focused on all three processes because he was interested in designing interpretive visuals.

Three Important Principles

You will learn three principles that will help you implement all the theories we've covered in this chapter: (1) figure/ground, (2) hierarchy, and (3) gestalt. These principles can be used to help you create or manipulate images that can be understood more easily. Although all three principles are used simultaneously, figure/ground in particular helps with selection, hierarchy with organization, and gestalt with integration. This is an oversimplified way to present what goes on perceptually, but it is a good way initially to learn visual design. It is also a great area for further research.

Figure/Ground: Helping the Learner Select Important Information

The figure/ground principle refers to the mind's tendency to organize information into figure and ground categories. As designers of instruction, our goal is to make figure/ground distinctions as clear as possible in order to reduce the amount of information that memory needs to process. If you make the most important information really noticeable, you make it easier for the learner to pay attention to the relevant content.

The principle of figure/ground is widely recognized in many professional disciplines. For example, the information design literature focuses on emphasizing content; to information designers, information is king. Edward Tufte (1990), an information designer, stresses the importance of emphasizing the instructional information (the data) over the data container.

There are many visual distractions on the page. We have a case of boxitis going on. The gradient fill in the last box makes the text too hard to read.

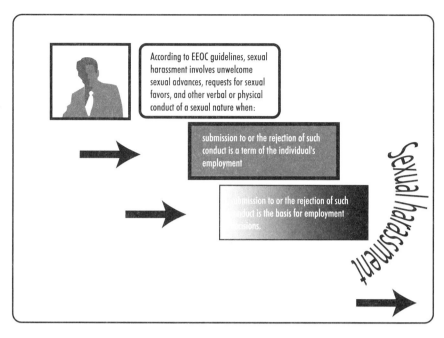

FIGURE 2-18 Example of figure/ground problem

Tufte (1990) describes a 1 + 1 = 3 phenomenon, the visual effect that takes place when two elements are combined and produce a third (1 + 1 = 3) element, which may or may not communicate. Figure 2-18 shows an example of a figure/ground problem. Notice how all of the arrows and fills make the message hard to see. In the bottom text box you see one element (text) plus another element (a gradient fill) that equals a third image (a combination of text and fill that is almost illegible.)

The graphic design literature focuses on creating optimal contrast. According to Mullet and Sano (1995), "contrast is essential for differentiating elements from one another — for allowing form to emerge from the void" (p. 52).

The message design literature describes perceptual processes that are at work in the learner's mind separating important from nonimportant information. Fleming and Levie (1978) suggest that "distinguishing between figure and ground is one of the most basic perceptual processes. Early perceptual processes are active in figure/ground organization" (p. 59).

The common theme of these different sources of advice is to make important information stand out. Loud backgrounds, competing typography, and clashing colors create an atmosphere that detracts from the important information rather than enhances it.

In the chapters that follow you'll learn how to use tools such as depth, color, and type, and actions, such as contrast, to create optimal figure/ground. You'll also learn more about figure/ground in Chapter 8, Figure/Ground Perceptions. All of these activities will lead to instruction that facilitates selection of important information.

Hierarchy: Helping the Learner Organize Information

The **hierarchy** principle is based on the mind's tendency to process and remember "chunks" of information that in turn are arranged hierarchically. To facilitate this process it is our job to shape information structures to show subordinate, super-ordinate, and coordinate relationships, including those related to time and direction. The use of outlines, arrows, and lists are common ways to establish hierarchy in a visual.

As with figure/ground, the hierarchy principle is considered a critical design principle by other disciplines. The information design literature speaks of layering and stratifying information. Tufte (1990) provides many examples of data enhanced by effective layering and separation, terms he uses to describe the relative organization of information:

> Among the most powerful devices for reducing noise and enriching the content of displays is the technique of layering and separation, visually stratifying various aspects of data" (p. 53).

The graphic design literature addresses creating pathways through content. According to Mullet and Sano (1995), "organization and visual structure provide the user with the visual pathways needed to experience a product in a systematic way" (p. 89.) The same authors note, "Organization begins with classification, which involves grouping related elements and establishing a hierarchy of importance for elements and groups." (1995, p. 93)

The message design literature stresses the importance of chunking information, suggesting that the designer may influence perception by organizing information in a way that essentially saves the mind from doing the same work. Fleming and Levie (1978) suggest that "early processing organizes perceptual units into groups, and groups into other groups in a hierarchical manner" (p. 63). When a designer chunks the information up front, that theoretically leaves less mental work for the learner.

Altogether the literature encourages the organization of information into hierarchical levels. Learner disorientation is prevented with clear hierarchical structures, implying subordinate, coordinate, and super-ordinate relationships and a sense of direction. Aligning coordinate information, using different intensities of color to designate importance, and using space to chunk content into distinct categories are all methods used to achieve a greater sense of hierarchy.

In the chapters that follow, you'll learn to use these tools and others to improve organization. You will learn more about hierarchy in Chapter 9, Hierarchy Perceptions.

Gestalt: Helping the Learner Integrate Information

The gestalt principle encompasses figure/ground and hierarchy principles. **Gestalt theory** is based on the belief that the whole is greater than the sum of its parts. For example, gestalt theory supports the idea that by combining text and visuals, we can produce more effective learning than if the two were taught separately.

Gestalt deals with how information comes together in a meaningful way. As with figure/ground and hierarchy, its importance is found throughout the design literature. Information design literature stresses the importance of content and detail presented in a manner that is easy to understand. As with other principles of design, Tufte (1990) stresses the importance of the data itself. Tufte espouses the importance of detail, culminating into a larger coherent structure. Simplicity is not the lack of detail but an organization of detail that make the information meaningful and clear.

Graphic design literature stresses the importance of experiencing a product systematically in order to make the information easy to understand. Graphic artists promote the use of grid structures for organizing information. Grid structures facilitate the development of consistent designs that users can experience in a harmonious way.

Instructional message designers stress the importance of grouping items into meaningful units. Greater understanding is achieved when parts, or elements of a message, are attended to as a whole, not selectively.

All three sources of advice (information design, graphic arts, and instructional message design) address the importance of creating a clearly understandable whole or big picture from individual parts. Learner disorientation may be prevented when the learner has a firm sense of the relatedness of the overall environment and the lay of the land. Repeating graphic elements and colors, using shapes to connect items, and placing items close together or far apart are all methods for creating gestalt.

In the chapters ahead you'll learn to use tools, such as type, shape, color, depth, and space, and actions, such as alignment, repetition, and proximity, to create better gestalt. You will learn more about gestalt in Chapter 10, Gestalt Perceptions.

Figure/Ground, Hierarchy, and Gestalt Together

You may wonder if there is much of a difference between figure/ground, hierarchy, and gestalt. They are difficult to distinguish in many instances and tend to overlap. Optimizing figure/ground helps create hierarchy, and with hierarchy comes greater gestalt. As noted earlier in this chapter, figure/ground and hierarchy are considered by many to be elements of gestalt. The approach of this book, though, is to treat these principles as distinct in order to assist the recognition of their individual power in designing instruction. The goal is to improve perception through greater distinctions, clearer hierarchies, and the creation of related information, achieved through any combination of the three principles.

Keep in mind that the underlying concept of the book is that you, as a designer, can manipulate visual information to improve learner perception and support cognitive processes. My belief is that the three principles of perception (figure/ground, hierarchy, and gestalt) take you a long way toward creating learner-friendly visuals for learning or performance.

SUMMARY

In Chapter 1 you learned that although the instructional world increasingly relies on visual communication, in many cases visuals do not help learning or performance. In all likelihood the belief that a picture is worth a thousand words has been interpreted too loosely, giving people the false confidence that any picture will do. A strong need exists for instruction related to creating visuals for learning and performance.

This chapter helps you build expertise in instructional visual design by sharing and explaining what we know from the research on learning from visuals. Significant research shows that learning is positively influenced by visuals. Three theories in particular help while you create instructional visuals: information processing theory, Pavio's dual-coding theory, and Mayer's multimedia theory.

The approach to creating visuals promoted in this book is based on a combination of these three theories. By focusing design of instructional visuals on the three types of memory (sensory, short-term, and long-term), you should be able to support the cognitive functions of selection, organization, and integration. Three principles of perception from gestalt theory (figure/ground, hierarchy, and gestalt) help you design for selection, organization, and integration. The following chapter moves from theory to action by describing *how* you create visuals using tools, actions, and perceptions.

FOR MORE CHALLENGE

Visit Chapter 2's Challenge section on the book's website. There you'll find several instructional problems that require your visual solutions. Compare your solutions to those of others.

DISCUSSION FOR DISTANCE LEARNING

Visit the book's website (Chapter 2 > Discussion) for discussion or chat questions.

REFERENCES

Alesandrini, K. L. (1984). Pictures and adult learning. *Instructional Science, 13*, 63–77.

Anglin, G. J., Towers, R. L., & Levie, W. H. (1996). Visual message design and learning: The role of static and dynamic illustrations. In D. H. Jonassen (Ed.), *Handbook of research for educational communications and technology* (pp. 755–794). New York: Simon & Schuster.

Arnheim, R. (1969). *Visual thinking*. London: Faber and Faber Limited.

Atkinson, R. L., & Shiffrin, R. M. (1968). Human memory: A proposed system and its control processes. In K. W. Spence & J. T. Spence (Eds.), *The psychology of learning and motivation: Advances in research and theory* (Vol. 2). New York: Academic Press.

Braden, R. A. (1996). Visual literacy. In D. H. Jonassen (Ed.), *Handbook of research for educational communications and technology* (pp. 491–520). New York: Simon & Schuster.

Broadbent, D. E. (1984). The Maltese cross: A new simplistic model for memory. *Behavioral and Brain Sciences, 7*, 55–94.

Duchestel, P. C., & Waller, R. (1979). Pictoral illustration in instructional texts. *Educational Technology, 19*(11), 20–23.

Fleming, M., & Levie, H. (1978). *Instructional message design*. Englewood Cliffs, NJ: Educational Technology Publications.

Griffin, R. E. (1994). Using symbols in business presentations: How well are they understood? In D. G. Beauchamp, R. A. Braden, & J. C. Baca (Eds.), *Visual literacy in the digital age*. Blacksburg, VA: International Visual Literacy Association. (ERIC Document Reproduction Service No. ED 370 602)

Griffin, R. E., Pettersson, R., Semali, L., & Takakuwa, Y. (1995). Using symbols in international business presentations. In D. G. Beauchamp, R. A. Braden, & R. E. Griffin (Eds.), *Imagery and visual literacy*. Blacksburg, VA: International Visual Literacy Association.

Levie, W. L. (1987). Research on pictures: A guide to the literature. In D. M. Willows and H. A. Houghton (Eds.), *The psychology of illustration*. New York: Springer.

Levie, W. H., & Lentz, R. (1982). Effects of text illustrations: A review of the research. *Educational Communications and Technology Journal, 30*(4), 195–232.

Levin, J. R. (1981). On the functions of pictures in prose. In F. J. Pirozzolo & M. C. Wittrock (Eds.), *Neuropsychological and cognitive processes in reading* (pp. 203–228). San Diego: Academic Press.

Lockhart, R. S., & Craik, F. I. M. (1990). Levels of processing: A retrospective commentary on a framework for memory research. *Canadian Journal of Psychology, 44*, 87–112.

Marr, D. (1982). *Vision: A computational investigation into the human representation and processing of visual information*. San Francisco, CA: Freeman.

Mayer, R. E. (1993). Illustrations that instruct. In R. Glaser (Ed.), *Advances in instructional psychology* (Vol. 5, pp. 253–284). Hillsdale, NJ: Erlbaum.

Mayer, R. E., Steinhoff, K., Bower, G., & Mars, R. (1995). A generative theory of textbook design: Using annotated illustrations to foster meaningful learning of science text. *Educational Technology Research and Development, 43*, 31–43.

Miller, G. A. (1956). The magic number seven, plus or minus two: Some limits on our capacity for processing information. *Psychological Review, 63*, 81–97.

Misanchuk, E. R. (1992). *Preparing instructional text: Document design using desktop publishing*. Englewood Cliffs, NJ: Educational Technology Publications.

Moreno, R., & Mayer, R. (2000). *A learner-centered approach to multimedia explanations: Deriving instructional design principles from cognitive theory*. Retrieved from http://imej.wfu/articles/2000/2/muex.asp

Mullet, K., & Sano, D. (1995). *Designing visual interfaces: Communication oriented techniques*. Englewood Cliffs, NJ: Sunsoft Press.

Norman, D. A., & Bobrow, D. G. (1975). On data limited and resource limited processes. *Cognitive Psychology, 7*, 44–64.

Ormrod, J. E. (1995). *Human learning*. Upper Saddle River, NJ: Merrill/Prentice Hall.

Ormrod, J. E. (2000). *Educational Psychology: Developing Learners*. Upper Saddle River, NJ: Merrill/Prentice Hall.

Pavio, A. (1965). Abstractness, imagery, and meaningfulness in paired-associate learning. *Journal of Verbal Learning and Verbal Behavior, 4*, 32–38.

Pavio, A. (1990). *Mental representations: A dual coding approach* (2nd ed.). New York: Oxford University Press.

Reiber, L. P. (1989). A review of animation research in computer-based instruction. *Proceedings of selected research papers presented at the annual meeting of the Association for Educational Communications and Technology*, Dallas, TX, Feb. 1-5. (ERIC Document Reproduction Service No. 308-832)

Reiber, L. P. (1994). *Computers, graphics, & learning.* Dubuque, IA: Brown & Benchmark.

Saunders, A. C. (1994). Graphics and how they communicate. In D. M. Moore and F. M. Dwyer (Eds.), *Visual literacy, a spectrum of visual learning.* Englewood Cliffs, NJ: Educational Technology.

Severin, W. J. (1967). Another look at cue summation. *AV Communication Review, 15*(4), 233-245.

Shepard, R. N. (1967). Recognition memory for words, sentences, and pictures. *Journal of Verbal Learning and Verbal Behavior, 6,* 156-163.

Sweller, J., & Chandler, P. (1994). Why some material is difficult to learn. *Cognition and Instruction, 12*(3), 185-233.

Tufte, E. R. (1990). *Envisioning information.* Cheshire, CT: Graphics Press.

Waugh, N. C., & Norman, D. A. (1965). Primary memory. *Psychological Review, 72,* 89-104.

Winn, W. (1993). Perception principles. In M. Fleming, & W. H. Levie (Eds.), *Instructional message design: principles from the behavioral and cognitive sciences.* Englewood Cliffs, NJ: Educational Technology Publications.

CHAPTER 3

The Building Blocks: Tools, Actions, and Perceptions (TAP)

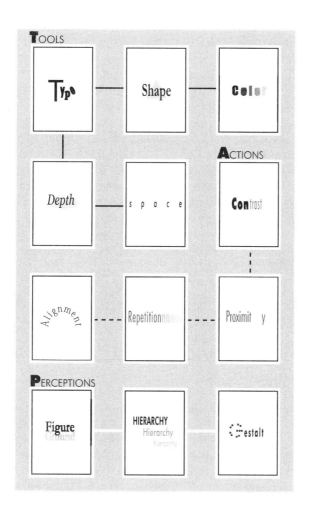

"There is a plethora of advice. Where do I start?"

Student

NOTES ABOUT THE OPENING VISUAL

The image on the previous page is a rectangle filled with labeled blocks. If you look closely, you'll see that five of these blocks are associated with Tools, four are associated with Actions, and three are associated with Perceptions. The initial letters of Tools, Actions, and Perceptions have been highlighted in boldface to create the mnemonic TAP. When you've mastered these tools, actions, and perceptions, you've mastered the basic skills behind creating instructional visuals. I'll use this cover image in the next seven chapters to show how we are building toward expertise block by block.

When creating this image I went through several versions (see Figure 3–1). Keep in mind that part of the creative process involves throwing away a lot of your first ideas. Chapter 11 features a chart that explains this part of the process, which can be a tough practice to master.

The first image in Figure 3–1 was my first idea. I made a black rectangle on layer 1 (see Figure 3–2). On layer 2, I created black text with a gradient fill (a black-to-white shading.) I made the space between lines of text really small so the text edges actually touch. I did this to create a textured image, something with lots of pattern and a tactile quality. I wanted this to be a really decorative image, not something that would be read. I wanted a little mystery, to indicate that things aren't always crystal clear and that tools, actions, and perceptions tend to bleed into each other, just as the image portrays.

As I developed the subsequent chapters, I began to realize the importance of using some type of image to organize all of the book information for the learner. Needed was an image that communicated the purpose of the chapter and its relationship to the rest of the book. Since all of these images seemed like pieces of a puzzle, the second image in Figure 3–1 was created. Since this image looked too busy, we modified it and eventually settled on the third image in Figure 3–1.

FOCUS QUESTIONS

- How do you get started?
- To whose design advice do you pay attention?
- What is the TAP model?
- How does the TAP model work?

KEY TERMS

ACTIONS   what you **do** with tools; actions include contrast (as in contrasting colors), alignment of type and visuals, repetition, and proximity

PERCEPTIONS   how your mind recognizes information using figure/ground, hierarchical, or gestalt patterns

TOOLS   the basic elements of design, including type, shape, color, depth and space

INTRODUCTION

Sylvia, the instructional designer/trainer, and Zack, the graphic artist/programmer, are in charge of workshops to help creative people find work that uses their creativity. They are using instructional materials created by the last person in charge of the workshop (see Figure 3-3). Sylvia and Zack decide to create a companion website to go along with the training workshop. Attendees can use the site to keep in touch with each other and order recent publications. Sylvia and Zack's first attempt looks like Figure 3-4. Sylvia doesn't know why she doesn't like

This was the first design. I liked the look of this visual because it shows how the words and the ideas behind them overlap.

This image shows how everything fits together like pieces of a puzzle.

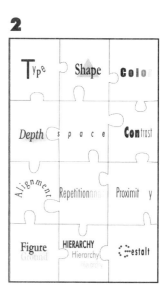

We eventually settled on this image because it was less busy.

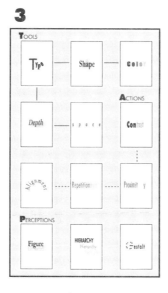

FIGURE 3-1   Initial ideas for the opening visual

it or what she should do about it to make it better. In all the design books she and Zack own, she finds no shortage of design advice. "I don't even know where to begin," she thinks.

While working on the redesign, Sylvia and Zack have these questions:

- Would this website make sense to someone who had attended the workshops?
- What do we do to make it easier to understand if it is confusing?
- Where do we start?

Many students and designers like Sylvia and Zack are confused by the many approaches to principles of design offered in how-to books. This chapter suggests an approach to make understanding design less overwhelming. The TAP approach uses learner-centered tools, actions, and perceptions to guide the visual design process.

Gradient fill applied

Layer 2 (The top layer.)
Text block

Layer 1 (The bottom layer.)
Black
rectangle

FIGURE 3–2 Steps toward the first idea

The workshop
materials looked
like this.

Out of the box thinking

Note paper

unconventional
unconventional
unconventional

Overhead Transparency

FIGURE 3–3 Original workshop materials

This website did not look right. The palette images did not match the workshop materials. The typeface seemed pretty conservative for a creative topic.

FIGURE 3–4 First step in designing workshop website

OVERVIEW OF TAP

TAP stands for tools, actions, and perceptions. Creating visuals for learning and performance involves using certain *tools* of design, to create *actions* that improve learner *perception*. These are abstract concepts now, but the rest of the book is dedicated to helping you understand what tools, actions, and perceptions are and how you use them to improve your design.

Tools

Tools, the first element of the TAP model, are survival basics. They are the core elements of design, the things that people reach for first instinctively without even thinking (see Figure 3–5). Color is intuitively used to highlight information, a circle is used to show a cyclical process, a line to connect thoughts or concepts. Color, simple shape, depth, space, and typography are all tools that are accessible and are frequently used by most trainers and educators.

Tools can be thought of as the basic design elements important for all designers. They can be manipulated using actions (contrast, alignment, repetition, and proximity), or they may influence perception directly. When one becomes skilled in design, tools alone help achieve one's design goals without even thinking of actions or perceptions—because one has cognitively automated the design process.

Sylvia and Zack use tools in the redo of the creativity website (see Figure 3-6). *Type* is used as a key graphic element. The "Keep it Creative" text is bold and creates emphasis. Though you see here black, white, and shades of gray, Sylvia and Zack actually use bright *colors*. A split complementary color scheme is used to convey the message of energy and excitement—important components of creativity. The person image is an energetic *shape* and matches the workshop graphic. The big, bold "Keep it Creative" type and the drop shadow used on the dancing image create depth that allows the viewer to immediately perceive the overall theme of creativity. The elements associated with creativity take up the

These are the
tools with which
you will
experiment.

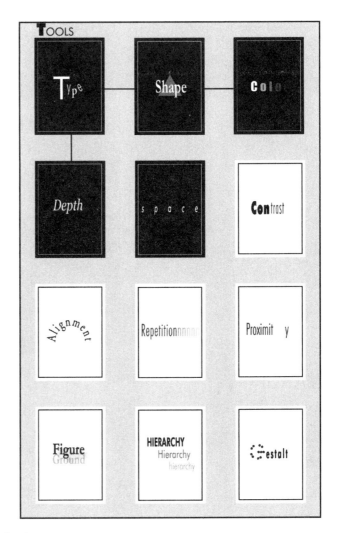

FIGURE 3–5   Tools of a designer

This matches the workshop materials
better. Notice how this image uses:

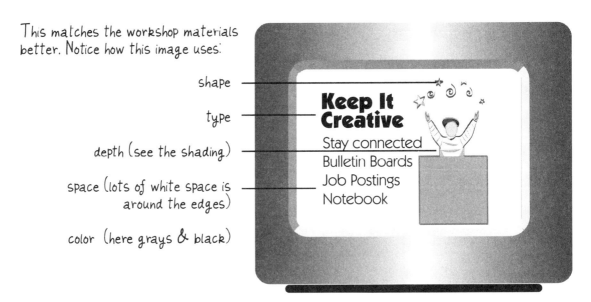

shape

type

depth (see the shading.)

space (lots of white space is
around the edges)

color (here grays & black)

FIGURE 3–6   Using tools to redesign the workshop website

These are actions. Think of yourself doing something with these. You contrast, you align, you repeat, and you move things close together or far apart.

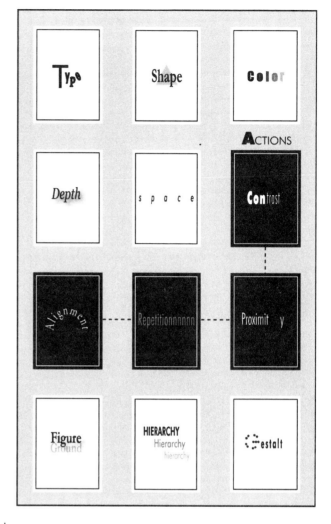

FIGURE 3–7   Actions designers apply

most space on the computer screen and are the most visually prominent. Finally, the background color, or *space*, falls more around the edges of the redesigned web screen, drawing the viewer's eye to the central image. In the original image, the background space seems to fall throughout the website, keeping the message a little unfocused.

Actions

Actions, the second component of the TAP model, deal with the physical changes or movements made to instructional information. Think of actions as something you do to tools to manipulate them. Actions (Figure 3-7) consist of alignment, contrast, repetition, and proximity, four design elements recommended by Williams (1994). Simply aligning, contrasting, repeating, and spacing elements close together or far apart can be powerful methods of improving visuals for learning and performance. While this seems too simple to be of much value, these four actions, when carefully applied, immediately yield professional and effective results.

In Sylvia and Zack's creative workshop scenario these actions are used to improve the overall image (see Figure 3-6). Sylvia and Zack used contrast when they made the overall message stand out better. The "Keep it Creative" text and the person image are made big and bold (*contrast*), taking up approximately 60 percent of the total screen space. All text lines

These are the perceptions you manipulate by using tools and actions.

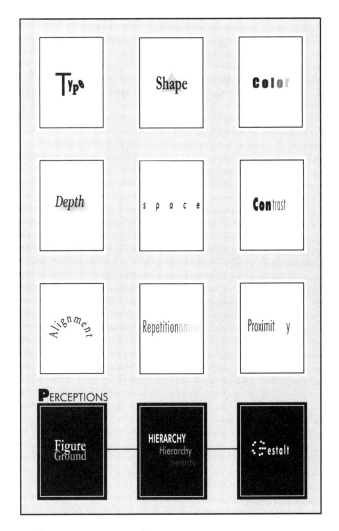

FIGURE 3–8   Perceptions designers can manipulate

in the image are *aligned* and moved close together (*proximity*) to create a greater sense of unity. Use of the same graphic element (the person) *repeats* the visual theme of the materials, making the website seem more connected with the workshop materials.

Perceptions

Perceptions, the *P* of TAP, were covered in Chapter 2. For review they consist of the three perception principles most critical for instructional designers: figure/ground, hierarchy, and gestalt (see Figure 3–8). Most of visual design problems that I see are related to figure/ground problems. Nine times out of 10 a novice designer tries to be "creative" and ends up "confusing"! The field of education and human performance technology has its own version of Edward Tufte's "chart-junk." We can call it *edu-junk*. "Chart-junk" refers to statistical presentations that rely on an abundance of clever or cute images to make their point. Tufte points out that most of the ink created in these presentations is not used for the actual data but for the data borders. Similar complaints are noted in the literature of information design (Tufte, 1990), graphic arts (Mullet & Sano, 1995; Williams, 1994), and message design (Fleming & Levie, 1978).

The second most common visual problem I see is related to a lack of hierarchy in information. Many designs are difficult to "read" with no organizational cues providing direc-

A.
This is blocky
and disjointed
and qualifies as
an example of
edu-junk.

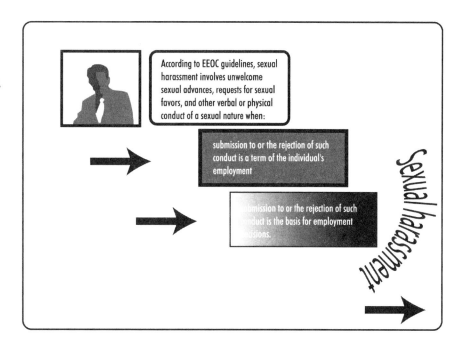

B.
This is better.
Most of the non-
essential
information has
been removed.

FIGURE 3-9   Increasing visual communication

tion. Notice in Part A of Figure 3-9, for example, the overuse of graphical cues (too many boxes, arrows, and ornamental text). We've got a bad case of boxitis or borderitis going on in this image. Who is the person in the top left corner, and what relationship does he have to the boxes of text? Part B of Figure 3-9 does a better job of unifying the image by reducing the use of unneeded graphics.

The third most common visual problem I see, which is often a function of poor figure/ground and hierarchical relationships, is that of gestalt. For now think of gestalt simply as harmony. Many visuals do not have any harmony or unified theme, making them difficult to understand.

Take a minute and try to spot the perceptual problems in the "before" images in part A of Figures 3–10 and 3–11. The "after" images (part B of Figures 3–10 and 3–11) are better because there is less there to detract from the overall message. You'll see better figure/ground, hierarchy, and gestalt in these "after" images.

The importance of keeping design simple is addressed in information, graphic, and message design literature for figure/ground, hierarchy, and gestalt principles of perception. In a nutshell, figure/ground is the principle that supports the importance of visually separating important from less important information. Hierarchy is the principle that endorses developing designs with clear directional cues. Gestalt is the principle that advocates the importance of showing learners the "big picture" and the relationship of the parts to the whole.

I've taken the liberty of making each of these categories separate in this book. Gestalt theory, however, considers figure/ground and hierarchy to be gestalt principles. I separate figure/ground, hierarchy, and gestalt because I find that these distinctions make it easier for students to learn design. A lack of adequate difference between figure and ground is the problem I see most often, followed by lack of hierarchy. Without attention first to figure/ground and then to hierarchy, it is hard to address gestalt. Gestalt, as you will learn in Chapter 10, is actually a term describing many design principles. Return to Chapter 2 if you need to review these perception principles.

Let's go back to Sylvia and Zack's project (see Figure 3–4) and think about it from a perception perspective. When Sylvia and Zack analyze their website with figure/ground, gestalt, and hierarchy in mind, they identify several problems. The first thing Sylvia and Zack question relates to figure/ground.

"What are we really trying to make stand out here?" asks Zack.

"Nothing stands out, does it?" Sylvia agrees. "Maybe we should make the 'Keep it Creative' text a little bit bigger."

"Yeah, it's not enough of a difference now to make much of an impact," Zack admits.

Sylvia and Zack also wonder about hierarchy.

"There isn't really a clear way to read the image either," Sylvia thinks aloud. "When looking at this, I don't know where to look next, or how I'm supposed to move through it. Is it to be read left to right, then down, or do I start on the left, move a little to the right and down, then move up, and then move right? Everything on the screen seems to have about the same visual weight."

"And, the whole thing just doesn't tie together that well," Zack says, addressing gestalt. "The creativity website doesn't seem related to the workshop materials. There's no continuity from workshop materials to website, outside of the word *creative*."

Sylvia agrees. "There are two different styles going on, the style of the workshop materials and the style of the website."

Together they set out to address their concerns, as described previously in the Tools and Actions section. In review, they made the words "Keep it Creative" even bolder, and they also positioned the headline so that it is the first thing a reader would see (at least a reader from a Western culture who starts in the top left position and reads to the right and down.) This addresses figure/ground (making the words big and noticeable) and hierarchy (establishing a reading order of top to bottom). They also make the website graphic similar to the one used in the workshop materials (see Figure 3–6). By connecting this new information site to the learner's previous experiences with the workshop, Sylvia and Zack are helping the learner integrate all the information. The overall gestalt, or relatedness of the materials, is improved.

It is time to take a break from reading. Suppose you've been asked to illustrate the concept of the 80/20 rule to a group of business professionals. The website shows a poorly designed visual (from the perspective of TAP) of the 80/20 rule. Following the instructions on the website, analyze the visual, and create a new example for the 80/20 rule. Some examples of the 80/20 rule you might use include: (1) 80% of people's time is spent on 20% of the tasks they need to complete; (2) 80% of

A. Vertical text is rarely a good idea since it is so difficult to read.

Do these boxes serve any purpose?

The steps of the recipe would be hard to follow since they are presented in a centered paragraph. Each new ingredient is hard to see.

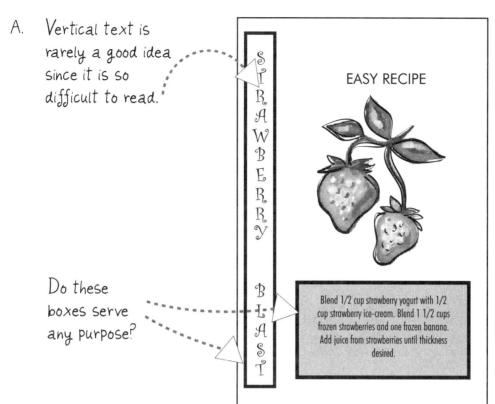

EASY RECIPE

S
T
R
A
W
B
E
R
R
Y

B
L
A
S
T

Blend 1/2 cup strawberry yogurt with 1/2 cup strawberry ice-cream. Blend 1 1/2 cups frozen strawberries and one frozen banana. Add juice from strawberries until thickness desired.

B. Here all of the graphic elements draw your eye to the most important information. If you were making this recipe it would be very easy to see how much of each ingredient is needed.

Strawberry
BLAST

Blend together:

1/2 c. strawberry yogurt
1/2 c. strawberry ice-cream
1 1/2 c. frozen strawberries
1 frozen banana
Juice from strawberries optional

FIGURE 3–10 Improving recipe instructions

A. All of the text in this image is hard to read. Although the clip-art has been softened to 30 percent black, it is not enough to make the text easily readable.

Buying Guide For Blender Beverages

Buy pineapples that have a raised diamond texture with a bright yellow color underneath the scales. Make sure you smell a sweet aroma. Avoid pineapples with brown and dried leaves.

Buy strawberries that smell sweet and are not moldy. Avoid berries with fine white hairs covering the skin near the top of the berry.

Buy bananas in any stage of ripeness. Bananas that have a slight fragrance and have small brown spots are best for blender beverages.

B. This information looks good and reads well with minimal graphics. This image would also look fine without any graphics.

The Buying Guide For **Blender Beverages**

Buy **strawberries** that smell sweet and are not moldy. Avoid berries with fine white hairs covering the skin near the top of the berry.

Buy **pineapples** that have a raised diamond texture with a bright yellow color underneath the scales. Make sure you smell a sweet aroma. Avoid pineapples with brown and dried leaves.

Buy **bananas** in any stage of ripeness. Bananas that have a slight fragrance and have small brown spots are best for blender beverages.

FIGURE 3-11 Improving buying guide instructions

sales are made by 20% of salespeople; (3) 20% of your clothes are worn 80% of the time. Create a visual solution to this information. Then visit the book website. Go to Chapter 3, and click on the web activity link to compare your solution to those of others.

If you are still somewhat confused about the relationship of tools, actions, and perceptions, think of these analogies. For example, you can think of something simple like hanging a picture on a living room wall. You usually grab a nail (a tool) and hammer it (an action) into either a stud or into a molly to view and appreciate the picture (perception). Or, consider this more direct example. If instruction doesn't read well because the two main colors clash and interfere with legibility, you would choose a new background color (a tool) to create better contrast (an action) to influence figure/ground distinctions (a principle of perception).

SUMMARY

Up until this point in the book you've learned that instructional visuals are important in educational and performance environments today. You have learned that in order to be effective, instructional visuals need to support three cognitive processes: selection, organization, and integration. By making information stand out and be noticed, you are addressing selection. By creating hierarchies and directions in information, you are addressing organization. By helping the learner make comparisons and see similarities, you are addressing integration.

Given that a vast number of skills and knowledge are needed to do these things, the book is organized using a Tools, Actions, and Perceptions (TAP) model. In short, the TAP model explains that *tools* of design (color, depth, shape, type, and space) are manipulated by *actions* (contrast, alignment, repetition, and proximity) that in turn influence *perceptions* (figure/ground, hierarchy, and gestalt).

The need for TAP is not based on scientific investigation or experimental research. Rather the need is supported by observations that are likewise mentioned in the literature of influential information designers, graphic artists, and instructional message designers. While the TAP approach may seem to be based on a formula, it is not. In contrast, TAP needs to be implemented heuristically. Tools and actions need to be experimented with, and blended creatively, much as an artist might work with a palette covered with different colors of paint.

The following chapters of the book follow the structure of the TAP model. First you learn the tools, next you learn the actions, and finally you learn how to optimize figure/ground, hierarchy, and gestalt. The next chapter, Type, introduces you to your first and most powerful tool—typography.

FOR MORE CHALLENGE

Visit Chapter 3's *Challenge* section on the book's website. There you'll find several instructional problems that require your visual solutions. Compare your solutions to those of others.

DISCUSSION FOR DISTANCE LEARNING

 Visit the book's website (Chapter 3 > Discussion) for threaded discussion or chat questions.

REFERENCES

Fleming, M., & Levie, H. (1978). *Instructional message design*. Englewood Cliffs, NJ: Educational Technology Publications.

Mullet, K., & Sano, D. (1995). *Designing visual interfaces: Communication oriented techniques.* Englewood Cliffs, NJ: Sunsoft Press.

Tufte, E. R. (1990). *Envisioning information*. Cheshire, CT: Graphics Press.

Williams, R. (1994). *The non-designer's design book*. Berkeley, CA: Peachpit Press.

PART II

Shaping Instruction to Facilitate Learning

CHAPTER 4

From Type to Typography

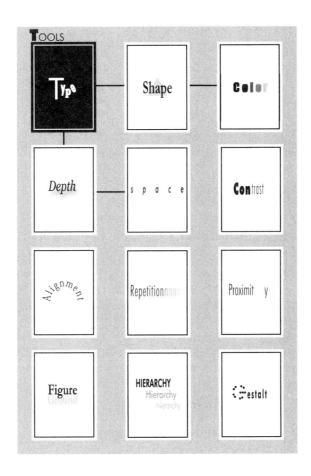

"Type is everywhere. Type exists. It is a fundamental part of our lives. These simple facts are essential to understanding how to communicate more effectively."

Erik Spiekermann and E.M. Ginger

NOTES ABOUT THE OPENING VISUAL

Notice how the words alone on this chapter cover have been used to communicate the meaning of different tools, actions, and perceptions. For example, the word *Type* is made up of letters that look different. These letters are arranged so that they aren't lined up evenly. This display shows you that type can change and that letters can be manipulated to express a message.

The word *Color* shows each letter in a different shade of gray, displaying that type can express color as well, even if in black and white. The word *Figure* in *Figure/Ground* appears to move forward because it is in a bold dark color and has a drop shadow behind it. The word *Ground* appears to move backwards because it is a softer gray color and is less dominant than the word *Figure*. These simple actions of showing contrast make the words *Figure/Ground* express their meaning. All of the words on the cover, with the exception of *Shape*, communicate their meaning visually.

FOCUS QUESTIONS

- What is a font?
- Are there rules of thumb for using type?
- Are serifs better than sans serifs for reading?

KEY TERMS

FONT   a computer-generated typeface for a specific point size. For example, Times New Roman 12-point is a font, as is Times New Roman 14-point. Bookman 8-point is a font, as is Bookman 72-point. The meaning of font has changed in the last decade to mean typeface

INSTRUCTIONAL TYPOGRAPHY   defined by the author of this text as the art and science of using individual letters, words, and passages of text to convey an instructional message

LEGIBILITY   how easy it is to read short bursts of text (Williams & Tollett, 1998)

READABILITY   how easy it is to read long passages of text (Williams, 1998)

TEXT   the main body of written or printed material, as opposed to display matter, footnotes, appendices, etc. (Carter, Day, & Meggs, 1985, p. 247)

TYPE   synonymous with *typography* in this book

TYPEFACE   is the formal definition of alphabetical and numerical characters that are unified by consistent visual properties (Meggs & McKelvey, 2000). Times New Roman, Arial, and Bookman are examples of the thousands of typefaces in existence.

TYPE FAMILY   all the varieties of a particular typeface, such as Arial Extra Bold, Arial Bold, Arial Narrow, Arial, and Arial Narrow Italics

TYPOGRAPHY   the art of the letterform (Carter, Day, & Meggs, 1985); typography involves composing the letterform (Meggs & McKelvey, 2000)

INTRODUCTION

Latisha, the community college instructor you met in Chapter 1, is working on her fall semester syllabus. A syllabus template has been provided for her to complete. After using the template however, Latisha is dissatisfied with its appearance (see Figure 4–1). She finds the

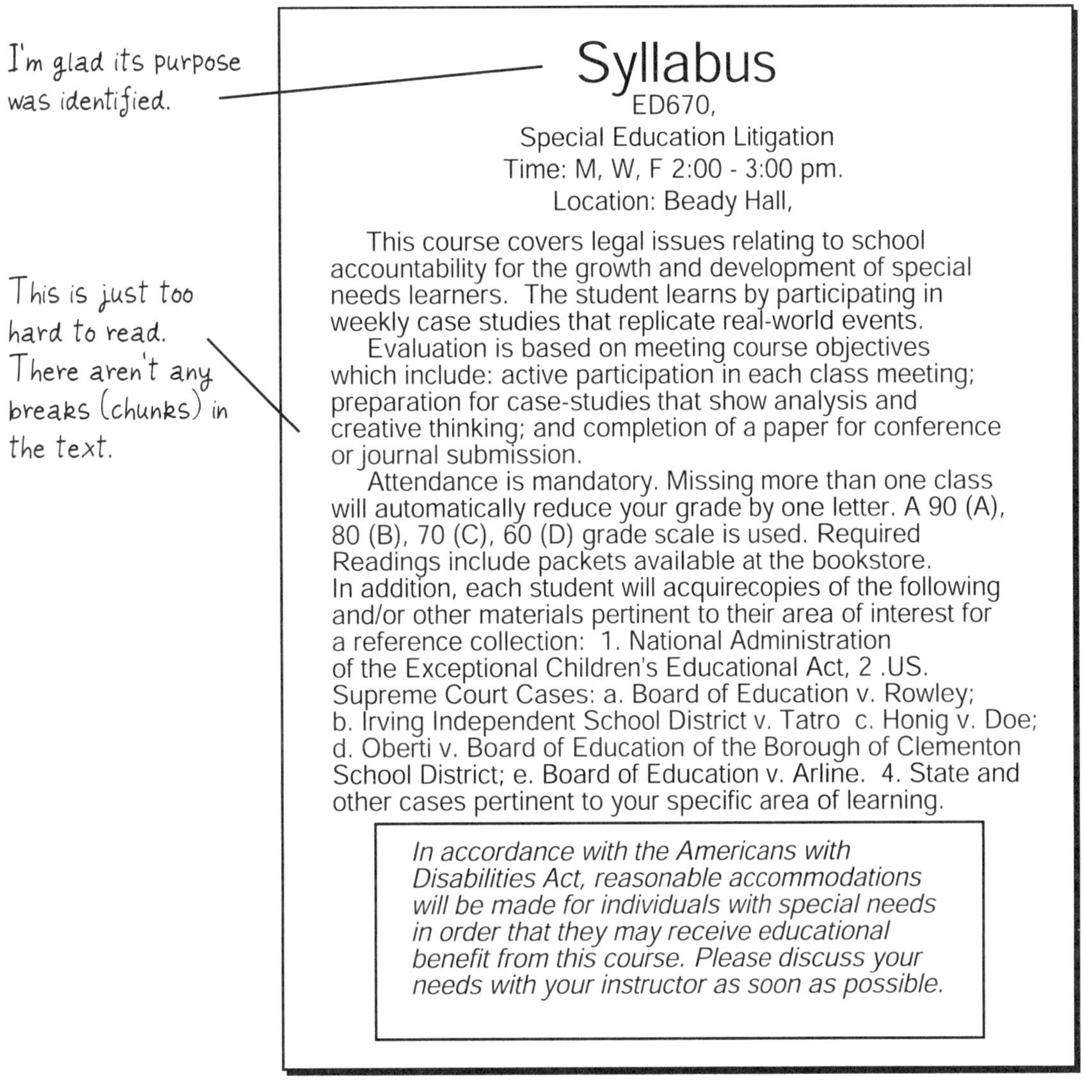

I'm glad its purpose was identified.

Syllabus
ED670,
Special Education Litigation
Time: M, W, F 2:00 - 3:00 pm.
Location: Beady Hall,

This course covers legal issues relating to school accountability for the growth and development of special needs learners. The student learns by participating in weekly case studies that replicate real-world events.
Evaluation is based on meeting course objectives which include: active participation in each class meeting; preparation for case-studies that show analysis and creative thinking; and completion of a paper for conference or journal submission.
Attendance is mandatory. Missing more than one class will automatically reduce your grade by one letter. A 90 (A), 80 (B), 70 (C), 60 (D) grade scale is used. Required Readings include packets available at the bookstore.
In addition, each student will acquirecopies of the following and/or other materials pertinent to their area of interest for a reference collection: 1. National Administration of the Exceptional Children's Educational Act, 2 .US. Supreme Court Cases: a. Board of Education v. Rowley; b. Irving Independent School District v. Tatro c. Honig v. Doe; d. Oberti v. Board of Education of the Borough of Clementon School District; e. Board of Education v. Arline. 4. State and other cases pertinent to your specific area of learning.

This is just too hard to read. There aren't any breaks (chunks) in the text.

> *In accordance with the Americans with Disabilities Act, reasonable accommodations will be made for individuals with special needs in order that they may receive educational benefit from this course. Please discuss your needs with your instructor as soon as possible.*

FIGURE 4–1   Standard syllabus

syllabus hard to follow and can't help but think that if she finds it confusing, the students will find it even more so.

As she looks over the syllabus, Latisha thinks, "Everything on the syllabus looks like one big gray box of text! Things aren't broken into visual groups. Assignments are mixed with course objectives and evaluation criteria. The typeface seems overly formal and distant. I want my students to feel comfortable and welcome."

Latisha has these questions:

- What font should I use to make the syllabus friendly?
- Should I change the way this is written?
- Should I use more than one font?
- Will inserting spaces here and there help students organize the information?
- How can I use headings to make the information more understandable?

Latisha wonders, however, if she would be breaking the rules by not following the template. On the one hand, she thinks, "The department wants the syllabi to be consistent. I'd be breaking rules." On the other hand, she thinks, "This syllabi doesn't communicate."

In the end Latisha decides to create a new syllabus format that is easy for the students to understand (see Figure 4–2). Several days after turning in her syllabus, her department chair stops her in the hallway. "Latisha, your syllabus is great. I'm surprised that just moving the text around makes it so much easier to read."

Latisha's department chair is experiencing the power of typography. Of all of the tools in this book, type is likely to influence your work the most. Unlike clip art and photographic images, type is a graphic tool easily accessible to everyone who has a computer. It is also a graphic tool that is copyright free, so unlike using other types of graphics, you do not need to worry about breaking any laws when you use type to enhance visual instruction.

There are countless books on typography, filled with appealing and motivating images (refer to Chapter 12, Resources for more information). This chapter distills much of the information contained in those books into instructionally relevant topics, including basic typography definitions, the use of type as a unique instructional tool, classification schemes for type, the anatomy of type, and basic computer skills for working with type (see the book website).

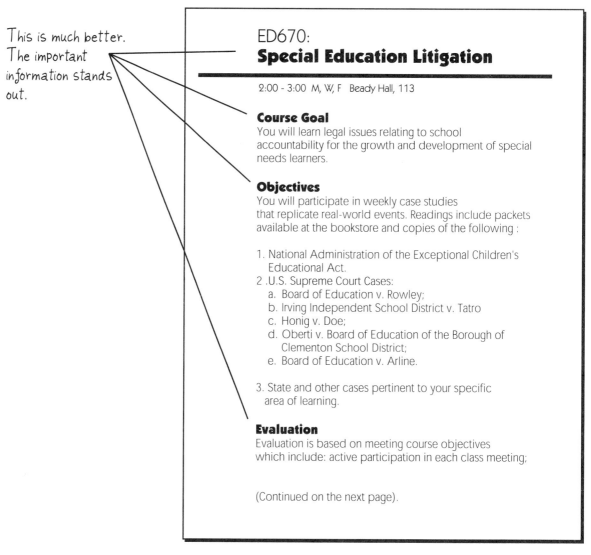

FIGURE 4–2   New syllabus format

WHY IS TYPE POWERFUL?

Type is perhaps the most versatile tool in this book. You can use type simply to create chunks of information that make following instructions easier, as in Figure 4-3. Or you can get complex with type, using it to express emotion or to enhance a message, as in Figure 4-4.

Careful choice of type is important. Compare the match between typeface and message in Figure 4-5. In Part A of the figure the message "*War Declared*" is set in an elegant typeface. The message "*Delicate Flowers*" is set in a bold typeface. "*War Declared*" should be set in the typeface that "*Delicate Flowers*" is set in, and vice versa (as shown in part B).

You can see some of type's organizational and communicative power in Figures 4-6 and 4-7. Type facilitates all the tools (Figure 4-6) covered in this book as well as all the actions (Figure 4-7).

Type is used to chunk this information into three overall steps. These steps (or chunks) make the information easier to approach.

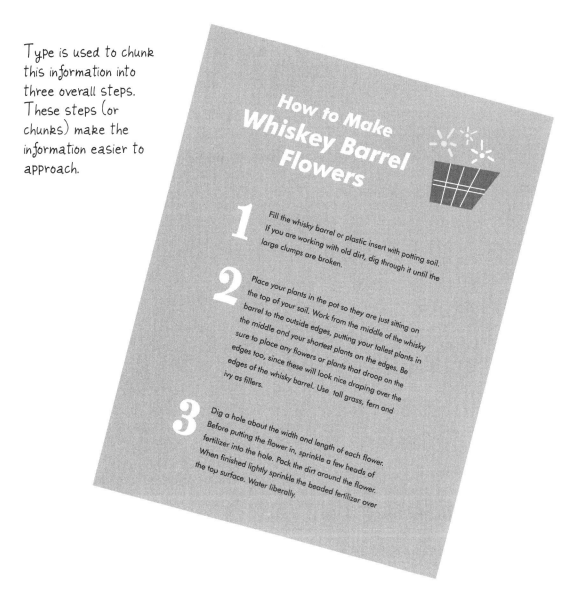

FIGURE 4-3   Simple use of type

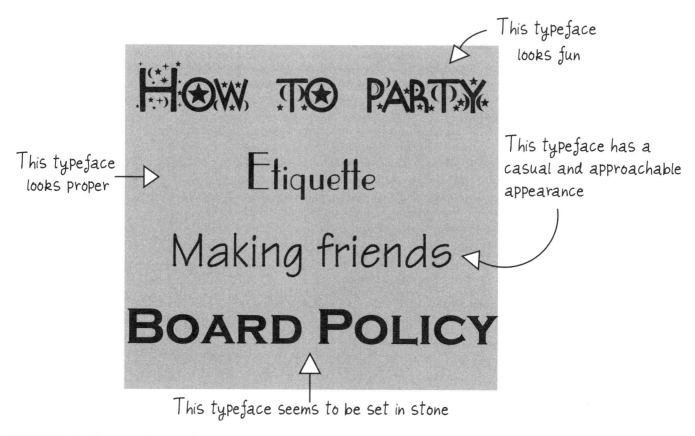

This typeface looks fun

This typeface has a casual and approachable appearance

This typeface looks proper

This typeface seems to be set in stone

FIGURE 4–4 More complex uses of type

A. These typefaces conflict with the meaning of the words.

B. These typefaces complement the meaning of the words.

War Declared

Supreme Court Ruling

DELICATE FLOWERS

Delicate Flowers

Supreme Court Ruling

WAR DECLARED

FIGURE 4–5 The right type for the message
Source: Created by Clark Parsons. Used with permission.

You can use type with other tools.

Shape

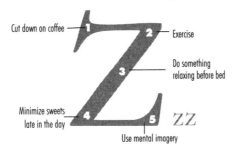

Your path to better sleep

Cut down on coffee — 1
2 — Exercise
3 — Do something relaxing before bed
Minimize sweets late in the day — 4
5 — Use mental imagery
ZZ

Type can be an organizing shape. The letter Z acts as a sequential path.

Color

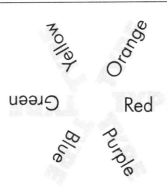

Yellow
Orange
Green
Red
Blue
Purple

Type can be any color on the color wheel.

Depth

TYPE TYPE

Type can show dimension and depth. Notice how the two types of drop shadows make the words appear to move forward.

Space

White space between text divides.

Type blocks can be carefully spaced to create chunks of memorable information. By using white space, you help create these chunks.

This is the second chunk of text. It is used to introduce a new topic.

This is the third block of text. It is used to introduce a new idea.

Type can be spaced so that chunks of information are created. These chunks help the learner categorize information.

FIGURE 4–6 Using type with other tools

You can manipulate type with actions.

Contrast

Con**trast**

Type can be thick or thin, dark or light.

Alignment

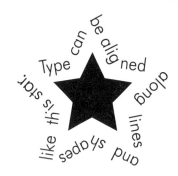

Type can be aligned to the edges of lines, shapes, and pictures.

Repetition

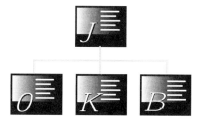

Repeating type creates harmony. Notice how the large letters are used on every box in the flow-chart, making them all look related.

Proximity

This sentence and the sentence below it look like they belong together.

This sentence looks like it belongs to the sentence above, even though it is in a different typeface.

Type that is far apart

seems unrelated. Even though this sentence is in the same typeface as the top sentence, it still seems unrelated.

When type is positioned close to other type, it appears related, as you can see in the left text block. When type is positioned far apart, it seems unrelated, as you can see in the right text block.

FIGURE 4–7 Using actions with type

WHAT ARE THE TYPES OF TYPE?

Most studies of type begin with learning about the different categories of type. Arial, Futura, Garamond, Bodoni, Dingbats, Webdings, Old English, Techno—the names of typefaces available for selection are nearly endless. To help organize the wide assortment of **fonts**, type is classified into categories based on characteristics of their anatomy. As you read through these different font groups, you'll notice that the tools and mediums available during the time in history they were developed determined the appearance of new type families. "The history of type is a history of technical constraints" (Spiekermann & Ginger, 1993, p. 115).

Although type has many different taxonomies or classification schemes, we'll use the following scheme that groups type into six groups: Black Letter, Roman, Square Serif, Sans Serif, Script, and Decorative (see Figures 4-8 through 4-16. Most people learning about type start the process unable to see much of a difference between the different groups. As you learn subtle variances in type groups, you will become more discerning with type selection from both an aesthetic and instructional perspective. As it turns out, typefaces from all of the groups can be used to enhance instruction. Knowing the different families can also help you select typefaces when faced with typeface names you do not recognize. By knowing that the edges of Square Serifs look blocky, you can look for a Square Serif substitute if you do not have any of the classic Square Serifs at your disposal.

WHICH TYPE IS BEST FOR INSTRUCTION?

After reading the past few pages you may be asking, "But which typefaces tends to be best for instruction?" The answer to that question is the "*It* Depends" rule (see Figure 4-17.) Like all design choices, a selection or action is accompanied by consideration of many different elements, all of them interacting to create a whole that is greater than the sum of the parts.

Characteristics of the instructional content, learner, delivery format, even colors of other elements in a learning environment interact, creating a variety of interaction effects that can all influence your selection of typeface.

A learner-centered methodology for making decisions of this nature is described in Chapter 11. The "ACE it" approach explains a process for involving the learner in your design decisions. Hartley (1996) has several good suggestions; he recommends that type decisions for instruction be made heuristically. Since individuals have widely varying opinions on typefaces (Misanchuk, 1992), Hartley provides a practical option: "It may be wiser to stick to conventional and familiar typefaces than to employ idiosyncratic ones" (p. 798).

Some typefaces have stood the test of time and are considered classics. Steven Heller (2000) describes a classic typeface this way, "In addition to all the functional and esthetic concerns, a typeface that continues to be used beyond its period of fashion, in my book that is a classic" (prologue). Classic typefaces used in this book (see Figure 4-18) are grouped into serif (characters with small strokes at the end of each stroke) and sans serif (characters without the small strokes) categories.

Classic serif typefaces include:

- Baskerville
- Bembo
- Bodoni
- Caslon
- Centaur
- Century
- Clarendon
- Garamond
- Times New Roman

Black Letter

Instructional Application

The Black Letter typeface has **limited application in instruction** and is usually only used for **decoration** — on training certificates, awards, and documents in drop-letter caps, as you can see in the examples column.

One could argue that small applications of Black Letter typefaces might be effective in creating a certain look and feel for a piece, perhaps giving it a timeless look or a formality. Drop cap applications can direct attention, too, which you will learn more about in chapters on figure/ground and hierarchy.

Though beautiful, it is **too difficult to read** when there are more than a couple of words, as you can see in the longer sentence at the end of the right column.

Some History
The Black Letter type family is one of the oldest typefaces, used in the days of Gutenberg. An elaborate, hand-drawn appearance characterizes Black Letter typefaces.

Examples

Frank typeface

Ornate hand drawn appearance

Good for certificates

The National Institute of Consulting Professionals formally recognizes

John Smith

Certified Consultant

Drop cap is good for directing attention.

n inadequate world-view can leave a person or a population unable to make solid and workable decisions. Problems cannot be solved, and the resulting environment is not conducive to either lasting success or satisfaction. There is little doubt that many of the failed or failing policies in todays society are like bedroom doors installed in a house with a faulty foundation.

A Black Letter Typeface

𝔉𝔯𝔞𝔫𝔨 𝔦𝔰 𝔲𝔰𝔢𝔡 𝔦𝔫 𝔱𝔥𝔦𝔰 𝔰𝔢𝔫𝔱𝔢𝔫𝔠𝔢.

A longer sentence set in Frank:

𝔄𝔫 𝔦𝔫𝔞𝔡𝔢𝔮𝔲𝔞𝔱𝔢 𝔴𝔬𝔯𝔩𝔡-𝔳𝔦𝔢𝔴 𝔠𝔞𝔫 𝔩𝔢𝔞𝔳𝔢 𝔞 𝔭𝔢𝔯𝔰𝔬𝔫 𝔬𝔯 𝔞 𝔭𝔬𝔭𝔲𝔩𝔞𝔱𝔦𝔬𝔫 𝔲𝔫𝔞𝔟𝔩𝔢 𝔱𝔬 𝔪𝔞𝔨𝔢 𝔰𝔬𝔩𝔦𝔡 𝔞𝔫𝔡 𝔴𝔬𝔯𝔨𝔞𝔟𝔩𝔢 𝔡𝔢𝔠𝔦𝔰𝔦𝔬𝔫𝔰.

(𝔈𝔦𝔨𝔩𝔢𝔟𝔢𝔯𝔯𝔶, 2000)

FIGURE 4–8 Overview of Black Letter type

Roman: Old Style

Instructional Application

Examples

Old Style typefaces are **widely used in instructional materials**. They are considered **very easy to read**. They are characterized by tapered or slanted serifs and inclined counters (you learn more about counters in the following pages).

Some History
The Roman typeface appeared in the days that Roman stonecutters chiseled letters into stone. Serifs (the cross strokes at the ends of letter forms) were used to keep the stone from chipping when the cutters ended the strokes.

There are three types of Roman type: Old Style, Modern, and Transitional. This section of the chart shows examples of Old Style typefaces.

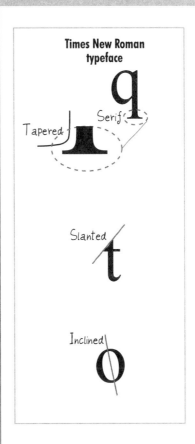

Some Old Style Typefaces

Garamond is used in this sentence.

Times New Roman is used in this sentence.

A longer sentence set in Times New Roman typeface:
An inadequate world-view can leave a person or a population unable to make solid and workable decisions.

(Eikleberry, 2000)

FIGURE 4–9 Overview of Roman: Old Style type

Roman: Modern

Instructional Application	**Examples**

Modern Roman typefaces have perpendicular serifs, upright counters, and often high contrast between lines. Although **striking in appearance**, they are considered **difficult to read** when there is moderate to large amount of body text.

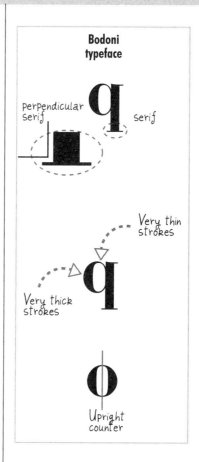

Bodoni typeface

Perpendicular serif

serif

Very thin strokes

Very thick strokes

Upright counter

A Modern Typeface

Bodoni is used in this sentence.

A longer sentence set in Bodoni typeface:
An inadequate world-view can leave a person or a population unable to make solid and workable decisions.

FIGURE 4–10   Overview of Roman: Modern type

Roman: Transitional

Instructional Application

Examples

Transitional typefaces have some characteristics of each of Modern and Old Style. They may have perpendicular serifs and low contrast between the lines. Or they may have tapered, slanted serifs with high contrast and upright counters. They are difficult to classify because of their combining attributes. Transitional typefaces are **considered very readable**.

Bembo typeface

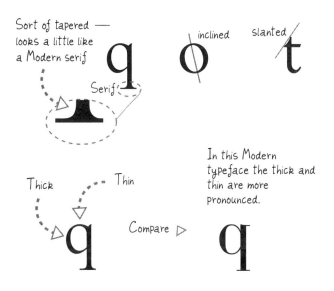

Some Transitional Typefaces

Bembo is used in this sentence.

Caslon is used in this sentence.

Centaur is used in this sentence.

A longer sentence set in Bembo typeface:
An inadequate world-view can leave a person or a population unable to make solid and workable decisions.

(Eikleberry, 2000)

FIGURE 4–11   Overview of Roman: Transitional type

Square Serif

Instructional Application	Examples

Square serifs, like Roman typefaces, are **widely used in educational materials** since they are considered **highly readable**. This typeface is **often found in children's books** for this reason. The typeface is often darker than the others, a quality some research finds to improve readability and to be preferred by readers. A new Web-based Square serif typeface, Georgia has been designed specifically to optimize screen reading.

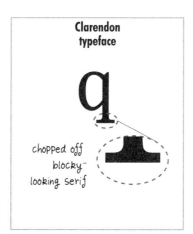

Clarendon typeface

chopped off blocky-looking serif

Some Square Serif Typefaces

Century is used in this sentence.

Clarendon is used in this sentence.

Georgia is used in this sentence. Georgia is a typeface designed for the Web.

A longer sentence set in Clarendon typeface:
An inadequate world-view can leave a person or a population unable to make solid and workable decisions.
(Eikleberry, 2000).

FIGURE 4-12 Overview of Square Serif type

Sans Serif

Instructional Application	Examples

Sans serif means "without serifs." Sans Serif typefaces do not have the little extensions at the end of characters.

Many consider Sans Serif type more **legible for computer-based instruction or presentation,** since the resolution of computer monitors is often not great enough to show serifs, making serif typefaces lose their legibility. This is a debated claim since there is not a large body of research to support such statements. Regardless of proof, Sans Serif typefaces are frequently **used as headings** in all types of instructional materials.

Two new Sans Serif typefaces have been designed to optimize screen display: Trebuchet and Verdana.

Univers typeface

no serif

Some Sans Serif Typefaces

Franklin Gothic is used in this sentence.

Futura is used in this sentence.

Helvetica is used in this sentence.

Trebuchet is used in this sentence.

Univers is used in this sentence.

Verdana is used in this sentence.

A longer sentence set in Franklin Gothic typeface:
An inadequate world-view can leave a person or a population unable to make solid and workable decisions.
(Eikleberry, 2000)

Some History
Fonts without wings are called "sans serifs." Some of the earliest sans serif fonts were cut in Italy in the early 1500s.

FIGURE 4–13 Overview of Sans Serif type

Script

Instructional Application

Like Black Letter, Script and Cursive type have **limited** application in instructional materials since they can be difficult to read in text of any length. They are often used to designate different voice (as I do throughout this book with this Juleswriting typeface.) As with Black Letter, script typefaces are used frequently in certificates, to designate a historical period of time, and in small places where ornamentation may be desired.

Script forms were considered "gimmick" fonts because they looked handwritten. Cursive (another word for Script) forms, however, go back to the earliest days of printing when monks used cursive forms to write. As printing caught on and spread, the monks adopted faster forms to keep up with the increased pace of their writing.

Examples

Brush Script typeface

g

Some Script Typefaces

Brush Script is used in this sentence.

Lucida handwriting is used in this sentence.

Freestyle script is used in this sentence.

A longer sentence set in Brush Script typeface:

An inadequate world-view can leave a person or a population unable to make solid and workable decisions.

(Eikleberry, 2000)

FIGURE 4–14 Overview of Script type

Decorative: Symbol

Instructional Application	Examples

Symbol typefaces and Dingbats **provide access to a variety of images that can be used for instructional purposes.** For example, if you were teaching keyboarding, you might make the image to the right that shows the middle row keys. These keys come from the Qwerty typeface, a symbol typeface. To the right you also see Webdings, another symbol typeface.

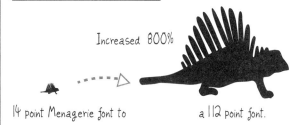

Qwerty typeface is used here.

The keys come from typing the letters a, s, d, f, g, h, j, k, k, l, ;, :

Middle row keys:

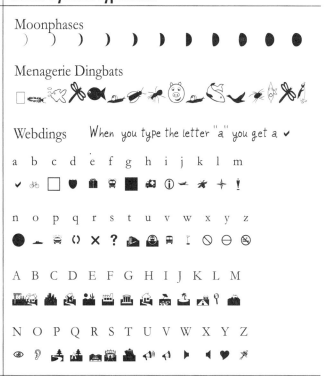

Increased 800%

14 point Menagerie font to   a 112 point font.

Some Symbol Typefaces

Moonphases

Menagerie Dingbats

Webdings   When you type the letter "a" you get a ✔

a b c d e f g h i j k l m

n o p q r s t u v w x y z

A B C D E F G H I J K L M

N O P Q R S T U V W X Y Z

FIGURE 4–15 Overview of Decorative: Symbol type

Decorative: Display

Instructional Application	Examples

Decorative typefaces are often **used for titles, headings, and other display purposes** because they are **tiring to read for anything that is very lengthy.**

While extensive use of decorative typefaces is generally discouraged in instructional materials, they can be used quite effectively in small amounts to **create a mood** or act in part as a **metaphor** for a topic

Some History

Decorative typefaces (also called Ornamentals) have been around since the 1800s. Recently the World Wide Web and the proliferation of digital type tools have made Decorative fonts some of the most developed fonts today. Even though there are a large number of these Decorative fonts, they do not share the widespread acceptance of the older more classic typefaces (see Figure 4.19 for a list).

Decorative typefaces are categorized into two groups: display and symbol. This section of the chart covers display typefaces.

Really Bad Typewriter typeface

Some call these Grunge typefaces

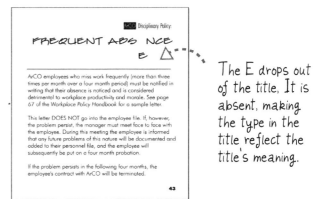

ArCO Disciplinary Policy:

FREQUENT ABS NCE

The E drops out of the title, It is absent, making the type in the title reflect the title's meaning.

ArCO employees who miss work frequently (more than three times per month over a four month period) must be notified in writing that their absence is noticed and is considered detrimental to workplace productivity and morale. See page 67 of the Workplace Policy Handbook for a sample letter.

This letter DOES NOT go into the employee file. If, however, the problem persist, the manager must meet face to face with the employee. During this meeting the employee is informed that any future problems of this nature will be documented and added to their personnel file, and the employee will subsequently be put on a four month probation.

If the problem persists in the following four months, the employee's contract with ArCO will be terminated.

43

Some Display Typefaces

Really Bad Typewriter is used in this sentence.

Ravie is used in this sentence.

Litterbox is used in this sentence.

A longer sentence set in Really Bad Typewriter typeface:
An inadequate world-view can leave a person or a population unable to make solid and workable decisions.
(Eikleberry, 2000).

FIGURE 4–16   Overview of Decorative: Display type

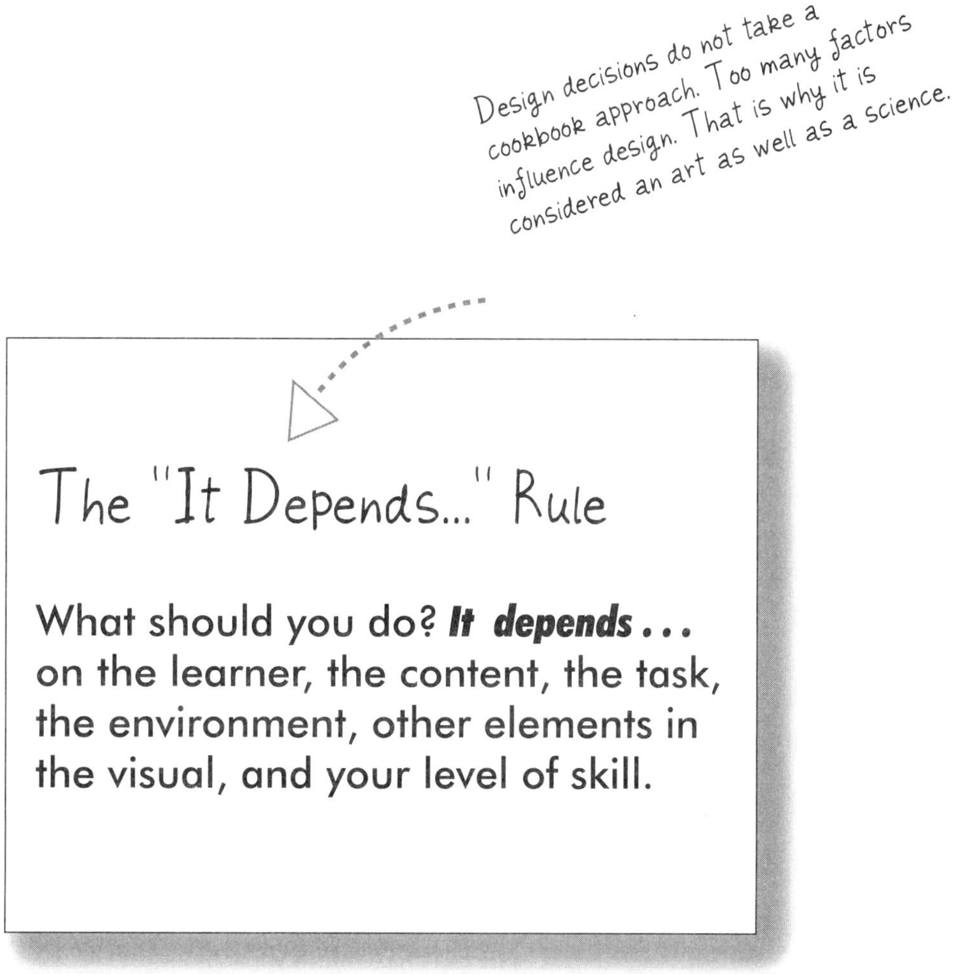

Design decisions do not take a cookbook approach. Too many factors influence design. That is why it is considered an art as well as a science.

The "It Depends..." Rule

What should you do? *It depends...* on the learner, the content, the task, the environment, other elements in the visual, and your level of skill.

FIGURE 4–17   Book design rule for type and other tools, actions and perceptions

Classic sans serif typefaces include

- Franklin Gothic
- Futura
- Helvetica
- Univers

I tend to use typefaces from this list almost exclusively. I like these faces for the reason most people do. They are readable and legible, and they are safe bets for instructional materials. To make instructional materials look more interesting and unique, I tend to mix the classic serifs with the classic sans serif faces (see Figure 4-19).

Black (1990) suggests that the unique properties of instruction be your guide to instructional typeface selection. If special character sets are needed, such as unique accents or mathematical symbols (see Figure 4-20), then a typeface that either provides these or works well with another typeface that does should be considered. If an instructional piece must be copied many times, then a typeface that maintains its legibility over frequent copies would be considered.

For most people, decisions about type boil down to the decision of whether to use serif or sans serif typefaces. There is a widespread belief that most people prefer reading body text set in a serif typeface. Popular books like *The Non-Designer's Web Book* (Willams & Tollett, 1998)

Classic Typefaces

You can't go wrong with a collection of these typefaces.

Serif	Sans Serif
Baskerville	**Franklin Gothic**
Bembo	Futura
Bodoni	**Futura Black**
Caslon	Helvetica
Centaur	Univers
Century	
Clarendon	
Garamond	
Times New Roman	

FIGURE 4–18   Classic type faces

recommend a serif typeface for extended **text**, suggesting that serifs are most appropriate when readability is a concern. **Readability** is defined as "how easy it is to read a lot of text, extended text, pages and pages of text" (Williams & Tollett, 1998, p. 214). (See Figure 4–21) for a discussion on legibility vs. readability. White (1988) and Hartley (1996) aren't as directive, citing research that fails to find any significant difference between serif and sans serif text related to readability. While White (1988) suggests that reading ease may be improved because the serif leads the eye from one letter to the next, this proposition has not been substantiated by research.

On the other hand, sans serif fonts have a reputation for clarity. Williams and Tollett (1998) suggest using a sans serif type to improve legibility. **Legibility** is defined as how easy it is to recognize short bursts of text, such as headlines and titles (Williams & Tollett, 1998). Many consider sans serif type more legible for computer-based instruction or presentation, since the resolution of computer monitors is often not great enough to show the serifs, making the typeface, especially when it is small, and difficult to read. Again, as with the readability literature, there is not a large body of research that substantiates these claims.

Miles Tinker (1963), who has done extensive research on typefaces, considers legibility and readability to be the same. Tinker investigated legibility by measuring speed of perception,

This would probably be easy for children to read because of the Clarendon typeface.

Many people have these typefaces so you'll see this combination a lot.

Franklin Gothic

Clarendon body text is used here to show you what it looks like when combined with the Franklin Gothic typeface as a heading.

Helvetica

Times New Roman body text is used here to show you what it looks like when combined with the Helvetica typeface as a heading.

Futura

Bodoni body text is used here to show you what it looks like when combined with the Futura typeface as a heading.

Univers

Caslon body text is used here to show you what it looks like when combined with the Univers typeface as a heading.

I've had really good results with this elegant combination, but only when I do not have a lot of body text.

This looks elegant but doesn't lose any readability.

FIGURE 4–19   Mixing classic serif and sans serif typefaces

FIGURE 4–20   Typeface with unique symbols

Symbol Typeface

a b c d e f g h i
α β χ δ ε φ γ η ι

j k l m n o p q r
φ κ λ μ ν ο π θ ρ

s t u v w x y z
σ τ υ ϖ ω ξ ψ ζ

What is the difference between legibility and readability?

Legibility
How easy it is to read **short bursts of text**, such as headlines, bullets, and signs. Sans Serif typefaces are preferred when legibility is the goal.

Williams and Tollet, 1998 (Not research based)

Readability
How easy it is to read a lot of text or *long text passages*. Serif typefaces are preferred when readability is the goal.

FIGURE 4–21   Legibility vs. readability

perceptibility at a distance, perceptibility in peripheral vision, visibility, eye movements, and other similar calculations. In Tinker's research, Roman typefaces had the best legibility and Black Letter the least, as measured by learner speed. The difference between Roman, Square Serif, and Sans Serif typefaces, however, was not significantly different. Black Letter typefaces were significantly linked to decreased reading speed. Even though reading speeds were higher for some Roman typeface (Garamond and Times New Roman) learners preferred the Square Serifs typeface Chelthenham, indicating preference for typefaces that are heavier in appearance. Black Letter typefaces were considered the hardest to read quickly and were the only typefaces where speed of reading and learner preference results matched.

What does this mean for you? First, since research shows no significant readability/ legibility differences between serifs and sans serifs, you can feel free to use what you and your audience prefer. Williams (1994, p. 87) suggests: "If the only sans serifs you have in your font family are Helvetica and Avant Garde, the best thing you can do for your pages is invest in a sans serif family that includes a strong, heavy black face." In other words, learn to use a big, wide sans serif typeface in combination with a lighter font. Try this strategy and you will see your pages or screen designs come alive with headings that are especially bold, making a nice contrast with body text that is lighter and more elegant (see Figure 4-22 Part A). Also consider using a serif typeface in the body text to provide extra contrast with the serif heading as in Part B.

Type Category Summary

Test yourself by matching the typeface with its description. Draw lines or fill in the blanks on Figure 4-23, and use the small chart at the bottom of the figure to check your understanding. Figure 4-24 is a quick overview of the type families and their recommended use for instructional materials.

In the next section you will find other important information about type for instructional purposes, such as attributes of type that make a difference in readability. For example, a lower case letter that is a little taller and wider than normal is considered easier to read. Additionally, several layout characteristics related to text are important to educators.

A.   B.

Look here
This body text does
not have much
contrast with
the heading.

Look here
This body text has
more contrast
with the heading.

Look here
This body text does
not have much
contrast with
the heading.

Look here
This body text has
more contrast
with the heading.

There is more contrast in B than in A
because of the mix of serif and sans
serif typefaces.

FIGURE 4–22   Typeface contrast

 It is time to take a break from reading and check out the website information (Chapter 4 > More info) on creating text blocks. There you will find an overview and step-by-step instructions for using either Microsoft Word or Adobe Illustrator text blocks.

 You can also take part in an activity that explores an important part of type we haven't covered yet—expressing emotion. Use just letters (no clip art) in this activity to describe the following words: collaboration, synergy, alienation, and bossiness (see Figure 4–25). Use the format you see in Figure 4–25 (the four boxes). Create a visual solution. Then visit the book website (Chapter 4 > Web activity) to compare your solution to those of others.

CAN YOU TALK TYPE?

"I'm not so sure about using Paris for instruction. Verdana's x-height is better."

"Paris *is* elegant, but I agree, we need something more readable for training."

What are these people talking about? You'll learn ahead that x-height refers to the height of a typeface's lowercase letters. Figure 4–26 shows how much x-height can range from typeface to typeface. The Verdana x-height for a 100 point lowercase *x* is twice the size of Paris 100 point lowercase *x*.

Things like x-height and serifs are called *type attributes*; these attributes are responsible for giving each typeface its unique appearance (see Figure 4–27). Not all of these attributes have an instructional impact (though x-height does!), but those that do will be described in some detail after we've identified all of the type attributes.

Test yourself

Match type category names to descriptions

Script   **A**   _____ Formal, old-fashioned, and used on certificates

Black Letter   **B**   _____ Highly readable on paper but serifs often disappear on a computer screen

Decorative   **C**   _____ Considered highly readable

Georgia   **D**   _____ Often preferred for computer display, particulary so when the font size is small

Square Serif   **E**   _A_ Looks like handwriting

Verdana   **F**   _____ Often more expressive than legible, encompasses symbols and dingbats

Roman Old Style   **G**   _____ A Web font with serifs

Sans Serif   **H**   _____ A Web font without serifs

Answers: Cover these up while you take the test.

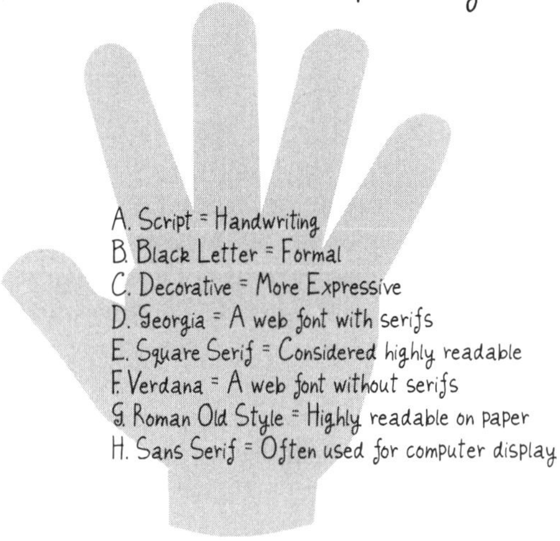

A. Script = Handwriting
B. Black Letter = Formal
C. Decorative = More Expressive
D. Georgia = A web font with serifs
E. Square Serif = Considered highly readable
F. Verdana = A web font without serifs
G. Roman Old Style = Highly readable on paper
H. Sans Serif = Often used for computer display

FIGURE 4–23 Typeface test

Family	Classics	Instructional Application
Black Letter	No identified classic 𝔒𝔩𝔡 𝔈𝔫𝔤𝔩𝔦𝔰𝔥 𝔱𝔶𝔭𝔢𝔣𝔞𝔠𝔢	Drop caps, directing attention, historical emphasis, certificates
Roman: *Old Style*	Garamond, Times New Roman	Very readable
Roman: *Modern*	Bodoni	Elegant, but can be difficult to read in long passages
Roman: *Transitional*	Bembo, Caslon, Centaur	Very readable
Square Serif	Century, **Clarendon**, Georgia	Very readable
Sans Serif	**Franklin Gothic**, Futura, Helvetica, Trebuchet, Univers, Verdana	Very legible, bold versions especially good for headings
Script	*No identified classic* *Kunstler Script*	Can seem approachable or formal
Decorative: *Display*	No identified classic Kristen typeface	Good for establishing mood
Decorative: *Symbol*	No identified classic ⬛ Webdings	Good for symbols and images

FIGURE 4-24 Instructional applications of typefaces

WHAT ARE THE ATTRIBUTES OF TYPE?

Let's explore each type attribute in more detail. The numbers in the following list refer to the labels in Figure 4-27.

1. *Ascender* — the part of a lowercase letter that rises above its body. The letters *b, d, f, h, k, l,* and *t* have ascenders.
2. *Descender* — the part of a lowercase letter that falls below its baseline. The letters *g, j, p,* and *y* have descenders.
3. *Caps height* — the height of an uppercase letter measured from the baseline.
4. *Ascender height* — the height of the tallest part of a letter.

Collaboration

Synergy

Alienation

Bossiness

FIGURE 4–25 Chapter 4 Web activity

Verdana is twice
as big.

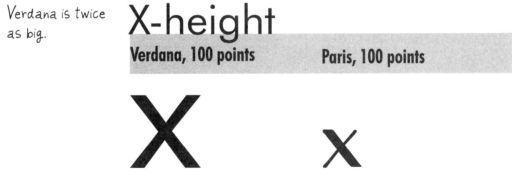

FIGURE 4–26 Comparing x-height

5. *X-height* — the height of a lowercase letter without ascenders or descenders. The height of the letters x (or $a, c, e, i, m, n, o, r, s, u, v, w, z$) gives you the x-height of a typeface. In terms of instructional impact, generally speaking, letters with larger x-heights are considered easier to read.

6. *Bowl* — the curved portion of a character that encloses a counter (the enclosed or partially enclosed area of a type character). The letters $a, b, c, d, e, g, h, m, n, o, p, q$ have bowls.

7. *Serif* — means wings. Serifs on a typeface are the small end strokes on a character. Most people seem to prefer serif type for reading large bodies of text.

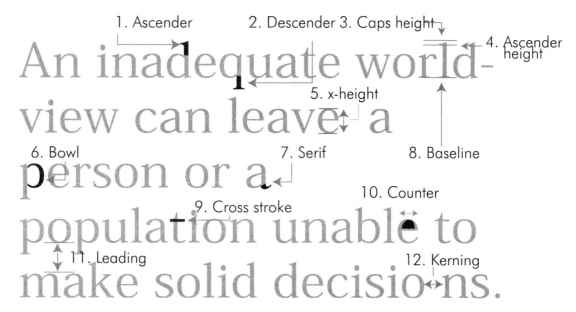

FIGURE 4–27   Type attributes

8. *Baseline* — the line on which the bases of upper and lower case letters rest, not including descenders.
9. *Cross stroke* — the horizontal stroke that crosses the vertical stroke of a type character.
10. *Counter* — the enclosed or partially enclosed area of a type character, including the letters $a, b, c, d, e, g, b, m, n, o, p$ and q. Readability is thought to increase with wider counters.
11. *Leading* — the vertical space between lines of text, called *line spacing* in some computer programs.
12. *Kerning* — the horizontal space between individual characters or letters in a word.

WHICH TYPE ATTRIBUTES ARE IMPORTANT FOR INSTRUCTION?

Of the attributes listed previously, five are important for instructional visuals: x-height, serifs, counters, leading, and kerning.

x-height

FIGURE 4–28   X-height

X-Height

Taller x-heights in text passages (Figure 4–28) can be easier for people to read because the additional height emphasizes the lowercase letters. A teacher creating instruction for children, would be wise to choose a typeface with a larger x-height, like Georgia (a typeface designed for the Web) or Clarendon, than one like Paris or Bodoni (see Figures 4–29 and 4–30).

FIGURE 4–29   Taller x-heights better for readers

All of these typefaces are 30 points. Clarendon has the tallest x-height.

Bodoni   Georgia   Clarendon

30 point typeface

The planets in our solar system are: Mercury, Venus, Earth, Mars, Jupiter, Saturn, Uranus, Neptune, and Pluto. To help you remember these names try to remember this sentence: My Very Earthy Mother Just Served Us Nine Pizzas.

This is the Paris 18 point typeface. Paris has a small x-height.

The planets in our solar system are: Mercury, Venus, Earth, Mars, Jupiter, Saturn, Uranus, Neptune, and Pluto. To help you remember these names try to remember this sentence: My Very Earthy Mother Just Served Us Nine Pizzas.

This is the Clarion 18 point typeface. Clarion has a large x-height.

FIGURE 4–30   Comparing readability of typefaces with different x-heights

Serif

a↵

FIGURE 4–31   Serif typeface

Serif or Sans Serif?

As you previously read, one widely held belief is that using a serif typeface (Figure 4-31) is best for long passages of paper-based text, and using sans serif typeface is best for computer displays and headings. Instructional technology research, however, has found no significant difference when comparing the effectiveness of serifs versus sans serifs for instructional materials, with one exception. Use of very small (under 10 points) serif typefaces is discouraged for computer displays because the serifs disappear (see Figure 4-32).

Some say that serifs are more readable on paper and sans-serifs are more readable on a computer screen. There isn't any research that supports these claims other than the research that shows that any serif type 10 points and lower can be difficult to read on a computer screen.

Garamond type. 18 point and 9 point.

Some say that serifs are more readable on paper and sans-serifs are more readable on a computer screen. There isn't any research that supports these claims other than the research that shows that any serif type 10 points and lower can be difficult to read on a computer screen.

Franklin type. 18 point and 9 point.

FIGURE 4–32   Serif vs. sans serif

Where does that leave you? Does this mean anything goes? To be safe, experiment with both serif and sans serif typefaces and test them out with representatives of your learner audience. Don't be too shy about using serifs on the Web either, particularly when you use the Georgia typeface designed specifically for the Web.

Counter

FIGURE 4–33   Counter space

Counters

There are two major differences between counters and x-heights. Whereas x-heights are the *height* of a lowercase letter, counters (see Figure 4-33) are the *width* of the enclosed part of uppercase letters (A, B, D, O, P, Q) and lowercase letters (a, b, d, g, o, p, q). Some consider wide counters to improve legibility and readability. Figure 4-34 displays the difference in counter widths for the Kabel and Futura Light Condensed typefaces.

Figures 4-35 and 4-36 show the effect of counter size on similar text passages. All in all, narrow counters are difficult to read, as both of these figures show.

At times, however, narrow counters are helpful for squeezing words into tight places (see Figure 4-37).

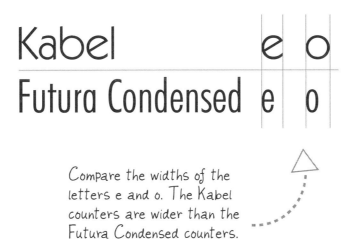

Compare the widths of the letters e and o. The Kabel counters are wider than the Futura Condensed counters.

FIGURE 4–34   Comparing typeface counters

Kabel An inadequate world-view can leave a person or a population unable to make solid and workable decisions. Problems cannot be solved, and the resulting environment is not conducive to either lasting success or satisfaction. There is little doubt that many of the failed or failing policies in today's society are like bedroom doors installed in a house with a faulty foundation.

Futura Condensed An inadequate world-view can leave a person or a population unable to make solid and workable decisions. Problems cannot be solved, and the resulting environment is not conducive to either lasting success or satisfaction. There is little doubt that many of the failed or failing policies in today's society are like bedroom doors installed in a house with a faulty foundation.

Which do you think is easier to read?

FIGURE 4–35   Comparing readability of typefaces with different counters

This is a text passage with large counters. You might try using large counters when you need text to be especially legible.

This is a text passage with small counters. You might try using small counters when you need text to fit into a narrow space.

This is 18-point Univers

This is 18-point Onyx

FIGURE 4–36   Choosing typefaces based on counter width

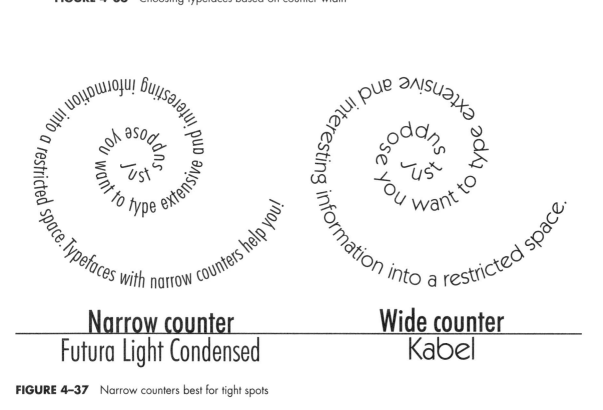

Narrow counter
Futura Light Condensed

Wide counter
Kabel

FIGURE 4–37   Narrow counters best for tight spots

Should You Change the Leading?

When you change leading, you either increase or decrease the vertical space between lines of text (see Figure 4-38).

Usually the leading is automatically set to be 20 percent larger than the point size of your font. Therefore if you've set your font size to 12, your leading will be approximately 20 percent larger, or 14.4. As a rule of thumb, the longer the line of text, the greater the leading should be.

By adjusting leading, you can subtly change the look and feel of instruction. For example, if you want to make your instruction seem more approachable to a group of people who typically do not like reading, try increasing the leading. They'll see more white space and may be less intimidated by the amount of text they need to read.

Leading is often used to adjust the spacing of text lines in projected slide displays. The software often sets the leading too high, as in Figure 4-39. Decreasing the leading (see Figure 4-40) separates the title more distinctly from the bullet points and groups both the title and bullet points.

Keep in mind that leading in either extreme (low or high) is not optimal for readability Figure 4-41 shows different leading combinations.

popul
↕ Leading
make

FIGURE 4–38   Leading, the space between lines

Too much leading here. The words in the title do not seem to belong together.

Importance of World-View

- Decisions

- Problem-solving

- Satisfaction

FIGURE 4–39 Slide display leading, version 1

Leading has been decreased here. Notice how the words in the title seem to belong together now. The same thing happens with the bullet points.

Importance of World-View

- Decisions
- Problem-solving
- Satisfaction

FIGURE 4–40 Slide display leading, version 2

Leading is too small here

Below is 11-point text with 7 point leading.

An inadequate world-view can leave a person or a population unable to make solid and workable decisions. Problems cannot be solved, and the resulting environment is not conducive to either lasting success or satisfaction.

Leading is too large here

Below is 11-point text with 18-point leading.

An inadequate world-view can leave a person or a population unable to make solid and

workable decisions. Problems cannot be solved, and the resulting environment is not

conducive to either lasting success or satisfaction.

FIGURE 4–41 Leading extremes

Rimar (1996), in his review of design guidelines for screen-based programs (computer-based training), suggests that readability and comprehension increases as leading increases. Double spacing, as opposed to single spacing, is recommended. More information about leading follows in the layout section of this chapter. For specific, research-based guidelines on how to set leading according to type size and line length, see Table 4–1 later in this chapter.

What is Kerning?

Kerning

io↔ns

FIGURE 4–42   Kerning, changing the horizontal space between letters

"Type from a computer is ugly," a typography instructor informs his class. He then adds, "To make type look good, you need to letter space." This instructor is talking about kerning. By kerning, or letter spacing, you can make words look better.

Kerning is the action of increasing or decreasing the horizontal space between individual characters or letters in a word (see Figure 4–42). Kerning is used mostly for type sizes larger than 30 points, and is generally performed to improve the appearance of a heading. In Figure 4–43 notice how the appearance of the word "WORLD" is improved by decreasing the kerning between the letters *W* and *O* and increasing the kerning between the letters *L* and *D*. Some research supports kerning. According to Rivlin, Lewis, and Davies-Cooper (1990), applying proper kerning improves appearance. Varying the width between letters, if done correctly, can also increase readability (Lynch 1994).

Kerning can also make things fit better. For example, when creating the chart to show the correspondence between letters of our alphabet and symbol characters (Figure 4–44), I used kerning to align the letters with the symbols. Without kerning the last letters in the list are not aligned, making the symbol for *x* look like it is the symbol for *y*.

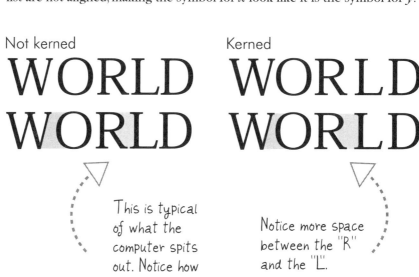

FIGURE 4–43   Kerning to improve appearance

How Does Type Affect Layouts?

According to Hartley (1996), "the way in which a designer uses space on a page greatly affects how easily the reader can understand and retrieve information from it" (1996). This statement applies equally to screen-based information. Issues such as text alignment, line length, type sizes, and cueing devices all impact the effectiveness of your instruction.

These symbols were not kerned. It is hard to tell here which symbol goes with which letter. For example, what symbol goes with z?

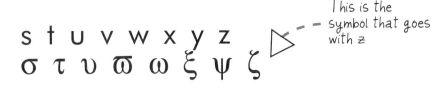

This is the symbol that goes with z

s t u v w x y z
σ τ υ ϖ ω ξ ψ ζ

These symbols were kerned in order to make them line up with the letters above

s t u v w x y z
σ τ υ ϖ ω ξ ψ ζ

FIGURE 4–44   Kerning to improve comprehension

Left aligned is considered the easiest to read.

Text where the **left** edge is **aligned**, leaving the right edge to fall unevenly from line to line, is considered ragged right, or left aligned. Ragged right, or left-aligned text, is considered to be the most readable and is highly encouraged for long instructional text passages over all other alignment types.

This is a ragged right edge.

This is a ragged left edge.

Right-aligned text does the opposite, like this paragraph. Here, the right side is aligned and the left side is ragged. Right-aligned text can be difficult to read in long passages so should be avoided in lengthy instructional text. Right aligned text, however, can add an element of interest and at times is useful when aligning text to a graphic or another column of text.

Right aligned text is considered hard to read

Centered text is the most formal, but it can be hard to read because of the ragged edges.

Text that is **centered** in a document falls exactly in the middle for each line of text. While it may be a quick way to create balance on a page (everything is centered evenly), it is hard to read, and it can look boring. Novice designers tend to overdo centered text for that reason. These designers think centered text improves the appearance of their work, when in reality it makes their work look less, rather than more, professional. Sometimes, however, centered text in instructional materials is perfectly appropriate, (especially when used for short segments of text, such as a title page) since centered text is often more formal.

Justified text is aligned on both edges, causing small gaps between letters. These small gaps can strain the eyes.

Text where both the right and left edges of text line up is considered **justified**. This type of alignment is usually avoided in instructional text since the small gaps created within the lines can be difficult to read. The learner's eyes will eventually get tired of the irregular spaces   between   words   (exaggerated   here   for   effect).

FIGURE 4–45   Examples of text alignment

Text Alignment

Alignment refers to the place where the body of text lines up along the edge of a page, screen, shape, or image. Figure 4–45 shows the four different types of alignment: left, right, centered, and justified.

Line Length

The following rules of thumb should help you select the length and size of your text. Optimal line length follows the "it depends" rule. Point size, page size, direction, and leading all play into the selection of line length. Different rules apply for text for Screen, paper, and other media. Generally speaking, if a typeface is small, the line length should be short (see Figure 4–46). People tend to dislike line lengths that are very short or very long. According to Tinker (1963), children under 10 years are most comfortable with line lengths between 2 and 3 inches.

Some suggest optimal line lengths based on the number of characters in the line, ranging from 35 to 75 characters. Given that leading plays a role in line length decision, these guidelines have limited usefulness. Tinker (1963) provides research-based guidelines that help you figure ideal leading settings for different line width and point size combinations. For example, Tinker recommends that for a line length of 5.5 inches and 12-point text the leading should be set between 13 and 16 points.

Table 4–1 simplifies Tinker's research for line lengths between 2.3 and 5.5 inches. Most computer programs default to these settings making it unnecessary to memorize these guidelines. To make things easy to remember use this guideline. Set leading 1 to 5 points larger than text when text is between 6 and 12 points.

Another rule of thumb for remembering an acceptable width of 4 to 5 inches is to use your palm as a guide (see Figure 4–47). Measure your palm until you have a good idea of where 4 to 5 inches falls. This practice, after all, is similar to using your feet to measure a foot. It comes in handy when you do not have a ruler nearby or when you simply need to eyeball whether something will fit within a column of text.

This shows how small type is easier to read when the line length is short.

Notice how small the typeface is in this sentence. It is 8-points, about as small as you can reduce a typeface and have it remain legible. It is much harder to read in long lines than short lines. Compare these two paragraphs. The top paragraph is harder to read because your eye doesn't get a break.

Notice how small the typeface is in this sentence. It is 8-points, about as small as you can reduce a typeface and have it remain legible. It is much harder to read in long lines than short lines. Compare these two paragraphs. The top paragraph is harder to read because your eye doesn't get a break.

Much easier to read!

FIGURE 4–46   Effect of line length on readability

TABLE 4–1   *Leading and text point size combinations for line lengths between 2.2 and 5.5 inches*

If your point size falls within this range …	then set your leading
6–9 points	1–4 points larger than the point size
Example Text size of 6 points	uses 8–10 point leading
10–12 points	1–5 points larger than the point size
Example Text size of 10 points …	uses 11–15 point leading.

Source: Adapted from Legibility of Print *(pp. 106–107), by Miles A. Tinker, Ames, IA: Iowa State University Press.*

FIGURE 4–47   Using your palm as a guide to line length

Other good advice related to optimal line length comes from Hartley (1996), who recommends that you break a line of text when it makes sense, based upon content and not some formula. For example, rather than conventional formatting in which text spans the length of a column or width of the page, text instead spans the length of an idea or thought. Take, for example, the following passage.

> My mother's parents were named Alonzo and Louise. She also has two brothers Frank Junior and Gene. Frank Junior and his wife Christy have two children, Stephanie and Brock. Gene and his wife Maggie have three children, Johnny, Janice, and Keighly. My mother's immediate family is made up of her husband Jackson and her three daughters, Carrie, Lazlo, and Bea.

> My mother's parents were named Alonzo and Louise.
>> She also has two brothers, Frank Junior and Gene.
>>> Frank Junior and his wife Christy have two children,
>>>> Stephanie and
>>>> Brock.
>>> Gene and his wife Maggie have three children,
>>>> Johnny,
>>>> Janice, and
>>>> Keighly.
>> My mother's immediate family is made up of
>> her husband Jackson and her three daughters,
>>> Carrie,
>>> Lazlo, and
>>> Bea.

Hartley also suggests a floating baseline—that is, breaking the bottom edge of text according to the content. Rather than filling up all of the pages, the text stops or breaks when the content warrants it.

Type Size

Type size is called point size in computer applications. The distance from the lowest point of the longest descender to the highest part of the tallest ascender is considered the point size. There are about 36 points in a ½ inch or 72 points in an inch. Notice how some type-faces are the same point size, but they look either larger or smaller based on x-height or counter size (look back at Figures 4–29 and 4–30).

Many other general rules address appropriate point sizes for legibility of different formats (projected presentations, computer-based training, and print-based instruction). Given the considerable difference in equal point sizes of different typefaces, these rules may or may not apply. Table 4–1 shows how point size can be selected based on line length and leading.

FIGURE 4–48   Testing slide/transparency legibility

FIGURE 4–49   Testing the legibility of computer screen text

For printed text and computer-based instruction, the most commonly recommended point size is 12 points. Tinker (1963) states that most type size in most textbooks falls between 10 and 12 points, with 11 the most popular. Headings are generally sized 14 points and higher.

For projected displays, a common guide is the 6 × 6 rule, which states that an overhead transparency should have no more than six lines of text and no more than six words in each line. Another guideline, the 6w × 2w rule, states that text must be legible a maximum of six screen widths distance and a minimum of two screen widths distance. Another recommendation is to hold your slide at arm's length (Figure 4-48) from your face. If you can read the slide text easily, the slide will probably be legible when projected.

If you are evaluating a slide from a computer screen, display the slide at 100 percent and back six feet away from the front of the screen (see Figure 4-49). If you can read the text from this distance, the text will most likely be visible when projected.

Another more scientific approach (Heinich, Molenda, & Russell, 1993) is to consider the dimensions of the room (see Figure 4-50). Estimate the furthest distance from which your slide will be viewed. For every 10 feet, increase the typeface ½ inch (remember 36 points is approximately ½ inch for many typefaces).

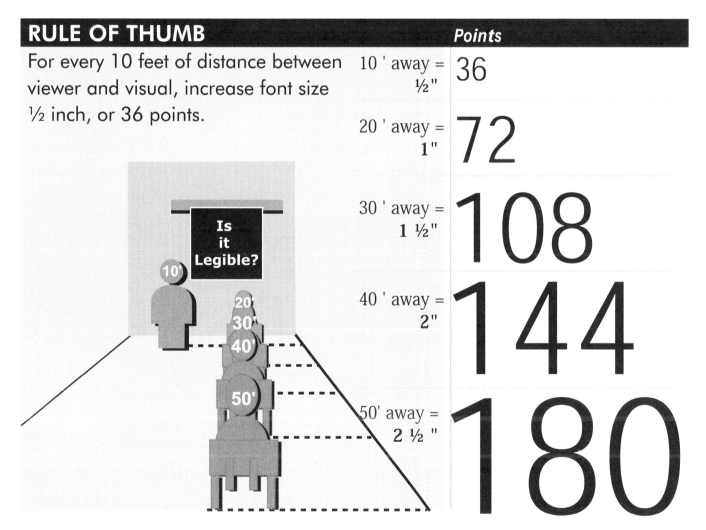

FIGURE 4–50   Guide for legibility of slides and transparencies

Cueing Devices

You can change type to signal or cue the reader to a change in your message. Changing colors, USING ALL CAPS, **bolding**, changing SIZE, changing leading, <u>underlining</u>, *italicizing*, using a contrasting typeface, and ***combining*** ANY NUMBER <u>of these cues</u> are examples of this practice.

One rule of thumb for typography is to limit the number of cues to one or at the most two combinations (notice how confusing the above sentence was to read.) Hartley (1996) suggests "a brief rule of thumb might be that there is no need to use three or more additional cues when one or two at most will do" (p. 799). Research on the effectiveness of cueing or directing information is contradictory with some finding learning gains from cues (Croft & Burton, 1995) and others finding impairment (Rivlin et al., 1990) Rimar (1996) states that to date there is minimal solid research on appropriate cueing methods.

Many use all capital letters to emphasize information, not realizing that it is hard to read more than a few uppercase words. A rule of thumb is to avoid using all caps, unless you are dealing with mathematics (Tinker, 1963) or are working with only a few words. ALL CAPITAL LETTERS ARE DIFFICULT TO READ, AS YOU CAN SEE IN THIS SHORT SENTENCE—AND IN THE SENTENCE THAT FOLLOWS. AFTER A WHILE YOUR EYES BECOME TIRED. HAVE YOU EVER NOTICED HOW HARD IT IS TO READ FOOD LABELS THAT ARE SET IN ALL CAPS?

Problems with readability associated with all caps can be explained in part by gestalt theory, which you'll learn more about later in this book. In all caps text, the eye tends to pass quickly over a word since all of the letters are the same height. Individual letters are not perceived as distinctly since they are not that different from each other (see Figure 4-51). Notice in Figure 4-52 how the top half of the word "millennium" is easier to figure out than the bottom half, for this same reason. In Figure 4-53, you can see how difficult the word "millennium" is to read when the dots over the "i's" are missing.

The all caps rule holds for italics as well. According to Raines (1989) italics should not be used for emphasis because people ignore them. *Avoid using italics in text. Italics are very difficult to read, as you can see in this short sentence and the sentence that follows. After a while your eyes become tired.* I have ignored this advice when italics are used for only a few words.

FIGURE 4–51   Comparing lowercase to uppercase readability

FIGURE 4–52   One advantage of lowercase text

Would you recognize this word without the dots?

millennium

millennium

FIGURE 4–53   Letter attributes that improve word recognition

Other types of cues include headings, such as the Summary heading that follows. Headings are also used to help learners understand the organization of content. Misanchuk (1992) recommends using no more than four levels of headings. If you have more than Four, you might consider restructuring your content. Three or fewer levels of headings are more effective, according to research by Lang (1987) and Miles (1987). Learners may have difficulty understanding the organization of text when more than three headings are used.

SUMMARY

Prior to reading this chapter, you learned about a tools, actions, and perceptions (TAP) approach to designing instructional visuals. The idea behind TAP is that tools can be used with actions to influence learner perception. Type is the first of five tools covered in the book; the others include shape, color, depth, and space.

In this book the word **type** is synonymous with **typography. Instructional typography** is defined as the art and science of using individual letters, words, and passages of text to convey an instructional message. Although typography is only one of the five essential tools for creating instructional visuals, it is perhaps the most powerful tool. Type can increase the organization of information and also communicate emotion. Not only can type be used to enhance the other tools such as shape, color, dimension, and space, it can be manipulated by actions of contrast, alignment, repetition, and proximity as well. You can select from any number of typefaces to enhance an instructional message; thousands are available for use.

Typefaces are classified into Black Letter, Roman, Square Serif, Sans Serif, Script, and Decorative **families**. Some categories, such as serif typefaces (Roman and Square Serif) and sans serif typefaces, have a preferred but not researched-based place in instructional materials. Serif typefaces are preferred for reading large passages of text, but there is no research to strongly support this preference. Likewise, sans serif typefaces are preferred for headings and computer displays, but again research doesn't strongly support or explain this preference either. Some characteristics of type, such as x-height and counter width, have some implication for instructional design, with larger x-heights and wider counters considered easier to read.

The "it depends" rule influences decisions about type. It recommends that designers consider the learner, the context, other elements in the visual, and the message as they make typeface selection decisions. A few other guidelines have been proposed, such as avoiding too many cueing devices, using classic typefaces, and considering the unique properties of the instructional unit prior to selecting a typeface.

The next chapter, Shape Tools, moves you into the second tool for creating visuals. Like type, shape is an easy tool to use, is copyright free, and can be used to make instruction easier to understand.

FOR MORE CHALLENGE

Visit Chapter 4's Challenge section on the book's website. There you'll find several instructional problems that require your visual solutions. Compare your solutions to those of others.

DISCUSSION FOR DISTANCE LEARNING

Visit the book's website (Chapter 4 > Discussion) for threaded discussion or chat questions.

REFERENCES

Black, A. (1990). *Typefaces for desktop publishing: a user guide.* London: Architecture Design and Technology Press.

Carter, R., Day, B., & Meggs, P. (1985). *Typographic design: Form and communication.* New York: Van Nostrand Reinhold.

Croft, R. S., & Burton, J. K. (1995). Toward a new theory for selecting instructional visuals (Report No. IR 016 996). In *Imagery and Visual Literacy, Annual Conference of the International Visual Literacy Association* (Tempe, AZ, October 12–16, 1994). (ERIC Document Reproduction Service No. ED 380 075)

Hartley, J. (1985). *Designing instructional text.* London: Kogan Page.

Hartley, J. (1996). Text design. *In* D. H. Jonassen (Ed.), *Handbook of research for educational communications and technology* (pp. 795–820). New York: Simon & Schuster Macmillan.

Heinich, R., Molenda, M., & Russell, J. D. (1993). *Instructional media and the new technologies of instruction.* New York: Macmillan.

Lang, K. (1987). *The writer's guide to desktop publishing.* London: Academic Press.

Lynch, P. J. (1994). Visual design for the user interface (1). *Journal of Biocommunications, 21* (1), 22–30.

Meggs, P. B., & McKelvey, R. (2000). *Revival of the fittest. Digital versions of classic typefaces.* New York: RC Publications.

Miles, J. (1987). *Design for desktop publishing.* San Francisco: Chronicle Books.

Misanchuk, E. R. (1992). *Preparing instructional text: Document design using desktop publishing.* Englewood Cliffs, NJ: Educational Technology Publications.

Raines, C. (1989). *Visual aids in business: A guide for effective presentations.* Los Altos, CA: Crisp Publications.

Rimar, G. I. (1996). Message design guidelines for screen-based programs. *Journal of Computer Assisted Learning, 12,* 245–256.

Rivlin, C., Lewis, R., & Davies-Cooper, R. (1990). *Guidelines for screen design.* Oxford, England: Blackwell Scientific Publications.

Spiekermann, E., & Ginger, E. M. (1993). *Stop stealing sheep and find out how type works.* Mountain View, CA: Adobe Press.

Tinker, M. A. (1963). *Legibility of print.* Ames: Iowa State University Press.

Tinker, M. A. (1965). *Bases for effective reading.* Ames: Iowa State University Press.

White, J. V. (1988). *Graphic design for the electronic age: The manual for traditional and desktop publishing.* New York: Watson-Guptill Publications.

Williams, R. (1994). *The non-designer's design book.* Berkeley, CA: Peachpit Press.

Williams, R., & Tollett, J. (1998). *The non-designer's web book: An easy guide to creating, designing, and posting your own web site.* Berkeley, CA: Peachpit Press.

CHAPTER 5

Shape Tools

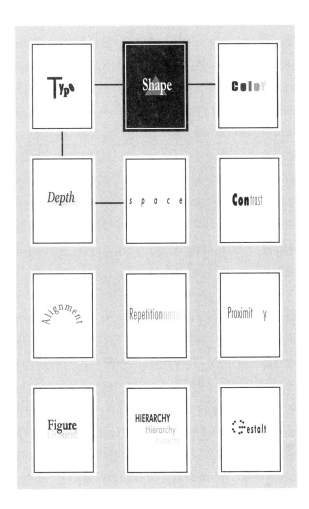

Get into shape.

NOTES ABOUT THE OPENING VISUAL

In this chapter you learn to use basic shapes in instructional visuals. Notice how most of the chapter cover image is made up of a simple shape, the rectangle. The underlying shape of the image is a rectangle, the elements on the shape are rectangles, and even the page is a rectangle. I wanted to convey the idea of building blocks with the chapter cover image. Squares might have worked, but I liked the harmony created using rectangles.

FOCUS QUESTIONS

- Are meanings attached to shapes?
- Can shapes be used to enhance learning?
- What is the display shape?
- What do I need to know about copyright laws?

KEY TERMS

ANTI-ALIASING   a process that blends the rough edges of a rasterized image, creating a soft transition between the image and its background

BIT   the smallest unit of information processed by a computer, a computer signal

CLIP ART   line art (art that consists of just lines) or photographs found in books, on disks (Toor, 1996), and on the Web

COLOR-DEPTH   the number of color-related bits (1-bit, 4-bit, 8-bit, 16-bit, and 24-bit) a pixel can store

COPYRIGHT   legal rights for reproducing a work granted by its creator

DISPLAY SHAPE   the shape of the background upon which an image is placed for viewing

GRAPHIC FILE EXTENSION   the last three characters in a file name that designate a particular type of graphic format (.bmp, .jpg, .eps, .tif, wmf)

PIXEL   short for picture element

PORTS   devices that accept data transferred to the computer, including wireless transfer as well as serial, parallel, USB, and IEEE 1394 transfer using cables

RASTER GRAPHICS   graphics made up of a collection of pixels, and edited by changing pixels; also called bitmap graphics

RESOLUTION   visual quality based on the number of pixels along the height and width of an image or display

SCANNERS   devices that pass a light-emitting element across an image to capture it in digital format

SHAPE   "any element that is used to give or determine form" (Peterson, 1997, p, 38)

VECTOR GRAPHICS   graphics formed by vectors (mathematical formulas) and edited by changing the outlines and fills of a shape

INTRODUCTION

Sylvia and Zack, the instructional designer and graphic artist/programmer you met in Chapter 1, are working on a computer-based training menu and have only one day to come up with a prototype. The computer-based training will include lessons for new employees in a food chain. Sylvia watches over Zack's shoulder as they brainstorm what the menu should look like.

While he is working Zack has these questions:

- What shapes should I use?
- Which shapes can I combine effectively?
- Which shapes will help me group and separate information?

Sylvia is amazed when Zack comes up with an elegant solution (see Figure 5-1) based mostly on shapes: lines, rectangles, ellipses, circles, and brackets.

Sylvia has learned an important design lesson. Simple shapes are often incredibly effective, both from a functional and aesthetic perspective. Like type, they are easy for the designer to use. She watches Zack as he changes the sizes and arrangements of the shapes until the image looks balanced (you'll learn more about balance in chapter 10 on gestalt). No doubt Zack's skill helps him accomplish the task quicker than Sylvia could, but she is right when she thinks, "I could do that."

Like Zack, I've found that simple shapes are about as versatile as typography. I introduce them as the second design element because next to typography they are my most useful tool. You'll find in many instructional situations that all you really need to use is type and shape. Together they are powerful. Make a point to find and study images that rely mostly on shape, and you'll be amazed at how many examples are out there. Look at corporate logos, business card design, brochures, wrapping paper, websites, and even design on coffee cups! Shapes are everywhere and are often stunningly simple.

Shape is formally defined as "any element that is used to give or determine form" (Peterson, 1997, p, 38). The form-giving function of shape explains its influence on learning. People tend to perceive shapes as wholes (or gestalt). Gestalt is often defined as shape. A shape is seen as a unit, and anything superimposed on a shape, or aligned to it, is likely to be seen as part of that unit. Therefore, a shape can be an effective way of presenting related but distinct information as one unit.

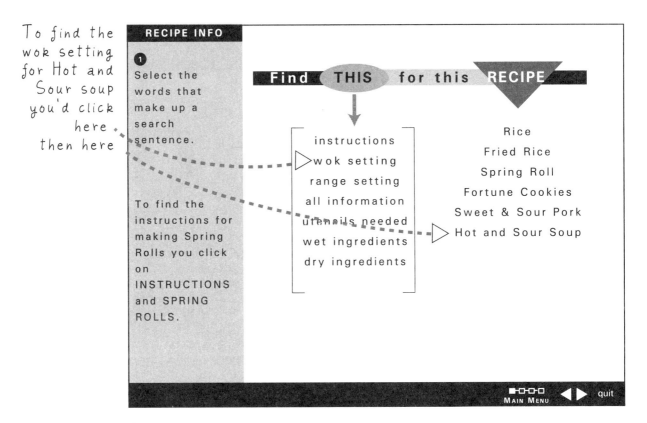

FIGURE 5–1   Food chain training menu

Consider an experiment by Pomeratz, Pristach, and Carson (1989). They showed how the mind automatically creates perceptual groupings. When people saw either:

two end parenthesis ((
or a left and right parenthesis ( )

(see top two lines in Figure 5-2, Part A) they grouped them as one unit; they saw the ((as one unit and the ( ) as one unit, even though each of these perceived units was actually composed of two distinct elements. When these people saw the two elements displayed on the bottom line of Part A, however, they didn't perceive them as one element but two, most likely because the underlying shape didn't seem like one shape (see Part B of Figure 5-2).

When you create visual instruction, you want to use shape to group or separate information according to your goals. In other words, you want to be able to come up with an overall shape that reads as a unit when you want something read as a unit. And likewise, you want to use shapes to divide information that you want to be seen differently. For example, take a look at Zack's menu in Figure 5-3. Notice how different information zones are set up by his use of rectangles? Zack uses rectangles to keep information in these zones apart from each other. He wants instructional information (see section a of Figure 5-3) to be kept separate from navigational information (sections b and c of Figure 5-3). He also wants to keep the navigation related to a cooking topic (section b) separate from navigation of the whole performance support environment (section c).

THE INSTRUCTIONAL FUNCTION OF SHAPE

You'll see how a variety of shapes are used to improve instruction in the pages ahead. Like type, most computer programs allow you access to drawing tools with which you can quickly create lines, circles, arrows, and boxes with minimal effort. Though common, these shapes have a timeless appeal. Just think about their use in many corporate logos and national flags (see Figure 5-4).

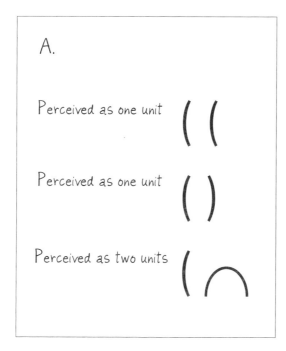 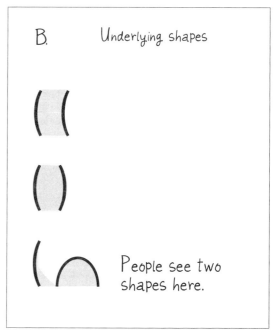

FIGURE 5-2 Shape perception

Source: Adapted from Attention and Object Perception by J.R. Pomeratz, E.A. Pristach, & C.E. Carson, In B.E. Shepp & S. Ballestero's (Eds.), Object Perception: Structure and Process. (pp. 35–90). Hillsdale, NJ: Lawrence Erlbaum Associates.

FIGURE 5–3 Information
zones in Zack's training menu

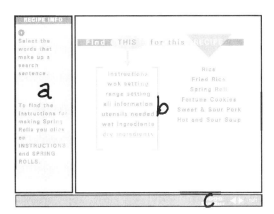

All of these flags
use simple shapes.

FIGURE 5–4 Common shapes in flags

Aside from their classic appearance, Hansen (1999) lists a variety of instructional attributes for circles, ovals, squares, rectangles, and lines (Figures 5-5 through 5-7). I've added my own list of instructional attributes for common and complex shapes (see Figures 5-8 and 5-9).

Simple Shapes

According to Hansen (1999) circles and ovals (see Figure 5-5) are used to: show unity, imply harmony, show processes, focus attention, and show elements of systems or subsystems. Since circles create a natural balance, they are easy elements for a beginner to use. Squares and rectangles (see Figure 5-6) act to contain information, facilitate comparisons, show hierarchy, and focus attention. Lines (see Figure 5-7) are used to separate and define, set boundaries, show motion and direction, make connections, show sequence, and show emotion and volume (Hansen, 1999).

Common and Complex Shapes

Common shapes (see Figure 5-8), including triangles, stars, swirls, arrows, brackets, and more, are used to provide direction, imply motion, organize and unify, make something look engaging or fun, and make connections (join items). More complex shapes come from clip art and digital images (images that have been converted to a digital form to be used on a computer.) **Clip art** can be obtained from publishers such as Dover Publications who sell thousands of copyright free images. The clip art image in Figure 5-9 that looks like a bad hair day comes from *Curious and Fantastic Creatures*, a Dover Publication. Images can also be scanned from drawings, photographs, and real objects or obtained from the Internet and software packages. You can even make up your own image by combining images (see the cow and zebra in Figure 5-9).

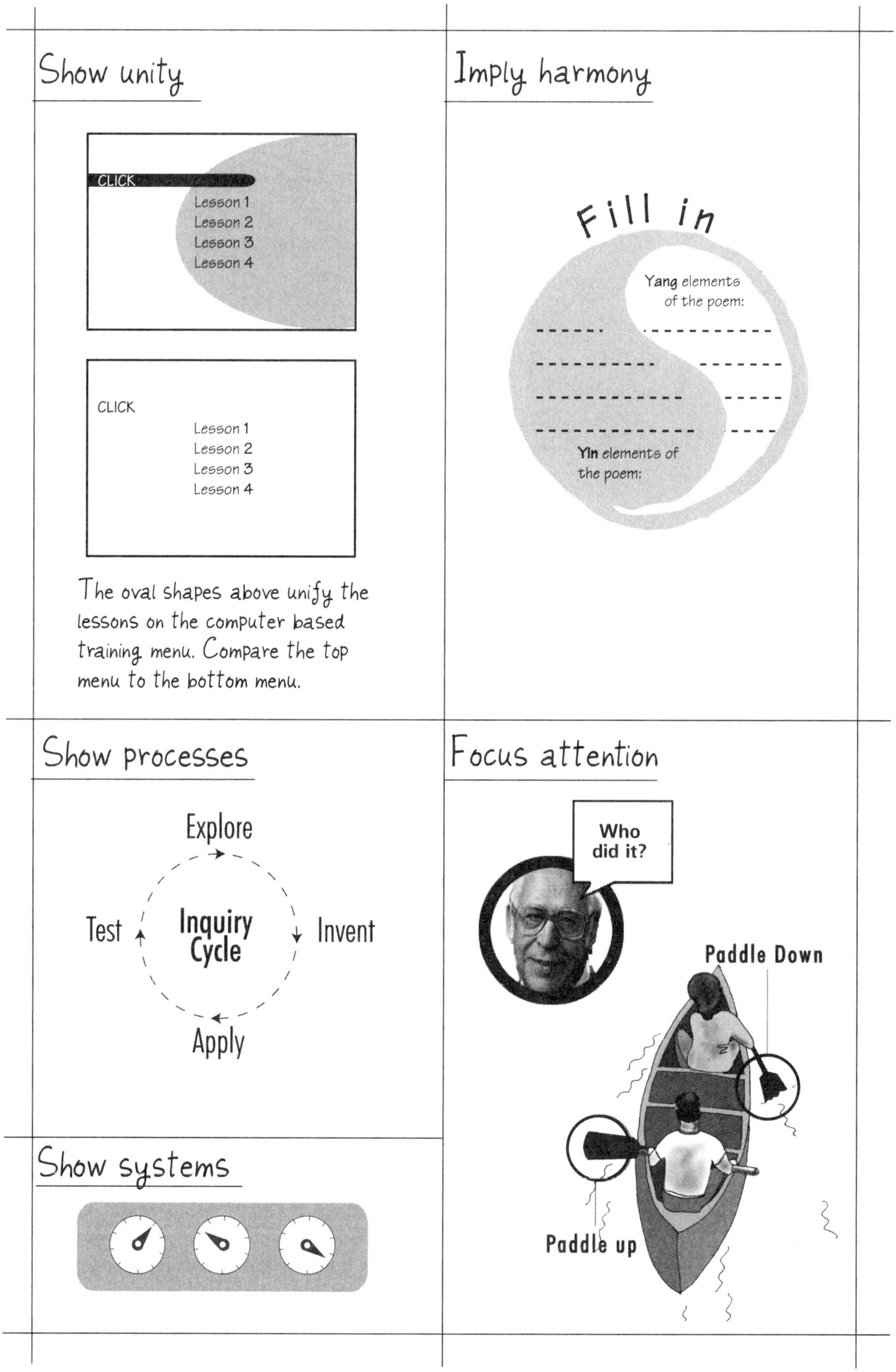

Show unity

CLICK

Lesson 1
Lesson 2
Lesson 3
Lesson 4

CLICK

Lesson 1
Lesson 2
Lesson 3
Lesson 4

The oval shapes above unify the lessons on the computer based training menu. Compare the top menu to the bottom menu.

Imply harmony

Fill in

Yang elements of the poem:

- - - - - -   - - - - - - - - - - -
- - - - - - - - -   - - - - - - - -
- - - - - - -   - - - - - - - - - -
          - - - - - - - - -

Yin elements of the poem:

Show processes

Explore

Test   Inquiry
Cycle   Invent

Apply

Show systems

Focus attention

Who did it?

Paddle Down

Paddle up

FIGURE 5–5 Common instructional purposes of circles and ovals
Source: Clip art © 1997 RomTech (dials, face)

108

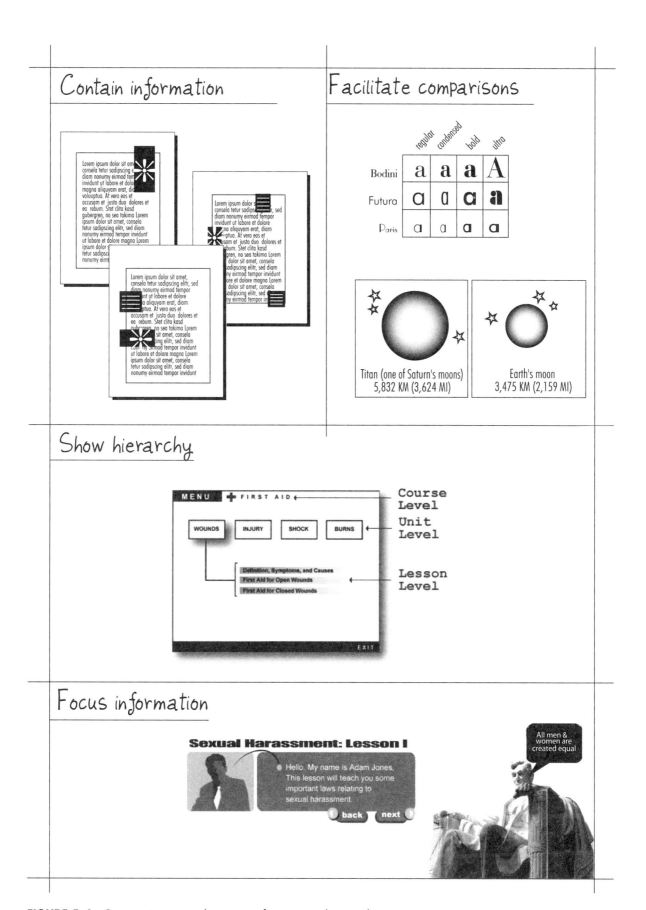

FIGURE 5–6 Common instructional purposes of squares and rectangles

Source: Clip art © 1997 RomTech (Lincoln Monument).

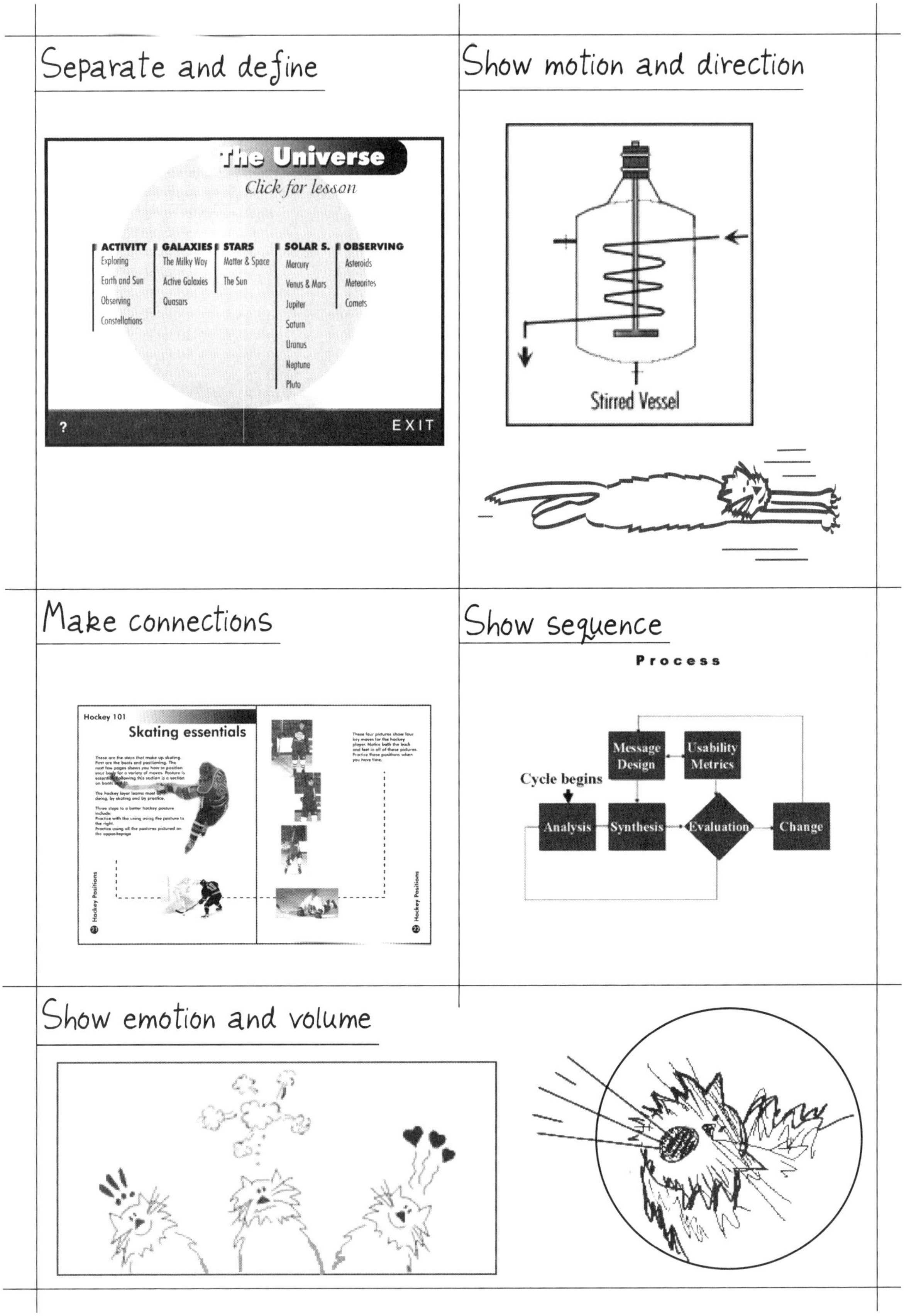

Separate and define

Show motion and direction

Make connections

Show sequence

Show emotion and volume

FIGURE 5–7 Common instructional purposes of lines

Source: Clip art © 1997 RomTech (stirred vessel).

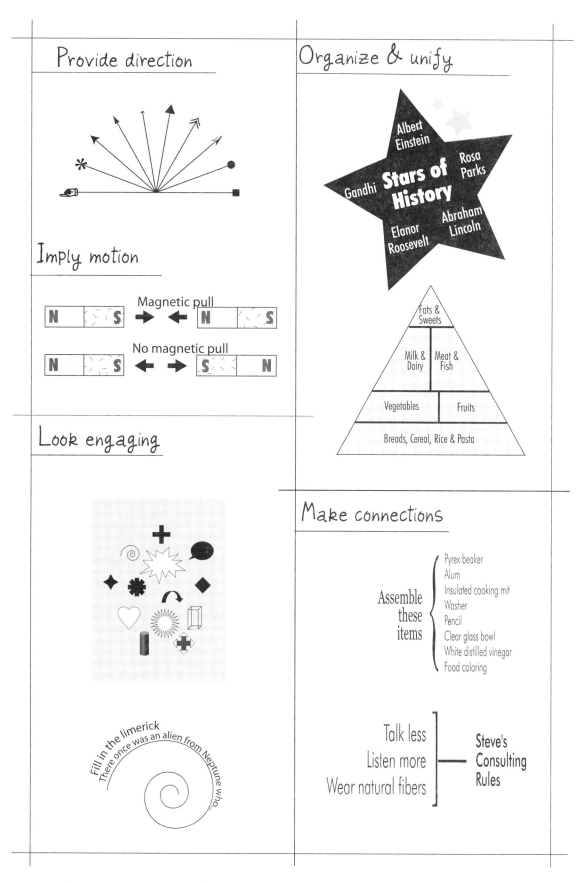

Provide direction

Imply motion

Magnetic pull

| N | S | → ← | N | S |

No magnetic pull

| N | S | ← → | S | N |

Look engaging

Fill in the limerick
There once was an alien from Neptune who...

Organize & unify

Albert Einstein

Rosa Parks

Gandhi **Stars of History**

Elanor Roosevelt

Abraham Lincoln

Fats & Sweets

Milk & Dairy | Meat & Fish

Vegetables | Fruits

Breads, Cereal, Rice & Pasta

Make connections

Assemble these items
- Pyrex beaker
- Alum
- Insulated cooking mit
- Washer
- Pencil
- Clear glass bowl
- White distilled vinegar
- Food coloring

Talk less
Listen more
Wear natural fibers
— Steve's Consulting Rules

FIGURE 5–8 Instructional purposes of other common shapes

Use clip art	Create new images

from Dover Publications

Clip art from the internet

A 3-D digital image

A digitized photopgarph

Something unusual

Computer
Graphics
lesson 1

FIGURE 5–9 Common instructional purposes of clip art (complex shapes)

WORKING WITH SHAPE

So far you've learned some instructional attributes of shape. Here you'll learn more about how to actually work with shape. A couple important considerations provide guidance. First you'll learn the importance of the underlying shape. Then you'll learn some of the nuances of bitmap and vector formats. Finally, you'll discover how you can either create or modify both simple and complex shapes.

Identifying the Display Shape

A good place to start with shape is to determine the underlying shape of your document or display. Elizabeth Boling (Heinich, Molenda, Russell, & Smaldino, 2000) suggests that early in the design process you identify the underlying shape for your instructional visual and then arrange your type and other design elements around that shape. Part of what determines that underlying shape is the **display shape**. Are you using a standard computer screen, a standard page size, or a nonstandard size? Hartley (1985, 1996) suggests that your design decisions start and revolve around this issue of display size.

I followed Hartley's advice when I created the cover image for all the chapters by considering what my end product would look like. Anything I created needed to work for both the book and the book's website. The book page size was easy since I'd be using a standard size (8½ × 11&] inches, either portrait or landscape layout). The website, however, was a challenge because not only did I need an image that looked good at different monitor resolutions, I'd need an image that would fit well on any pages that might be printed from the website.

When you create an image for use on the computer, you do not know how the user's display is set; it might be set for 640 pixels × 480 pixels or 800 pixels × 600 pixels. (**Pixels** are tiny squares through which a computer image is displayed.) To be on the safe side, most designers create for the 640 × 480 setting because it works for both situations. If you create something in an 800 pixels × 600 pixels setting and your learners use it on a 640 pixels × 480 pixels setting, your image will not fit on their screens and learners must scroll in order to see everything. On the other hand if you create something that is 640 pixels × 480 pixels and the learners' screens are set to 800 pixels × 600 pixels, the image will fit within the screen with plenty of space left over. (Sometimes what you create looks pretty small, though.) These days, more people are using the 800 × 600 setting; therefore, the 640 × 480 rule may no longer apply as much as it did. Though the following information applies to 640 × 480 resolution, you can easily apply the information to an 800 × 600 resolution.

Figure 5-10 shows you the dimensions of a 640 × 480 screen. If you want to design just a screen of information, you actually need to design for a space smaller than 640 × 480. As you can see in Figure 5-10, a recommended dimension for your design is 595 pixels × 295 pixels. Additionally, if you want people to print information from the website, you need to consider the dimensions of a printed page as well. Designs that are created to span the width of the computer screen will not fit on a printed page. Figure 5-10 shows the recommended dimensions (535 pixels × 700 pixels) for pages that display on the Web but are intended for printing. Given this information, I created a shape that worked well within the dimensions shown in Figure 5-11.

Shapes to Fit the Display

You've just learned that the underlying shape of your display will be an important determinant in how you eventually design. Generally speaking, you'll choose shapes and layouts that complement the underlying display shape. For now, consider these rules of thumb (see Figure 5-12). Tall and narrow displays require tall and/or narrow graphics or a layout that complements the tall and narrow shape of the background. Perfectly square displays tend to work well with symmetrical arrangements, and wide and shallow displays work well with

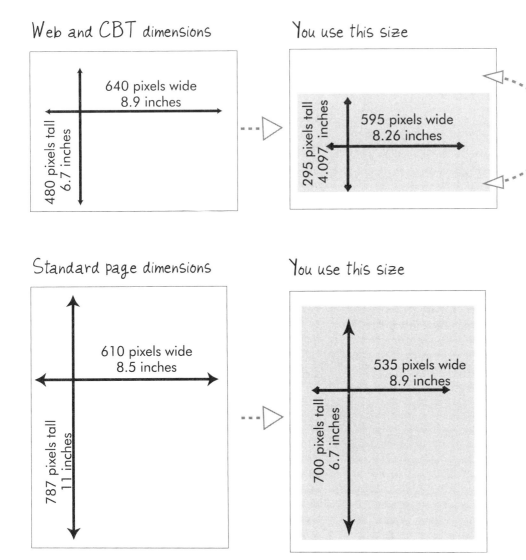

Web and CBT dimensions

640 pixels wide
8.9 inches

480 pixels tall
6.7 inches

You use this size

595 pixels wide
8.26 inches

295 pixels tall
4.097 inches

You use these dimensions when you create instruction for the computer screen. The extra spaces acccommodate the browser and other panels that are usually part of the computer screen.

Standard page dimensions

610 pixels wide
8.5 inches

787 pixels tall
11 inches

You use this size

535 pixels wide
8.9 inches

700 pixels tall
6.7 inches

FIGURE 5-10   Display shapes for computer screen visuals

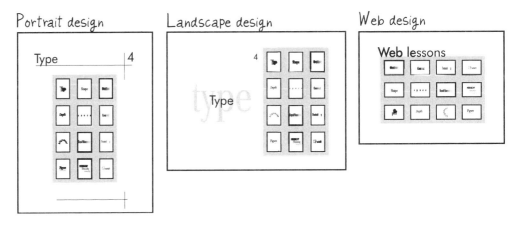

Portrait design

Type   4

Landscape design

4
Type

Web design

Web lessons

FIGURE 5-11   Versatile design for paper and computer display

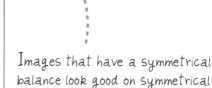

Tall thin images look good on tall & narrow displays.

Images that have a symmetrical balance look good on symmetrical displays (like this square).

Wide images look good on a wide display.

FIGURE 5-12   Shapes that fit the display

images that have either wide or shallow (or both wide and shallow) attributes. Though they are oversimplified, these guidelines are satisfactory for the purposes of this chapter. You'll learn more about working with the background display space in Chapters 6 and 10.

Shape Formats

Whether you create shapes or use shapes and images provided by others (such as clip art), you need to know about file formats. A file format is just internal information that tells the computer program how to work with your shape or graphic. Typically you'll work with two types of files, **vector graphics** (shapes made up of outlines) or **raster graphics** (shapes made up of a series of dots). Knowing how to work with both formats is important because you'll find advantages and disadvantages to each type depending upon your situation. Figure 5-13 compares how vector and raster graphics are defined, created, and modified.

It's time for a break in reading. Suppose you need to create an instructional overhead on butterflies. How would you use simple shape to create the image given the following information?

Create a visual solution to the information that follows. Then visit the book website (Chapter 5 > Web activity) to compare your solution to those of others.

Vector and Raster

Vector image created by tracing the bitmap cat to the right in a draw program

Raster image created by scanning a cat pin and touching up in a paint program

Definition

Vector graphics (or object-oriented graphics) are images created by outlines based upon mathematical formulas. Filenames with .wmf, .eps, .pct and .cdr (among others) extensions are vector files.

Raster graphics (or bitmapped graphics) are images made up of dots. These dots are simply pixels that are either filled or not filled. Filenames with bmp, .tif, .pnt, and .pcx extensions (among others) are raster files.

How they are created

Vector graphics are created by drawing programs such as Adobe Illustrator™ and Corel Draw™. You create vector graphics by drawing outlines that can be left hollow or filled.

Raster graphics are created by paint or photo editing programs such as Adobe Photoshop™, Corel Paint™, and Painter™. You create raster graphics by painting or drawing shapes.

How they are edited

Vector graphics are edited by changing the edges of the outline. Some skill is required to work with the Bezier curves and handles that allow you to make these changes.

Raster graphics are edited using erasers, paintbrushes, and smudge tools that are used to edit the image's pixels. Editing with these tools is fairly intuitive, working much like real-world pencils and paintbrushes. A feature called anti-aliasing removes some of the jagged edges of raster images. Anti-aliasing blends the edges of a rasterized image, creating a soft transition between an image and its background.

Clarity

Vector graphics are used when a clear image is needed (often for print publications) or when a graphic image does not need a lot of fine detail (like the detail you see in a photograph). Because vector images are resolution independent, their size can be changed without loss to image clarity.

Raster graphics are used for continuous tone images like photographs (images that have many subtle gradations, colors, and details). Raster graphics are resolution dependent, representing a fixed number of pixels; thus when they are increased in size, they lose image quality because the pixels are stretched out and lose clarity. Raster graphics have a slightly fuzzy appearance because they are made up of pixels (tiny squares). If you look closely at the edges of the graphic, you will see the pixel edges, called "jaggies" because they have a zigzag appearance.

FIGURE 5–13 Introduction to vector and raster graphics

While you are visiting the book website, check out the information on creating shapes using Microsoft Word and Adobe Illustrator software. Go to Chapter 5 > More info for this information.

A butterfly starts out as an egg attached to some leaves or part of a plant. The egg is a tiny round or oval object that may just look like a little ball, but the egg contains microscopic elements, such as ribs. Eggs are usually laid next to food that the caterpillar will eventually eat.

The caterpillar (or larva) is the long wormlike stage of the butterfly. If you look closely, you'll see that the worm is covered with patterns and stripes and even small hairs. The caterpillar is busy feeding and growing in this stage.

The chrysalis (or pupa) stage is where the caterpillar tissues change into insect structures. Because the chrysalis is brown or green, it blends into nature while it makes this transformation.

The adult (or imago) is the colorful butterfly with which you are familiar. At this stage the butterfly can take part in creating eggs of its own. Butterflies have courtship, mating and egg-laying rituals. The adult butterfly may also change locations and start breeding butterflies in a new habitat.

CREATING/MODIFYING COMPLEX SHAPES

The types of shapes covered so far are ones you make yourself using a software drawing or paint program. You can also work with more complex shapes by:

- Using clip art
- Modifying clip art with a draw or paint program
- Creating your own images using a scanner or a digital camera

Using Clip Art

Clip art is line art (art that consists of just lines) or photographs found in books or on disks (Toor, 1996). Most clip art is advertised as royalty free or copyright free, although there are often restrictions for using some images (Farace, 1998). The final section of this chapter covers copyright issues in greater detail.

Clip art is easy to use. You usually just insert it into the document on which you are working. For example, if you are using a word processing program such as Microsoft Word™, you do one of two things (these directions assume you are familiar with using a computer or have visited the chapter Web activity):

1. Insert > Picture > Clip art (this inserts clip art images that come with Microsoft Word™)
2. Insert > Picture > From File (this requires you to locate clip art that you've saved on disk or that is stored on a CD-ROM).

If you are using a draw program such as Adobe Illustrator™, you work with clip art in one of two ways:

1. You place the image using File > Place
2. You open the image using File > Open

Occasionally when you try to insert a picture, it doesn't appear on screen. This happens when the program you are using does not recognize the format of your file. For example, if you have a file called dog.bmp and your program doesn't recognize .bmp files, the dog.bmp file will not show up. Programs like Corel Draw, Adobe Illustrator, and PhotoShop, however, can change the format from dog.bmp into dog.jpg or whatever formats you need. You simply open the files and select a Save As… or Export the files, choosing the desired format. Table 5-1 lists some common formats by their **graphic file extension** and where they are used.

The final chapter of this text, Resources, provides more information about finding good clip art.

TABLE 5-1 *Some common file formats and their uses*

Extension	Name	Used in
.bmp	Bitmap	**Electronic presentations** (Microsoft PowerPoint) **Documents** (Microsoft Word) **CD-ROMs** and multimedia not used over the Internet
.eps	Encapsulated PostScript	**Print publications and illustrations**
.gif	Graphic Interchange Format	**Web-based documents** for images that have a continuous or flat color (see Figure 5–14)
.jpeg	Joint Photographic Experts Group	**Web-based documents** for photographic images or images that have noncontinuous colors — that have a variety of shades or gradations (see Figure 5–14)
.pdf	Portable Document Format	**For use with Adobe Acrobat**® for both screen and page output
.tiff	Tagged-Image File Format	**Print documents** when high quality and precision is required; tiff files can be changed (made either larger or smaller) without losing precision

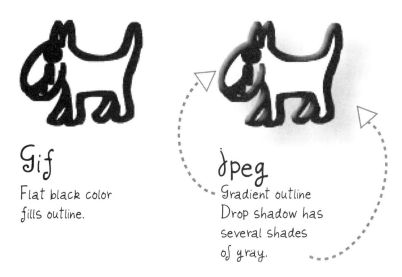

Gif
Flat black color fills outline.

Jpeg
Gradient outline
Drop shadow has several shades of gray.

FIGURE 5-14 Examples of electronic graphic files

Modifying Clip Art

One of the best things you can learn to do is to modify clip art by adding words, changing colors, adding arrows, taking out distracting images, and making other changes to suit your purpose. You can quickly make simple instruction look professional by changing the colors in the clip art to match those of your headings and lines (rules), and vice versa. Figure 5–15, for example, shows how map clip art was changed for instructional purposes.

Creating Your Own Images Using Scanners and Digital Cameras

Scanners and digital cameras share the same technology and continue to improve at increasingly affordable prices, making it easier than ever to create your own images. Although an in-depth discussion of the technical specifications related to scanners and cameras is beyond the

Step by step

These instructions show how images can be modified,

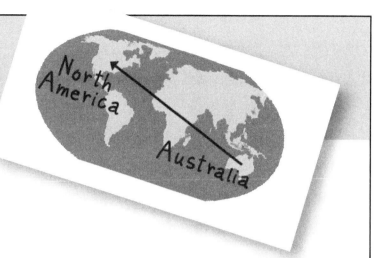

A teacher created this graphic to emphasize the distance between Australia and North America.

1 Clip art is located.

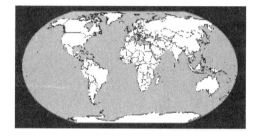

2 Distracting information is eliminated.

3 An arrow and the words Australia and North America are added.

FIGURE 5–15 Modifying clip art

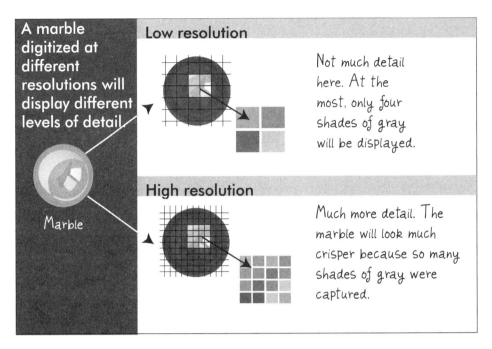

FIGURE 5-16 Low vs. high resolution

scope of this book, at minimum you should be familiar with the meaning of resolution. **Resolution** becomes important not only for scanners and digital cameras, but for any type of computer display. Some projects require a high resolution in order to look good, such as printed documents. Other projects, however, look fine with a low resolution, such as websites.

The number of pixels across and down an image determines resolution. An image with a resolution of 1,280 pixels $\times$ 1,280 pixels has a total of more than 1 million pixels (1,280 pixels $\times$ 1,280 pixels = 1,305,600 pixels) and is considered megapixel. An image with 2 million pixels has a resolution of 2 megapixels, and so on. The more pixels that make up an image, the better the image quality.

It might help to think of it this way. Imagine that you are holding up wire mesh screen. Wherever wire threads intersect, you have a square. Think of each square as a pixel. Consider that you have two types of screens, one with 100 squares, and another with 200 squares. Suppose you are looking through these two screens at the same marble (see Figure 5-16). Each square in the 200-wire mesh screen captures a smaller unit of detail in the marble than does the other screen. This same thing happens when images are digitized. When you are able to capture a dark blue in one square and a light blue in the one next to it, your final picture will have more precision than if you capture a blend of the two, which is what happens with digital cameras and other imaging devices. The quality of your output is dependent on how many pixels your digital device can capture. The more pixels you have, the better your display quality.

How much resolution you need is determined by how you plan to display images. If you intend to use your images for the Internet, your resolution does not need to exceed 72–96 pixels per inch (ppi), since most monitors are not set up to display greater resolution. If you want to print your image, you will need a better quality image with a higher resolution. For most print applications a 300 dot per inch (dpi), file is the standard. Pixels per inch and dots per inch are many times used interchangeably. DPI refers to the number of dots of ink used to print text and graphics; the more dots, the better and sharper the image. PPI is the image resolution. It is how a device, such as a monitor, displays an image. The quality of the image on screen is determined by the number of pixels that can be displayed in a given area. For our purpose, dpi and ppi are the same thing, they are the number of little dots that make up the image. To put it more in perspective, if you want to shoot a 4×6 inch photo that is print quality (300 dpi), you'll need 300 pixels for every inch of output. You will need a 1200 (3×400) $\times$ 1800 (6×300) pixel image. If you multiply the two numbers you get the resolution you will need from a digital camera:

$1200 \times 1800 = 2{,}160{,}000$ pixels, or 2.16 megapixels

You will want a digital camera with at least 2.6 megapixels to make a 4×6 inch photo.

Using Scanners and Digital Cameras

Let's turn now to the many useful and creative ways that scanners and digital cameras can be used. Your **scanner** can create images from a number of things:

- photographs
- drawings
- sketches
- objects like pencils, fabrics, nails, and more

Scanners are a good way to add visual depth into your instructional materials. By depth I mean the detail and shadows that can make information look real or more noticeable. When you scan, you are essentially taking a picture of the object you are scanning, and in the process you get a lot of visual detail. I suggest you read the book *Start with a Scan* (Ashford & Odam, 1996) because it has many motivating examples of how a scanner can be used creatively to make effective and appealing visuals.

Scanners are easy to operate, too. Instructions vary, so you need to follow those found with the scanner model you use. Just to show you how easy they are to use, however, I've sketched the generic steps involved in operating a scanner in Figure 5-17.

Digital cameras are also a good way to add visuals to your instruction, and they are particularly handy for personalizing instruction. Not only can you take pictures of the exact training or school environment, but you can take pictures of the trainees or students, too.

Digital cameras operate like scanners. You take a picture (the scan) and then move the picture from the scan into your computer. There are several ways to do this, and it is getting easier as the technology improves. The oldest method is to hook the camera up to the computer using a cable that uploads (sends the image from the camera to the computer) using one of several ports (devices that accept the image data.) The most common ports are serial ports (older and slower), parallel ports (commonly used for printers), USB ports (Universal Serial Bus, which are newer and faster), wireless ports (transferred using infrared technology), and IEEE 1394 ports (USB ports "on steroids") (Kobler, 2001, p. 35). Depending upon the camera, you either operate software that transfers the images from the camera to the computer (see Figure 5-18), or the technology does this for you with the press of a button. Printers today are accepting images directly from camera disks, making it easy to print images.

Most new cameras allow you to save your images directly onto removable disks (also called removable memory), which include 3½ inch computer disks, CD-ROMS, or smaller camera-specific disks (also called cards). When removed, these disks fit into either a 3½ inch drive, CD-ROM drive, or some type of peripheral designed specifically for the card. Some of these cards must be inserted into a larger disk shell or sleeve, which slides into the 3½ inch disk slot on your computer. Other manufacturers require the small disks to be placed in specifically designed peripherals (see Figure 5-19).

Popular types of removable memory cards include CompactFlash™, SmartMedia™, and the Memory Stick by Sony™. Figure 5-20, Part A shows a 65MB CompactFlash disk inserted into a SanDisk drive. Part B shows the relative size of a CompactFlash disk when compared to a quarter and a 3½ inch floppy disk.

Scanners

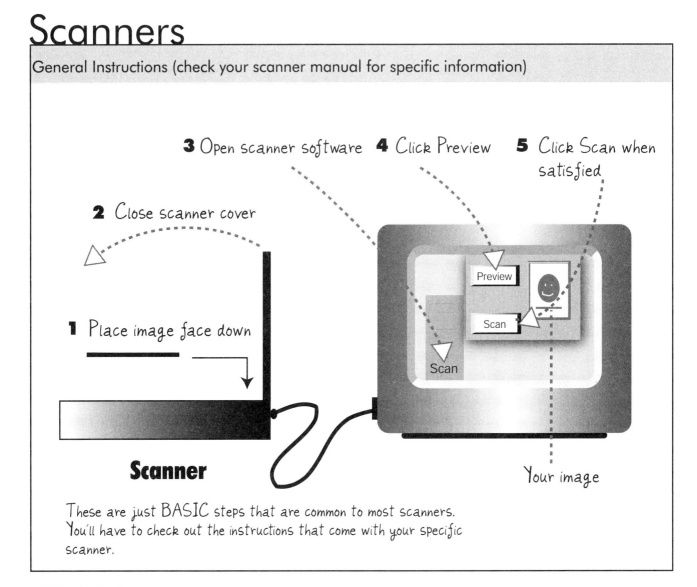

FIGURE 5-17   Operating a scanner

COPYRIGHT

We have one more topic to examine before concluding this chapter. As you work with complex shapes from clip art, scanning, and digital cameras, you need to be aware of copyright laws and what is legal and not legal for you to use.

What Do You Need to Know about Copyright for Instructional Visuals?

Consider this scenario. Antonio creates an instructional game on the World Wide Web similar to a widely marketed and popular game board called Money Madness, except his game teaches a different topic, Voluntary Simplicity. His game quickly becomes popular and is in-

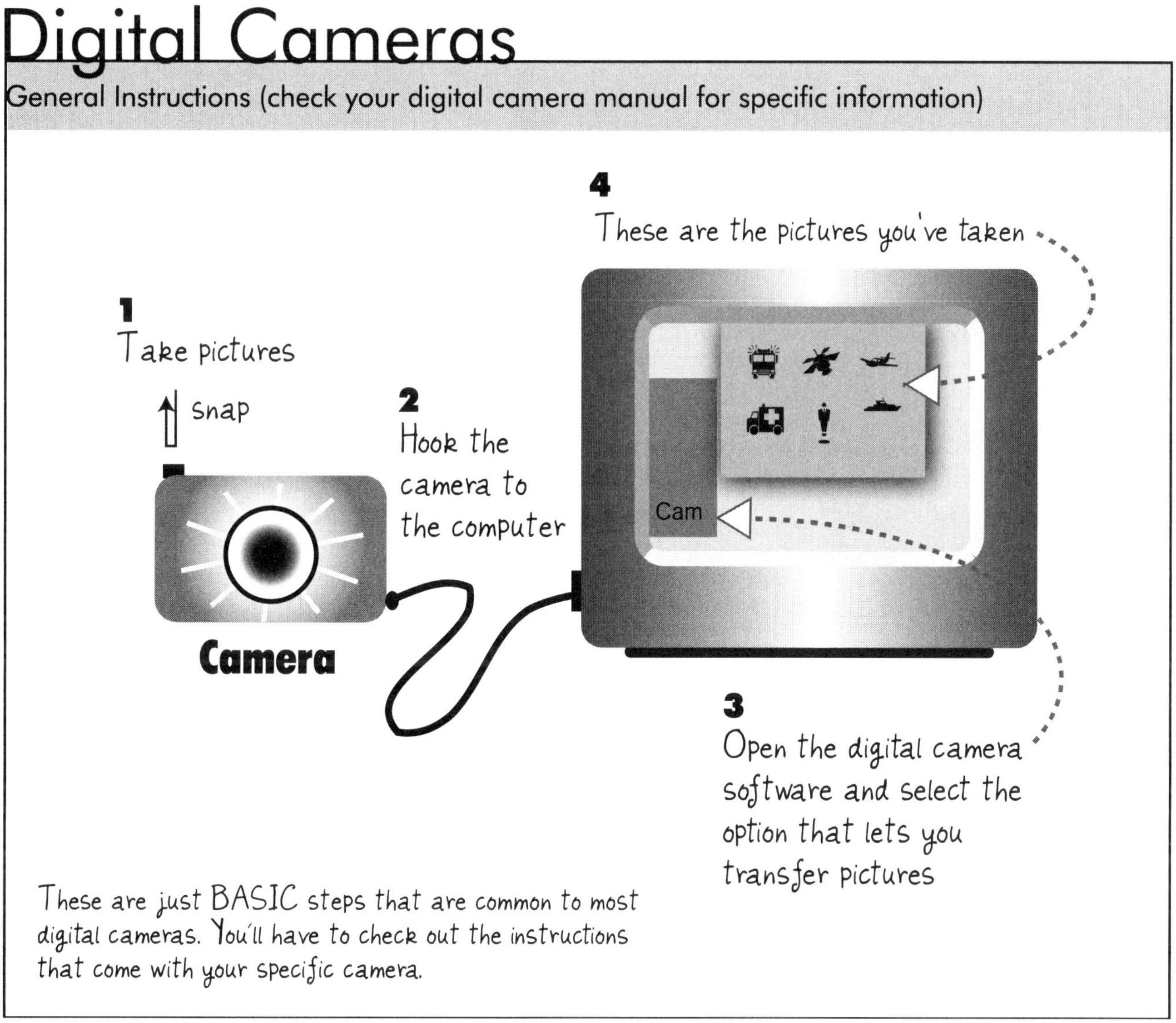

Digital Cameras

General Instructions (check your digital camera manual for specific information)

4
These are the pictures you've taken

1
Take pictures

snap

2
Hook the
camera to
the computer

Cam

Camera

3
Open the digital camera
software and select the
option that lets you
transfer pictures

These are just BASIC steps that are common to most
digital cameras. You'll have to check out the instructions
that come with your specific camera.

FIGURE 5-18   Operating a digital camera

creasingly accessed by teachers in his building who have suggested that he publish the game on his own. Antonio has two concerns, though: (1) that someone will steal his idea and publish it before he does, and (2) that perhaps *he* has violated copyright laws by imitating some of the ideas of Money Madness.

Latisha is writing a book and has asked several people to help her with the illustrations. Some of her students bring her exceptional work, but she isn't sure of how original it is. Her students are honest with her, telling her that they did copy the work, but digitally changed it beyond recognition. Latisha wonders if she should use their work or not.

Like Antonio and Latisha, you may be concerned about copyright from these two perspectives. First, you want to be sure that work *you* create is protected by copyright laws from other individuals who might want to replicate it for financial gain or credit that belongs to you. And second, you want to be sure that the materials you work with are copyright free or that you are legally covered when using the materials.

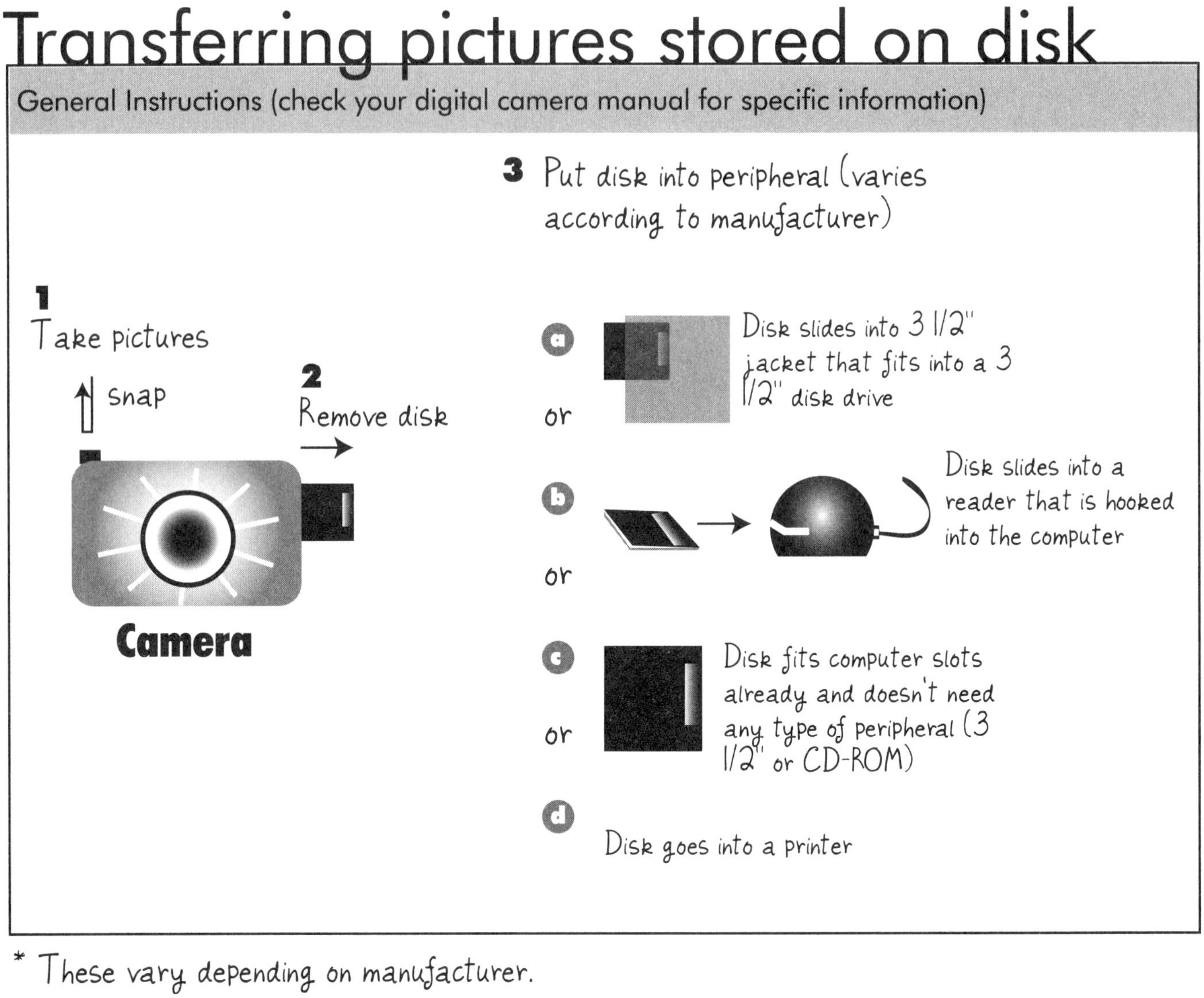

Transferring pictures stored on disk

General Instructions (check your digital camera manual for specific information)

3 Put disk into peripheral (varies according to manufacturer)

1 Take pictures

↑ snap

2 Remove disk →

Camera

a   Disk slides into 3 1/2" jacket that fits into a 3 1/2" disk drive

or

b   Disk slides into a reader that is hooked into the computer

or

c   Disk fits computer slots already and doesn't need any type of peripheral (3 1/2" or CD-ROM)

or

d   Disk goes into a printer

* These vary depending on manufacturer.

FIGURE 5–19   Transferring images from a digital camera

Copyright Protection of Your Own Work

The easiest way to understand copyright is to imagine yourself as someone who has created something that others want. Do you want your work to be used by others or not? Do you want to give others the permission to copy and redistribute your work? Do you want to be financially compensated or recognized? Copyright laws allow you to legally make these decisions and to seek compensation when others use your work without permission. Copyright is a form of protection provided by the laws of the United States to creators of original works of authorship. When you copyright your work, you alone can authorize the reproduction of any type of instruction (print, video, images, etc.) you create. You can protect yourself in the event that people try to steal your work.

You may be surprised to learn that anything you create is automatically considered copyright protected the moment it is created. Copyright is secured when your work becomes concrete, either visually or aurally (through some type of auditory device), including images, books, manuals, computer training videos, and computer-based training units. You do not have to mark your work with a copyright symbol or register your work with the U.S.

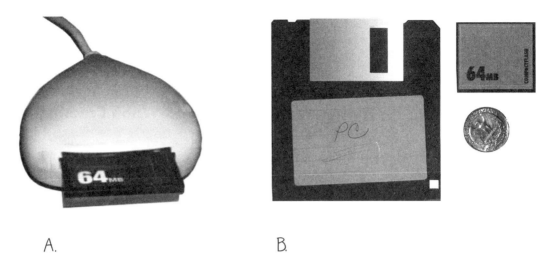

A.   B.

FIGURE 5-20   Digital camera memory cards

Copyright Office to gain protection. You do, however, have the option of including a copyright symbol or notice on your work. The copyright notice basically informs the public that your work is copyrighted. You also may choose to register your copyright with the U.S. Copyright Office (*www.loc.gov/copyright*). The key advantage to including a copyright notice and registering your copyright is extra legal protection.

If you are a little confused at this point about what copyright gains you, you are not alone. Copyright laws are somewhat ambiguous. On one hand the law states that anything you create is considered copyrighted, which means you are automatically legally protected the moment you create something. You do not need to mark it with copyright symbols or register it with the U.S. Copyright Office for the materials to be considered legally protected. On the other hand, however, the U.S. Copyright Office suggests registering the copyright for extra security in a court of law. By registering your copyright you make it part of public record and secure extra protection in a court of law. The exact value of a copyright seems somewhat vague. One wonders about the legal strength of an unregistered copyright. Perhaps the best advice is to play it safe and include a copyright notice and register the copyright when warranted.

You might also wonder what is and isn't considered copyrighted. The following are copyrightable:

- literary works
- musical works
- dramatic works
- pantomimes and choreographic works
- pictorial, graphic, and sculptural works
- motion pictures and other audiovisual works
- sound recordings
- architectural works

The following are not copyrightable:

- nontangible work (work that is not visible, recorded, or aural)
- titles, names, short phrases, and slogans
- familiar symbols or designs
- mere variations of typographic ornamentation, lettering, or coloring
- mere listings of ingredients or contents

- ideas, procedures, methods, systems, processes, concepts, principles, discoveries, or devices, as distinguished from a description, explanation, or illustration
- common information (for example: standard calendars, height and weight charts, tape measures and rulers, and lists or tables taken from public documents or other common sources)

Following Copyright Laws When Creating Your Work
Not-for-profit work

Although copyright owners have the power to limit use of their work, a "fair use" exemption to the copyright law allows educators and students a looser interpretation of the law if the materials they use promote learning, scholarly activity, and free speech or discussion, and if they meet certain conditions. The law lists the following factors as critical for determining whether a particular use of a copyrighted work is a permitted fair use:

- the purpose and character of the use, including whether such use is of a commercial nature or is for nonprofit educational purposes;
- the nature of the copyrighted work;
- the amount and substantiality of the portion used in relation to the copyrighted work as a whole; and
- the effect of the use upon the potential market for or value of the copyrighted work. (Stanford University, 1998)

This fair use exemption, like the rest of the copyright law, is quite vague and open to interpretation. In order to help educators be adequately sure that they are not in violation of the copyright law, a group of publishers and educators (the consortium of College and University Multimedia Centers, for one) assembled to create a set of fair use guidelines. If educators stay within these guidelines, they can be reasonably sure they are acting legally and have the backing of this large group of publishers and educators. In a nutshell, nonconsumable materials (nonprofit) have the following fair use guidelines:

Print Materials

Teachers or trainers are generally allowed:

- a single copy of any type of print materials (an article, a poem, an illustration)
- multiple copies (not exceeding the number of students in the class) **only** when a spontaneity condition is met (the teacher uses the materials at the "last minute")
- a limit of 250 words for a poem that is distributed under the spontaneity exception
- 10 percent (or a maximum of 1,000 words) of prose distributed under the spontaneity exception.

If in doubt, seek copyright permission from the publisher of the work. A form is available for requests at the Copyright Clearance Center; call (978) 750–8400 or go to *www.copyright.com*. You will need to specify the title, author, and/or editor, and edition, the exact number of pages and copies, page numbers and chapters used, how you plan to use the information, what form it will be in (classroom handout, newsletter, etc.), and whether the material will be sold.

Software

One backup of a computer program is permitted; language modification is approved if a language specific program is not available. A copy of software is not permitted over a network nor is making multiple backups.

Multimedia

Students and teachers may use copyrighted multimedia materials that are referenced and included under the fair use exemption of the U.S. Copyright law. Copyrighted materials may be used for education, portfolios for future employment, or evaluation materials. Educators and students may use:

- materials for up to two years after the first instructional use without receiving permission to use the copyrighted material
- 10 percent or 3 minutes of motion media
- 30 seconds of music
- 5 images per artist
- 2,500 fields in a database

These rules apply to distance learning environments as well. Take, for example, Antonio posting several paintings on his website. According to the fair use law he can legally do that if he meets all the criteria; he should use no more than five images per artist and show the images no longer than two years. Since Antonio isn't using the images to make a profit, his reproductions of those works should be permitted.

For-profit work

If you are creating instructional material for profit, you are advised to consider carefully the copyright laws and receive permission of the copyright owner to do any of the following:

- reproduce the work
- prepare derivatives of the work
- distribute copies of the work
- display the work publicly

In general, if a work has been in the public domain for more than 75 years, it is considered legal to use without a fee. As with all the copyright provisions, however, the rules are difficult to interpret, and it may be hard to determine the age of an image or its copyright status without a great deal of work. If the image is in a book that is more than 75 years old, then the image could be assumed to be copyright free, unless some organization or individual who has extended the copyright status assumes that image's copyright. For example, if the book is 75 years old, but the creator of the image is still alive, then the image would not be considered copyright free.

In many cases, one does not know when the work was created, who created the image, whether the creator or creators registered the image, and whether the creator or creators is still alive. Copyright laws are based upon whether the image was created before or after January 1, 1978, and whether the creator was an individual, several individuals, or a sponsoring organization or party. In addition to these facts, in order to determine copyright status one must know whether the work was registered and by what date, as well as if the authors are still alive.

Works originally created on or after January 1, 1978, are copyright protected from the moment of creation plus an additional 70 years after the author's death. In the case of "a joint work prepared by two or more authors who did not work for hire," the term lasts for 70 years after the last surviving author's death. For works made for hire, and for anonymous and pseudonymous works (unless the author's identity is revealed in Copyright Office records), the duration of copyright will be 95 years from publication or 120 years from creation, whichever is shorter.

Works originally created before January 1, 1978, but not published or registered by that date are now given federal copyright protection: the life-plus-70 or 95/120-year terms stated previously apply to them as well. The law provides that in no case will the term of copyright for works in this category expire before December 31, 2002, and for works published on or before December 31, 2002, the term of copyright will not expire before December 31, 2047.

The laws for copyright for works that were created and copyright registered prior to January 1, 1978, are somewhat difficult to interpret. Copyright status can last anywhere from 28 years to a total term protection of 95 years, based upon renewal extension status. Most works are copyright protected for at least 75 years, but under certain conditions a total protection of 95 years applies. Therefore, it can be difficult for an individual to determine.

Because of the potential risk, the advice is to use only images you know to be copyright free. Since this book in part teaches you how to use digital technology to create instructional visuals, you are more than aware of the ease in which you can revise an original work beyond recognition. It is fairly easy to scan a photograph out of a magazine and make enough changes to make the work unrecognizable even to the original artist/creator. Most individuals feel that in altering an image, a new and completely different image has been created, thus justifying the practice. In the end, the decision to alter or not becomes one that is often made in the context of expedience. One must get a project done quickly and to do so requires a little "cheating." In all likelihood, you will not be sued for changing an image beyond recognition; however, I'd like to urge you to avoid the temptation. Plenty of available copyright-free images can be modified beyond recognition.

To err on the side of caution, you should be aware that some clip art isn't as "free" as it may appear. Be sure to read the fine print that accompanies clip art to make sure it is also royalty free, meaning you do not have to pay to use it. You will often find the fine print on the CD-ROM envelope or jacket cover. Some clip art companies require their permission to use their images in for-profit endeavors, even if they are educational. For example, a clip art manufacturer is not likely to give you permission to create a Web site where people can download their clip art. Some clip art manufacturers also will not let their clip art make up a substantial portion of your product.

Sources of Copyright-Free Images

Excellent sources of royalty-free art are widely available and safe to use. First are typefaces. The names of the typefaces are copyrighted (such as Futura and Garamond), but the actual typefaces are not. As you learned in Chapter 4, typography is a powerful graphic element.

Next, find out if your library or local bookstore has a collection of Dover Publications, which publishes more than 700 books in its Pictoral Archives series containing more than 250,000 images.

Dover Publications
31 East 2nd Street
Mineola, NY 11501

Also, check out the Library of Congress's prints and photos division.

Library of Congress
Prints and Photos Division
Independent Avenue at First Street, SE
Washington, DC 20540

What about Copyright-Free Web Clip Art?

The best advice I can give about using clip art is to start out assuming that all images are copyright protected, and then do some research to prove otherwise. Many clip art collections on the Web advertise "free" clip art. Free can be interpreted in two ways: (1) the clip art really is copyright free, and it is available at no cost, or (2) you are free to copy the clip art, at no expense, but at your own risk of copying someone else's work. If in doubt, contact the owners of the website. If they do not respond, or if they do not know the origins of the art, you'd be better off not using it. If they respond with the name of the creator, write the creator to verify permission before using it (sometimes this is easy if an e-mail address is provided). A good practice is to make copies of all permissions for your files, in the event that you are questioned about the source of your images. Carefully review these permissions, and make sure they cover your specific situation. For example, when using images from the Web, I contacted several people to find where they obtained their images and if I had permission to use them in this book. I printed those e-mail correspondences and have them on file, just in case there is any question of legal rights to their use.

As stated at the start of this copyright section, the best advice is to put yourself in the shoes of the image creator. Just remember, it can take several hours or days to create clip art, and the owners of that work have the rights to its use and deserve to be paid or recognized as they see fit. Chapter 12 lists several sources of websites advertising copyright-free clip art and some websites that offer images for a small fee, allowing your use without concern regarding copyright.

What about Antonio and Latisha?

Now that you have read all of this information about copyright, what would you do if you were Antonio and Latisha in the opening paragraph on this topic? Antonio wonders if he is protected if others steal his Voluntary Simplicity game idea and if he himself might be guilty of the same transgression since he is using the idea from a commercially produced game board. Latisha wonders if she should use her students' images when they have admitted using images that were not copyright free.

Antonio and Latisha have valid concerns and should take some action. First, Antonio's idea could be copied by someone else since it is an idea, and ideas are not copyrightable. The actual format of that idea (the way the game looks and the strategies used), however, is under copyright from the moment Antonio created it, but only if it is completely different than the original game. Antonio's best bet is to check with a copyright lawyer. Latisha is right to be concerned as well. She faces a moral decision. Since the images have been changed beyond recognition, it is unlikely that she will be sued. However, if she wants to be extra careful, she, like Antonio, should seek the advice of a copyright lawyer. At minimum she should look at the original state of the images that were modified.

Copyright laws are perplexing. In the past year I've gone to three professional presentations on the subject. Surprisingly, all three speakers had the same advice: (1) if in doubt, hire a copyright lawyer, and (2) check the following website for current information: www.lcWeb.loc.gov/copyright/

SUMMARY

Shape is the second of five tools (type, shape, color, dimension, and space) used to create effective instruction. Many designers recommend starting a design project by first thinking of shape including the overall shape of the project—a square or rectangular page, for example — and the underlying shape that goes onto the page.

The importance of shape is often overlooked. Shape can be used to communicate instructional information. Simple shapes like circles, squares, and lines help learners see relationships, direction, and sequence. Common shapes like swirls, stars, arrows, and brackets help communicate emotion, imagination, and groupings. Complex shapes, such as digital images and photographs, help when realistic images are needed. Rapid improvements to scanners and digital cameras make it easier than ever to create complex images.

When access to images is as simple as it now is, consideration of copyright laws becomes important. Educators are protected somewhat under a fair use exemption of the copyright law, but the exact interpretation of the law is vague and experts in copyright recommend legal advice be sought when serious copyright questions arise.

FOR MORE CHALLENGE

Visit Chapter 5's *Challenge* section on the book's website. There you'll find several instructional problems that require your visual solutions. Compare your solutions to those of others.

DISCUSSION FOR DISTANCE LEARNING

Visit the book's website (Chapter 5 > Discussion) for discussion topics related to this chapter.

REFERENCES

Ashford, J. & Odam, J. (1996). *Start with a scan: A guide to transforming scanned photos and objects into high quality art*. Berkeley, CA: Peachpit Press

Farace, J. (1998). *Stock photo smart*. Gloucester, MA: Rockport Publishers.

Hansen, M. (1999). *Visualization tools for thinking, planning, and problem solving*. Cambridge, MA: MIT Press

Hartley, J. (1985). *Designing instructional text*. London: Kogan Page.

Hartley, J. (1996). Text design. In D. H. Jonassen (Ed.), *Handbook of research for educational communications and technology* (pp. 795–820). New York: Simon & Schuster Macmillan.

Heinich, R., Molenda, M., Russell, J. D., & Smaldino S.E. (2000). *Instructional media and the new technologies of instruction*. New York: Macmillan.

Kobler, R. D. (2001). PC photos and video [Special issue]. *Smart Computing in Plain English Learning Series, 7*(11).

Lynch, P. J., & Horton, S. (1999). *Web style guide: Basic design principles for creating web sites*. New Haven, CN: Yale University Press.

Peterson, B. L. (1997). *Using design basics to get creative results*. Cincinnati, OH: North Light Books.

Pomeratz, J. R., Pristach, E. A., & Carson, C. E. (1989). Attention and object perception. In B. E. Shepp & S. Ballestero (Eds.), *Object perception: Structure and process* (pp. 35–90). Hillsdale, NJ: Lawrence Erlbaum Associates.

Stanford University. (1998). Letter from Provost Condoleeza Rice, October 30. Retrieved December 8, 2001, from http://fairuse.stanford.edu

Toor, M. L. (1996). *The desktop designers' illustration handbook*. New York: Van Nostrand Reinhold.

Williams, R., & Tollett, J. (1998). The non-designer's web book: an easy guide to creating, designing, and posting your own web site. Berkeley, CA: Peachpit Press.

CHAPTER 6

Color, Depth, and Space

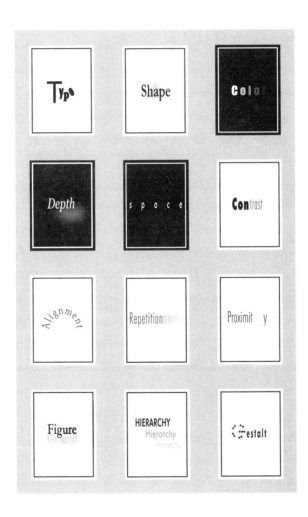

"All communication between the readers of an image and the makers of an image must now take place on a two-dimensional surface. Escaping this flatland is the essential task of envisioning information—for all the interesting worlds (physical, biological, imaginary, human) that we seek to understand are inevitably and happily multivariate in nature. Not flatlands."

Edward Tufte

NOTES ABOUT THE OPENING VISUAL

The chapter cover uses color, depth, and space as design tools. Black, white, and gray show contrast; depth is achieved with drop shadowing; and space is used to position type and shapes.

Though working with color, depth, and space takes practice, there are quick ways to use these tools effectively. For one, a white background always looks good with small areas of colors (even grays); you can hardly go wrong with this approach. If you want more visual or instructional emphasis, you might try drop shadows for depth since they make images look like they are floating above the paper.

Figure 6–1 shows how a drop shadow was created for a triangle shape, but you can use these simple steps for just about any shape (letters and words too). With some computer programs you don't even need to follow any steps, you just select the object you want shadowed and click on a drop shadow icon. Instructions on the book website show you how to create other types of drop shadows.

FOCUS QUESTIONS

- How do I choose colors for instructional purposes?
- Should I base decisions on the psychology of color?
- Can color improve instruction?
- What is depth? Does it have an instructional impact?
- What is white space? Is it always white?

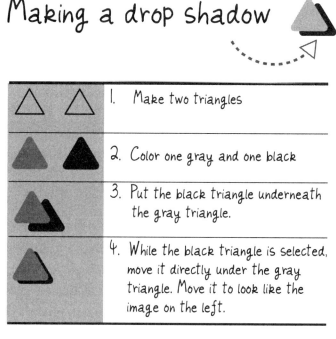

FIGURE 6–1   Drop shadow

KEY TERMS

BRIGHTNESS   the intensity of light in a color (just think of the sun as being a bright yellow, and butter as a dull yellow); brightness is also called *luminance* or *value* (Misanchuk, Schwier, & Boling, 2000) (Please refer to the book website for examples.)

CHROMA   see the definition for saturation (Please refer to the book website for examples.)

CONTRAST   the relative brightness of two colors (A section of the book website shows you examples of color contrast.)

DEPTH   refers to size, dimension and texture.

HUE   the term that describes color as we know it: red, green, violet, etc.; we tend to use *color* instead of *hue* (Please refer to the book website for examples.)

LUMINANCE   see the definition for brightness (Please refer to the book website for examples.)

SATURATION   the depth of color, also called *chroma*; if a color is saturated, the hue is strong (Please refer to the book website for examples.)

VALUE   see the definition for brightness (Please refer to the book website for examples.)

INTRODUCTION

Latisha, the community college instructor/part-time technical writer you met in Chapter 1, has been asked by a local hospital to redo some of the print materials, among them a daily menu design (Figure 6–2, Part A). Apparently some of the patients are complaining that the menu is too hard to read. As Latisha looks over the menu, she finds the strong contrast between black and white lines jarring. Additionally, the menu items are presented in all caps, making individual letters and words difficult to perceive. To a hospital patient under the

Even a healthy person would find menu A too much.

A

B

On pain killers.

FIGURE 6–2   Original hospital menu

influence of anesthesia and morphine, the menu could hardly be considered readable, (see Part B of Figure 6-2). Latisha wonders why patients needs to dial in their food order, if that is what is meant by the instructions next to French Toast to "press 52." When Latisha asks, she learns patients receive the menu, and then the kitchen calls them to take their order. Either the patient or the nurse can take the call, depending on the status of the patient, but the patient doesn't type in any numbers, so these instructions are not needed.

Latisha also has these questions:

- How can I use color to separate or chunk information?
- Which colors should I use?
- Should I use drop shadowing or images that have some depth to them?
- How can I use space to make the information easier to read?

With this information in mind, Latisha sets out to redesign the menu (see Figure 6-3). In her redesign she uses dark colors to emphasize important items—the main meals of breakfast, lunch, and dinner—drop shadows to emphasize meal times, and space to separate breakfast, lunch, and dinner. Latisha makes the menu elements that won't change (the words "Breakfast," "Lunch," and "Dinner") the most decorative. Since these decorative elements will not be edited, the kitchen staff will only need to change the menu items, making the daily menu easy to use, but remaining attractive.

This chapter covers three tools that Latisha used in her redesign of the hospital menu: color, depth, and space. These tools are generally used to focus attention, provide direction, and help the learner see the big picture. Given the restriction of printing the book in black and white, the topic of color is covered using limited colors: black, white, and gray.

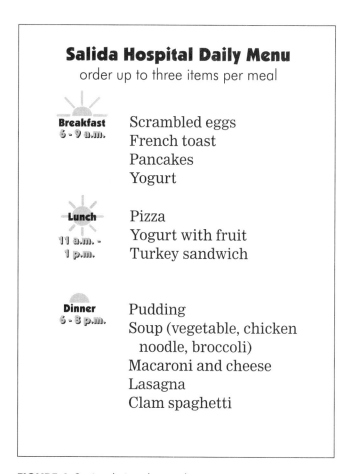

FIGURE 6-3 Latisha's redesigned menu

How Does Color Impact Instruction?

Color alone can make or break the appearance and effectiveness of instructional visuals. If you are like most people, the thought of using color in your instructional visuals is appealing. With the accessibility of affordable printers, projection devices, and software, the ability to create color-enhanced visuals is easier now than ever. Used effectively, color can enhance both the aesthetic and instructional quality of educational or support materials.

What Does Color Do for Instruction?

Edward Tufte (1990) describes four functions of color, or **hue,** in information design. The first function is color as a method of labeling or differentiating information. Maps often make extensive use of color. A subway map might use blue to designate the location of restrooms, red to designate all stops on a particular line, and green to identify where tokens can be purchased. The blue colored lines in many road maps are used to identify two-lane back roads that distinguish these "blue highways" from the red or black interstate highways. Ski areas label the difficulty of different runs using color and shape. A green circle means "easy" or "for beginners." A blue square means "intermediate." A black diamond means "for experts only."

The second function of color is to show quantity or measurement. In a pie chart, colors are often used in pieces of the pie, showing the relative percentages of certain items. Island maps use different saturations of blue to designate deep and shallow areas, with deeper areas colored a stronger, deeper blue. A diagram showing the spread of AIDS over time uses a stronger saturation of color to show a greater number of causalities.

The third function is the use of color to represent reality. For example, medical illustrations show the color of healthy versus unhealthy fingernails. Your dentist has posters showing examples of healthy versus unhealthy gums. If you were in a wine tasting class, you'd learn the difference between chardonnays and cabernets by their red and white colors. Architects use colored pencils on blueprints to help clients visualize plans. A wardrobe planner uses colored fabric swatches to help her client choose clothing.

The fourth function—color as decoration—refers to color and aesthetic appeal. We see this function of color every day on television, in printed materials, and on the Web. Color is used because people tend to prefer color to black and white, finding color motivating, soothing, stimulating, and capable of evoking emotions (Schwier et al., 2000).

Does Research Prove That Color Helps Learning?

Despite the enthusiasm and high regard educators tend to have related to color, the research on learning from color is mixed. Color research finds that use of color facilitates cognitive processes involved in learning, such as memory support, recall of information, and promotion of interaction between learners and content (Schwier et al., 2000). Other research finds that color can be distracting and inhibit performance (Shneiderman, 1992).

You might be surprised, too, that there are almost as many research-based reasons against the use of color in instruction as there are for it (Schwier et al., 2000). In their review of the literature, Schwier, Misanchuk, and Boling list reasons why color is and is not considered instructionally beneficial.

Reasons for using color include:

■ Color may be necessary (medical students need to know the color of healthy versus unhealthy tissue).

■ There are many research-based advantages for color. Schwier et al. list 19 references in all, only a few of which are listed here. These advantages include the ability to: "attract and control attention, add visual cues, locate information, link logically related data,

show associations, tie together related items that are scattered, aid in differentiation and discrimination among elements, facilitate subtle discriminations in complex displays, help interpret related and unrelated information, facilitate identification, speed searches for objects, increase task speed, express quality or quantity, rank items, highlight student errors, differentiate between required and optional data, aid decision making."
- Learners prefer color.

Reasons against using color include:

- Color may not be necessary.
- Researchers have found color to be distracting (Horton, 1991; Livingston, 1991) and confusing (Shneiderman, 1992). Chapman (1993) contends, "If color is added to a presentation and not functionally related to the task, its presence can act as a deterrent to performance" (p. 14).
- Learners may not have the technology to access color adequately.

You may have noticed that the "necessity of color" topped both of the lists. In a review of the research by Dwyer and Lamberski (1983), the influence of color on learning was highly dependent on the learning task at hand. This finding is in harmony with Tufte's recommendation to use color to represent reality. For the designer this means using color when color is a critical element of the learning or performance context. For example, if you were creating a job aid for inserting a colored ink cartridge into a printer, you'd probably use black and white for everything else but the location of the cartridge. If you were teaching people to identify the perfect color of green for fresh broccoli, you'd be smart to use the same green in your instruction. If you were teaching a group of medical students the color of a particular skin rash, you would need to show it. If you were teaching about color, you should use color (irony intended). The book's website teaches about color by showing you the color wheel, color contrast, and color examples.

Dwyer and Lamberski's research (1983) also found time and age to influence the power of color as an instructional tool. In their research, the effectiveness of color cues in instruction was dependent in part on the time available to learners to process those cues. Learners who have more time to study a color-coded visual are more likely to see why and how the various color codes have been used. For example, think of a subway map. If you have 15 minutes before the next train arrives, you'd have time to study the color coding assigned to different city routes. But, if you had only minutes to study the map, and you were unfamiliar with the route, you might not understand the importance of the color cues.

The time variable may be why color is not always as helpful for children as for older people. Dwyer and Lamberski's research suggests that children have problems pacing themselves through colored information and may need an adult to help them learn from the color. For example, if a child is learning to use a website that is color coded, the teacher (or tutorial) may have to point out how the child can use the color to navigate through different parts of the website.

HOW DO YOU CHOOSE COLOR?

If you decide to use color, you might find choosing and making it work well a challenge. Unless you've worked with color extensively, it is a good idea to leave complex color design to the experts. The encouraging news is that black, white, gray, simple primary (red, blue, and yellow), or secondary colors (purple, green, and orange) are amazingly versatile and effective in instruction and are easy for most people to use. They are especially easy to use if you use large spaces of white or gray with small sections of color. For example, imagine this page as white, with all of the headings in blue, and maybe page numbers on a small circle filled with yellow. This is a great rule of thumb, but it won't work for all situations. How do you decide on color the rest of the time? I have three suggestions that go with the major theme of the book. Choose color based on how you want the learner to perceive information. This means you choose color to:

1. make important information stand out (figure/ground).
2. establish an order of importance (hierarchy).
3. help the learner see the "big picture" (gestalt).

Choose Colors to Make Important Information Stand Out (Figure/Ground)

Color facilitates **contrast** and by doing so can help the learner differentiate between important and less important information. Heinich, Molenda, and Russell (1993) recommend these color combinations for effective contrast, in order of preference:

- black on yellow
- green, red, or blue on white
- white on blue
- black on white
- yellow on black

While these are recommended for maximum contrast, it doesn't always translate to maximum readability. A page of white text against a bright red background would hardly be readable. Yet the same combination is quite effective for a traffic sign. Once again, choices should be made according to the "It Depends" rule introduced in Chapter 4.

Another way to create contrast is to use warm and cool colors. Cool colors such as blues and purples seem more formal and distant, while warm colors such as red, orange, and yellow may seem more informal and approachable. Not surprisingly, warm colors are known to advance and cool colors to retreat. If you want an element in instruction to stand out, you'd use a warm color. You might even use a cool background color in the same instruction to make the warm element stand out even more. When creating contrast, it helps to think of color's two properties, chroma and value.

Chroma, also called **saturation,** refers to the intensity of a color. High chroma colors (think of a really bright red in a box of crayons) create more contrast because they are more intense and tend to advance when you look at them. Therefore, the instructional designer would want to use these colors to make important information stand out and be noticed. Since high chroma colors are strong, the designer can get away with using less of them. Color half of the butterfly in Figure 6–4 using two or three high chroma (bright) colors, then color the other half using several low chroma (less bright) colors.

While chroma refers to intensity, **value** refers to a color's **brightness.** Darker colors tend to stand out and lighter colors tend to recede. Darker colors, then, might be used for information that is important and needs to stand out. If you want the background to stand out, as does the ellipse shape in Figure 6–5, a stronger value is used. If you want the foreground to stand out, as would be the case when reading text, a lower value is used. One rule of thumb is to use strong values for images that do not take up a lot of space and lower values for images that do take up a lot of space.

Choose Color That Will Establish an Order of Importance (Hierarchy)

Color can suggest a ranking or sequential order (Horton, 1994). Color facilitates hierarchy by allowing you to create separate categories or layers of information. These categories can show levels of importance or the progression of data. You can use dark-to-light or dull-to-bright sequences to show increasing significance or importance. For example, in a table of

Color this with markers or crayons.

FIGURE 6–4   High vs. low chroma

contents, book sections might be highest chroma color, book chapters a mid chroma color, and chapter topics might sit on top of a low chroma color fill (see Figure 6-6). If you do not have color, shades of black (see Figure 6-7) can suggest sequential order.

Choose Colors That Help the Learner See the Big Picture (Gestalt)

Color can tie complex information together in aesthetic, organizational, and psychological ways. A variety of color selection schemes can contribute to the learner's sense of gestalt. The following section describes four types of color selection schemes, based on: (1) the color wheel, (2) inspiration from nature or art, (3) custom palettes provided with templates, and (4) psychological associations.

Choose Colors Based on Rules of the Color Wheel

The color wheel is simply an organization scheme that arranges color in a selected order. Some of the schemes are *spectral* (the order produced by nature, as in a rainbow), whereas others are more artistic, chosen because the color arrangements evoke a more harmonious response from people. For example, a spectral color composition designates red, green, and blue as primary colors, from which all other colors evolve. An *artistic* scheme, on the other hand, designates red, yellow, and blue as the primary colors. In this book we'll use the artistic organization scheme. See the book's website for color images.

Take a moment to fill in Figures 6-8 through 6-16 with colored markers or crayons as indicated on the diagrams. By doing so, you will be able to see some of the color schemes discussed (you can also look at the website.)

Primary colors are the three pure colors (red, blue, and yellow) on the color wheel (see Figure 6-9). All other colors start from a mixture of these colors, and black and white. The artistic color scheme arranges red, yellow, and blue equidistant on the color wheel.

Secondary colors are the colors (orange, green, and purple) created by mixing equal amounts of adjacent primary colors on the color wheel (see Figure 6-10). For example, a mixture of equal parts of blue and yellow creates green.

RULE OF THUMB

Use strong values for backgrounds that fill a small area (see the top ellipse). Use low value colors for backgrounds that fill large area (see bottom text block).

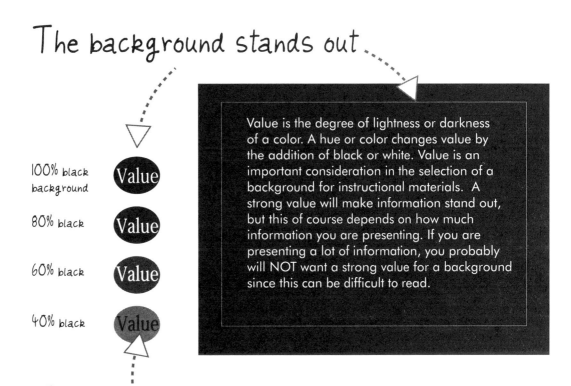

The background stands out

100% black background

80% black

60% black

40% black

Value

Value is the degree of lightness or darkness of a color. A hue or color changes value by the addition of black or white. Value is an important consideration in the selection of a background for instructional materials. A strong value will make information stand out, but this of course depends on how much information you are presenting. If you are presenting a lot of information, you probably will NOT want a strong value for a background since this can be difficult to read.

The words stand out

Value is the degree of lightness or darkness of a color. A hue or color changes value by the addition of black or white. Value is an important consideration in the selection of a background for instructional materials. A strong value will make information stand out, but this of course depends on how much information you are presenting. If you are presenting a lot of information, you probably will NOT want a strong value for a background since this can be difficult to read.

FIGURE 6–5   Color value

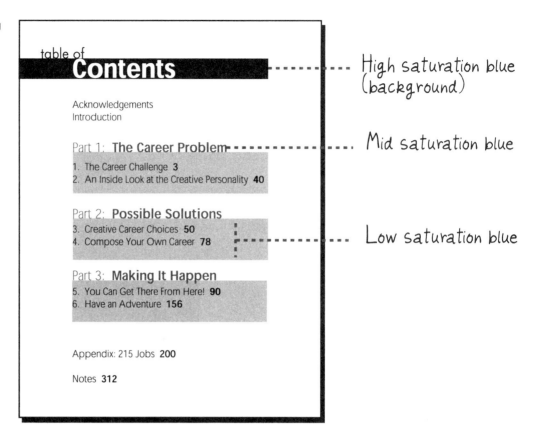

FIGURE 6–7 Shades of black suggesting hierarchy

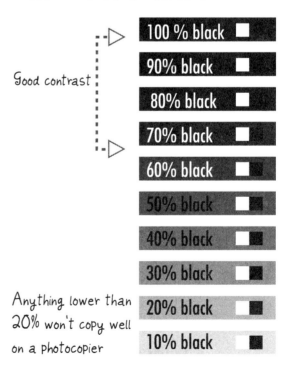

FIGURE 6–8 The color wheel

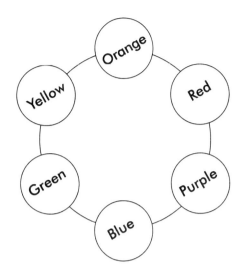

Fill in with markers or crayons

FIGURE 6–9 Primary color scheme

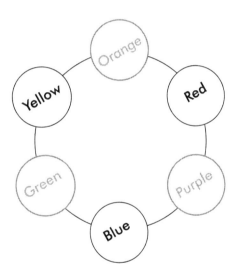

FIGURE 6–10 Secondary color scheme

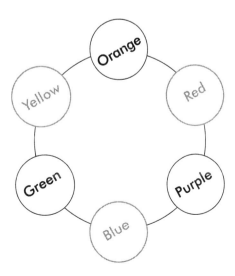

FIGURE 6–11 Tertiary color scheme

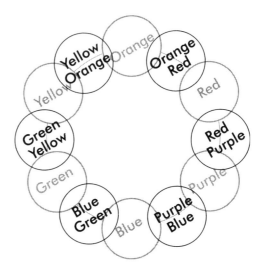

FIGURE 6–12
Complementary color scheme

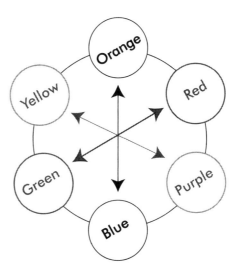

Tertiary colors are the colors (yellow-orange, green-yellow, blue-green, purple-blue, red-purple, orange-red) created by mixing adjacent primary and secondary colors (see Figure 6–11).

Complementary colors (yellow and purple, green and red, and blue and orange) are the colors that fall directly across each other on the color wheel. See Figure 6–12.

The rule of thumb for using complementary colors in instructional materials is to use them with caution. Although the name implies that they look good together, they only do so when combined carefully. Used in equal amounts, complementary colors compete for attention and can be visually jarring. The best approach for novices is to use predominantly one color and use the complement of the color for highlights, or small sections where you want contrast. Try experimenting with different proportions of the colors in a visual. For example try a 5% red, 50% green and 45% white combination. Or, try a 20% red, 60% green, and 20% white combination. I find yellow and purple are often the easiest to use effectively. Red and green are probably the hardest to use. Check the website example for a good example of complementary color schemes.

Monochromatic color schemes are an easy scheme for novices to use. A monochromatic scheme uses different tints or shades of the same color (see Figure 6–13). A tint is created when different percentages of white are added to a color. A shade is created when

FIGURE 6–13
Monochromatic color scheme

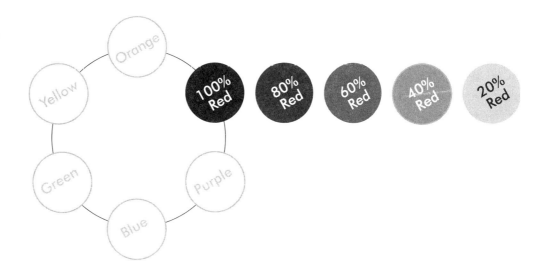

FIGURE 6–14 Analogous
color scheme

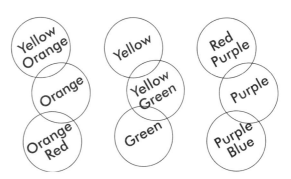

FIGURE 6–15 Split
complementary color scheme

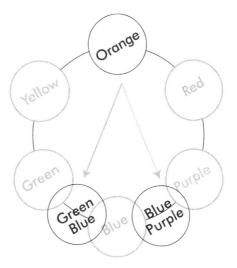

different percentages of black are added to a color. One note of caution, though, related to instructional visuals: Monochromatic color schemes often do not show enough contrast.

Analogous colors are next to each other on the color wheel, such as yellow, yellow-orange, and orange. See Figure 6-14.

Split complementary schemes use the colors on each side of a color's complement. For example blue with orange-yellow and red-orange. See Figure 6-15.

FIGURE 6-16 Warm and
cool colors

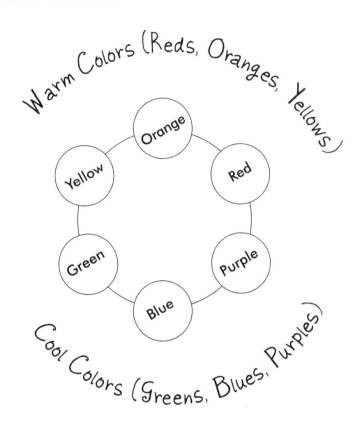

FIGURE 6-17 Color schemes
suggested by nature

Nature as inspiration

Warm and cool colors are those colors that are either on the warm side or the cold side
of the color wheel. Warm colors are on one side of the color wheel and include the reds, yellows, and oranges. Cool colors are on the other side of the wheel and include blues, greens,
and violets. Warm colors advance whereas cool colors recede. When emphasizing instructional information, warm colors can be used since they tend to advance and will be noticed
first. See Figure 6-16.

Choose Color Based on Inspiration from Nature and Art

Tufte (1990) suggests using colors found in nature, especially those on the lighter side, such as blues, yellows, and grays of sky and shadow (see Figure 6–17). He recommends using large background areas in muted colors to allow brighter colors to stand out more vividly. He also advises distributing colors throughout your work to give it better unity.

An approach I like to use involves finding color combinations from works of art, the Internet, advertisements, and design books. For example, I have a picture of Vincent Van Gogh's *The Chair* (Figure 6–18) above my desk. The colors I initially see are complementary golds, terra cotta, and blues. But when I compare the colors to the paint chips in my computer programs, I find that the colors are usually very grayish, or as Tufte says, muted. These are colors I wouldn't have picked without the help of the picture.

Choose Color Based on Color Palettes Found in Templates

Several books (see Chapter 12, Resources) suggest artist-created color schemes. These books provide specific values that you can use to duplicate the colors exactly with your computer. These color schemes are a great help, but they don't completely take care of everything for you. You still need to spend time with them. You may be given the right colors, but you still must figure out how much of each color to use.

The same can be said for the custom palettes that are part of software programs. These palettes have predetermined color schemes for background colors, text, drop shadows, and highlights. Even though the software companies claim that artists designed these color sets, they aren't effort free, as some of the combinations are questionable.

Choose Color Based on Psychological Associations

Colors evoke emotional responses (Horton, 1994). Walking into a room with blue walls can seem cold and somewhat formal. Blue, green, and some shades of purple are considered cold colors and can be used to calm, soothe, and reassure. Walking into a room with soft yellow walls can do the opposite, feeling warm and inviting. Yellow, orange, and red colors are considered warm colors and can be used to arouse, alert, and excite. Many of these emotional reactions to color depend upon color values and saturations. For example, while a soft yellow may be inviting and soothing, other yellows are known to provoke irritability in architectural settings.

FIGURE 6–18 Van Gogh's *The Chair*

Art as inspiration

Colors not only carry moods, they also have symbolic meaning (Nelson, 1989). Often the meaning of color varies between cultures. White is associated with weddings in Western cultures and with mourning in some Eastern cultures. Table 6-1 shows how the same color can mean many things. For example, green means both growth and disease blue dependability and transparency, and red both happiness and bloodshed.

While some of the associations in Table 6-1 may be more common than others, these associations are clearly not universal, and often with other elements on a page, the associations are simply not even influential. For example, a black background with bright vibrant colors would hardly be considered sinister; nor would a white background with vibrant colors be considered bland.

In several color preference studies (Roper and Pantone, undated), most people's favorite color is blue, followed closely by green, purple red, and black. People's least favorite colors are yellow and orange. Pantone's study shows color preferences for different marketing groups. For example adolescents liked orange and "slime green." People coined as "influentials" (the type of people others go to for advice) favored the color red.

 It's time for a break in reading. The book website asks you to redesign an instructional visual to make the color more effective. To see the image, create a solution, and compare your solution to others, go to the book website (Chapter 6 > Web activity). Be sure to check out all of the information on different types of color schemes (Chapter 6 > More info) as well.

TABLE 6-1 *Color and Mood/Meaning*

Color	Meaning/Mood
Red	Passion, power, zeal, happiness, aggression, impulsiveness (the American Automobile Association considers red-car drivers to cause more accidents because of their carefree nature, according to Nelson, 1989), danger, shame, optimism, warmth, extroversion, fire, bloodshed; can evoke a fight or flight response (Boyle, 2001)
Orange	Often misunderstood and misused, popular with children, energetic, festive, good for celebrations and happy events, knowledge, civilization, friendliness, deference, pride, warmth, gregariousness; considered a least favorite color along with yellow
Yellow	Warmth, cowardice, intelligence, brightness, clarity (in Western cultures), sacredness — as it approaches the color of gold (in the Orient and Europe, according to Nelson, 1989), treachery, novelty, idealism, introspection (Horton, 1994), madness (Vincent van Gogh used a lot of yellow), good cheer; bright yellow is the most visible color (Boyle, 2001) and is considered a least favorite color along with orange; provokes irritability in architectural settings
Green	Growth, freshness, health, hope, but also associated with guilt, disease, nausea, terror (Nelson, 1989); among the most cited favorite colors (Boyle, 2001)
Blue	Serenity, tranquility, dependability ("true blue"), constancy, used in many logos (Boyle, 2001), aloofness ("blue-blood"), sobriety, fear, sky, water, ice (transparent) (Nelson, 1989), depression
Violet	Considered both a warm and cold color (red brings out the warmth, blue the coolness), royalty (in some countries only royalty could wear—and afford—purple), nobility, sorrow, loneliness, vanity, nostalgia, wit, spirituality, regret (Horton, 1994); good for targeting creative types (Boyle, 2001)
White	Purity, truth, in the Orient used for mourning (Nelson, 1989), bland
Black	Depression, sorrow, gloom, death, sensuality, elegance, sophistication, elite, sin, dignity, morbidity, sinister
Brown	Earth, dirt, chocolate, coffee (Boyle, 2001), duty, parsimony, reliability, bareness, poverty (Horton, 1994)

DEPTH

In this book **depth** refers to size, dimension, and texture. Depth plays a critical role in making information stand out (figure/ground). The images on the book's website show the use of shadowing, size, texture, and color to achieve depth. If you visit the book's website (Chapter 6 > More information), you will find some instructions on how to create depth using Microsoft Word and Adobe Illustrator.

Shadows give an image depth, as in Figure 6-19, where the title is drop shadowed. If too many elements use drop shadowing, however, the technique loses its impact (see Figure 6-20). You can also use shading and figure shadowing, as in Figure 6-21. Notice how shadows can be stark or light (and from different light sources).

Size communicates importance (see Figure 6-22). Figure 6-23 helps a learner see the relative size of a microchip by comparing it to a penny. Comparisons of this nature are helpful because you help the learner assimilate new information into memory using what is already in memory.

Texture adds depth and makes items stand out. Texture is the presence of a rough or patterned surface. For example, sand is textured, water is not. Corduroy is textured, satin is not. Notice how Part A of Figure 6-24 approaches you while you look at the image as compared to Part B.

Perspective creates depth. If you ever find yourself with a boring image, just use perspective to liven up the image. Diagonal alignment adds energy to an image. An image shown from an unusual perspective as the building in Figure 6-25 helps the message stand out because it points to the title. Photographs are an easy way to employ perspective. Another way is to use 3D tools now offered in many presentation packages.

FIGURE 6–19   Drop shadows to add depth

Drop Shadow
No Drop Shadow

Too many drop shadows can be distracting and hard to read.

FIGURE 6–20   Overuse of drop shadows

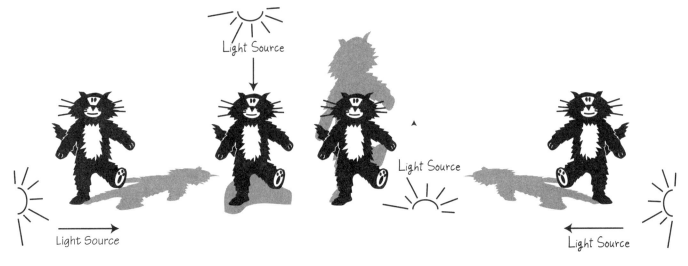

FIGURE 6–21 Shadows at different angles

Size and weight establish importance.

Important

Not important

FIGURE 6–22 Communicating importance through size

FIGURE 6–23
Communicating relative size

This is the actual size of a microchip. Putting it next to a penny helps you see its relative size.

This fly stands out because it has more texture (detail).

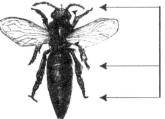

Limbs spread germs

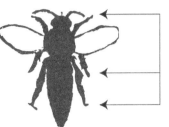

Limbs spread germs

A.

B.

FIGURE 6–24 Adding depth through texture

Notice how the diagonal lines in the building lead your eye toward the words? White space is used effectively in this image, too.

Taking Care of Business
General Manager
Roles & Responsibilities

FIGURE 6–25   Creating depth with perspective
Source: Clip art © 1997 RomTech.

Good contrast here.

Idaho

FIGURE 6–26   Using color for emphasis

Check out the instructions on creating one-point perspective and drop shadows (using Microsoft Word and Adobe Illustrator) at (Chapter 6 > More info).

Color makes things stand out, as you learned earlier. Using a strong color against a muted background will make the strong color dominant, as is the state of Idaho in Figure 6–26.

SPACE

Space is a design tool that many don't recognize as a tool. Space is called *white space, negative space*, and *counter space*. White space doesn't have to be white either; it can be any

FIGURE 6–27 Directing the eye with "white" space

This white space is actually gray.

FIGURE 6–28
Communicating a sense of timing with space

From The Flight of the Bumble-Bee
N. Rimskij-Korsakov (1844 - 1908)

color that makes up the background of an image. Space is the element between visual elements; it is the part of an image that is often ignored. Though considered unused space, space has an important role in instructional visuals. Space can direct the eye to important information by chunking and separating instructional elements, as in Figure 6-27.

Hartley (1985) considers space an important tool for clarifying text:

> It is space that separates letters from each other. It is space (with punctuation) that separates phrases, clauses and paragraphs from each other; and it is space (with headings and sub headings) that separates subsections and chapters from one another. (p. 27)

Hartley maintains that space has three instructionally related benefits. Consistent spacing helps

1. increase the rate of reading because readers are more able to see redundancies.
2. access the more personally relevant pieces of information.
3. the reader see the structure of the document.

As discussed in Chapter 4, Hartley recommends a "floating page," a page that ends not according to a predetermined bottom margin but according to where the content naturally ends.

Space can impart a sense of timing, with items that are spaced further apart communicating distance in time. Consider the arrangement of musical notes (see Figure 6-28).

Space also helps balance images on a page or screen. Balance is considered the distribution of information, or the achievement of equilibrium. You use space to work with balance by moving information into places to achieve either a symmetrical arrangement or an asymmetrical arrangement. Symmetry often conveys a sense of calm and professionalism (see Figure 6-29). Everything is in equilibrium; all elements are equal. Symmetrical arrangements, however, can be static and boring. Asymmetrical arrangements tend to create more interest since elements are thrown off balance (see Figure 6-30).

FIGURE 6–29 Adding balance through symmetry

How do you work with white space? White space is challenging at first because it is hard to "see." Yet to work effectively with white space, you must see it. One technique to try is to stand back from a design and look at it while squinting. Squinting allows the white space to be viewed as a separate visual element. If the white space looks odd, perhaps there are areas of trapped white space or rivers of space (see Figure 6–31). The goal is to create a good balance between the white space and the other elements that make up the visual. This takes practice, and eventually you'll develop a good eye for white space.

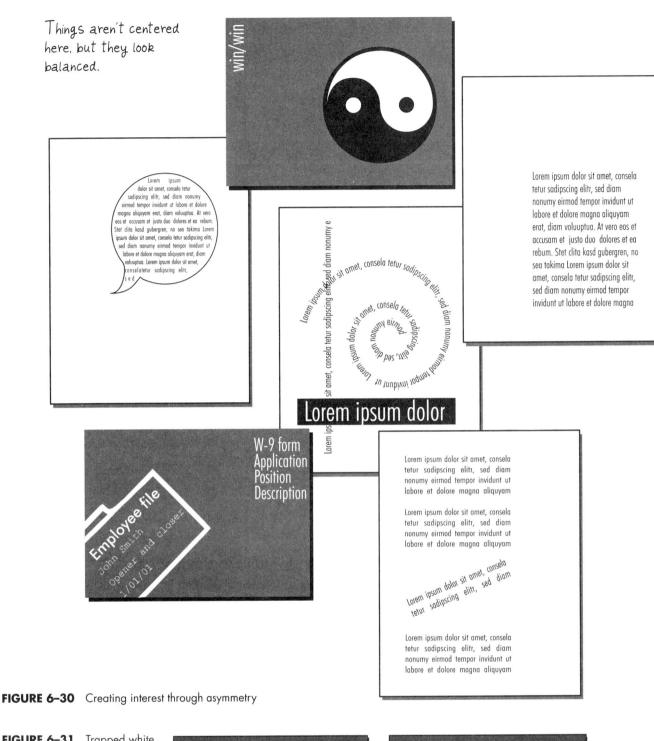

Things aren't centered here, but they look balanced.

FIGURE 6–30 Creating interest through asymmetry

FIGURE 6–31 Trapped white space

Trapped space

SUMMARY

This chapter concludes our look at design tools by describing and demonstrating how color, depth, and space enhance instructional visuals. Color has aesthetic as well as instructional impact and is useful for creating a mood, drawing attention, and organizing information into groups. Though color takes time to master, there are some easy and effective ways for nonartists to use color. Using white backgrounds with a small amount of primary color is easy for most people. Color schemes, colors from nature, and color combinations found in artwork are effective ways to select color combinations as well.

Depth is a tool that uses size, texture, and perspective to direct learner attention. Diagonal shapes instantly add energy to an image. Photographs and other images that have a textured, detailed, or shaded appearance create an illusion of depth and often create more visual interest or direct learner attention.

White space (or the background color) is the final tool covered in this chapter. Though often ignored, space is considered a design tool as important as type, shape, color, and depth. Space can direct a learner's attention and create symmetrical or asymmetrical balance. Many learners prefer images and text passages that use plenty of white space because they feel less overwhelmed by the volume of information presented.

This concludes the section on Tools. The next chapter on actions describes things you can *do* with the tools to improve instruction.

FOR MORE CHALLENGE

Visit Chapter 6's *Challenge* section on the book's website. There you'll find several instructional problems that require your visual solutions. Compare your solutions to those of others.

DISCUSSION FOR DISTANCE LEARNING

Visit the book's website (Chapter 6 > Discussion) for threaded discussion or chat questions.

REFERENCES

Boyle, C. (2001). *Color harmony for the web: A guide for creating great color schemes on-line*. Glouchester, MA: Rockport Publishers.

Chapman, W. (1993). Color coding and the interactivity of multimedia. *Journal of Educational Multimedia and Hypermedia, 2*(1), 3–23.

Dwyer, F. M., & Lamberski, R. J. (1983). A review of the research on the effects of the use of color in the teaching-learning process. *International Journal of Instructional Media*, 10, 303–328.

Hartley, J. (1985). *Designing instructional text*. New York: Nichols.

Heinich, R., Molenda, M., & Russell, J. D. (1993). *Instructional media and the new technologies of instruction*. New York: Macmillan Publishing Company.

Horton, W. (1991). Overcoming chromophobia: A guide to the confident and appropriate use of color. *IEEE Transactions on Professional Communication, 34*(3), 160–171.

Horton, W. K. (1994). *The icon book: Visual symbols for computer systems and documentation*. New York: John Wiley and Sons.

Livingston, L. A. (1991). The effect of color on performance in an instructional gaming environment. *Journal of Research on Computing in Education, 24*, 246–253.

Misanchuk, E., Schwier, R., & Boling, E. (2000). CD-ROM, *Visual design for instructional multimedia*, Self-published.

Nelson, R. P. (1989). *The design of advertising*. Dubuque, IA: Wm. C. Brown.

Roper & Pantone. Color preference study. On-line. Available at *http://www.freevote.com/booth/jamie*.

Shneiderman, B. (1992). *Designing the user interface: Strategies for effective human-computer interaction* (2nd ed.). Reading, MA: Addison-Wesley.

Tufte, E. R. (1990). *Envisioning information*. Cheshire, CT: Graphics Press.

CHAPTER 7

Actions: Contrast, Alignment, Repetition, and Proximity

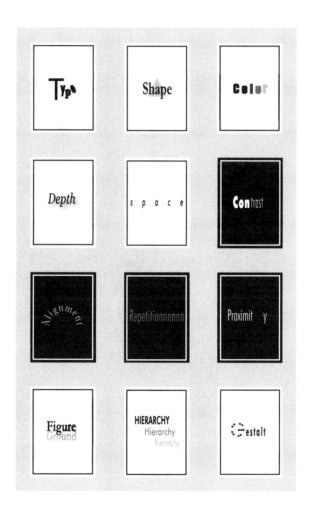

"[Contrast, alignment, repetition, and proximity] won't make you a brilliant designer, and they won't land you $20,000 web designer contracts, but they will keep you from embarrassing yourself in front of millions of people."

Robin Williams and John Tollett

NOTES ABOUT THE OPENING VISUAL

This chapter explains the critical role that contrast, alignment, repetition, and proximity play in instructional visuals. The chapter cover image uses all of these actions. Try to guess where each action took place and if it served any instructional purpose, then compare your thoughts to Figure 7–1.

Although the cover image uses all four actions, you do not need to use all four actions in an image. Sometimes you'll just use one or two, because that is all you need. In many images the actions overlap. For example, you might align a word with another word using an alignment tool like the one shown in Figure 7–2 (you'll learn more about this tool on the book's website). If you find that after aligning the words, they make a bigger, bolder impact, you've also created contrast. The point is that these tools overlap quite a bit.

FOCUS QUESTIONS

- Why are these concepts (contrast, alignment, repetition, and proximity) considered actions?
- Do you use all four actions in every visual?

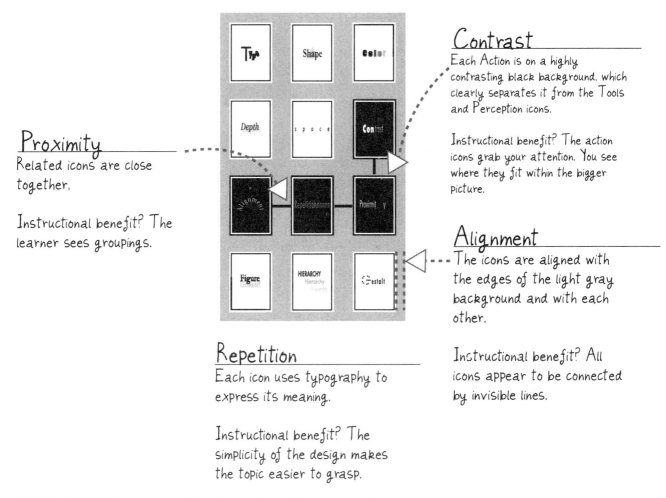

Proximity
Related icons are close together.

Instructional benefit? The learner sees groupings.

Contrast
Each Action is on a highly contrasting black background, which clearly separates it from the Tools and Perception icons.

Instructional benefit? The action icons grab your attention. You see where they fit within the bigger picture.

Alignment
The icons are aligned with the edges of the light gray background and with each other.

Instructional benefit? All icons appear to be connected by invisible lines.

Repetition
Each icon uses typography to express its meaning.

Instructional benefit? The simplicity of the design makes the topic easier to grasp.

FIGURE 7–1 Building instructional benefits into design of opening visual

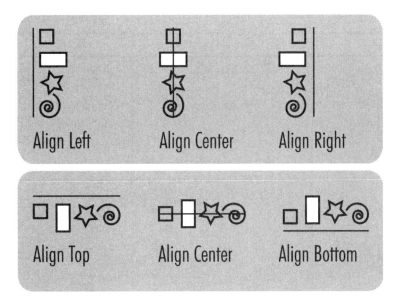

FIGURE 7–2   Alignment tool

- Do these actions improve instruction?
- How do you use these actions?

KEY TERMS

ALIGNMENT   lining things up along an edge or imaginary path
CONTRAST   making things different, such as making the shape or color different
PROXIMITY   moving things close together or far apart
REPETITION   reusing elements or using similar elements

INTRODUCTION

Sylvia has just been asked to do a small redesign project for a local paint company that wants to encourage sales by showing people how to apply faux paint finishes to walls, furniture, and anything else that might benefit from a decorative look. The store owner shows Stephanie a flyer she thinks might work (see Figure 7–3). "Of course," she says, "we're hiring YOU to redo this because we think you can turn this into something better." Sylvia asks the owner, "Who will be using this? Is there any particular group of people you want to attract?" The owner thinks for a few seconds, then replies, "I'd say artsy/craftsy. You can make it look fun, but don't go overboard."

As Sylvia looks over the flyer in Figure 7–3 and thinks about how she wants to redesign the information, she asks herself these questions:

- How do I make people notice the different painting techniques?
- How do I make the information look organized?
- How do I rewrite this so the information is organized and helpful?
- How can I make the page unified when there are so many techniques and descriptions?

Sylvia has just asked four questions that are related to the design actions covered in this chapter. Her first question deals with the importance of contrast, the second deals with alignment, the third repetition, and the fourth repetition and proximity. Contrast, alignment,

Materials for Faux Painting

Material	Painting Technique	Creating the look
Paint	Paint is the primary ingredient in all of the faux techniques.	The most important thing to consider when dealing with paint is the color. Use either complementary or contrasting colors to achieve your desired look.
Glaze	Glaze is used to create translucent effects in many techniques including color washing, sponging, ragging, etc.	If you are using a latex glaze, mix it with a colored paint, 4 parts glaze to one part paint. If you are glazing over that, next use 8 parts glaze to one part paint.
Brush	Brushes are especially important in the color wash painting techniques.	If you are color washing, first cover wall with a coat of paint. Then, dip your brush in glaze and randomly brush in crisscross strokes across your wall.
Roller	Rollers are necessary for many techniques that need a base color before applying the technique. However, they can also be used to create effects.	To create a faux technique with rollers, roll different colors in horizontal stripes vertically on your wall. Let the different colors "bleed" into each other at the edges.
Sponge	Sponging is one of the most common paint techniques. It is also one of the easiest for the novice to achieve.	First, have a base coat on your wall. Then, dip sponge in another paint color or glaze mixture and distress wall.
Rag	Ragging is used to achieve a variety of effects depending on the fabric used in the technique.	Either bunch rag up or twist into roll. Dip in paint and either distress or roll across your wall.

FIGURE 7-3 Original faux painting flyer

Source: Used with permission of Erin Hunt.

repetition, and proximity are all considered design actions because they require that you *do* something to one or more elements of a visual. When you create contrast, you make two or more elements very different from each other by manipulating them to increase the difference in size, color, or shape, among other things. When you align, you move elements around to line up on various edges. When you take an element and re-create some aspect of it, you are using the repetition action. You can repeat color, typeface, shapes, and other things. When you move elements close together or far apart, you are using the proximity action.

Look over Figure 7-3 and see if you can see places where the actions of contrast, alignment, repetition, and proximity might improve the flyer. Then look at Sylvia's redesign (Figure 7-4). Can you see where she employed contrast, alignment, repetition, and proximity? If you can't, you will. In this chapter we'll look at:

1. how the icons in the opening visual represent contrast, alignment, repetition, and proximity
2. how Sylvia used contrast, alignment, repetition, and proximity in her redesign
3. how the same information can be applied to a completely different instructional visual

This is a good time to point out that the research behind the instructional effectiveness of contrast, alignment, repetition, and proximity (CARP) is limited, perhaps because these actions are so widely acknowledged as useful for creating harmony or gestalt in a visual. I'll make more of a connection to CARP's role in perception in Chapter 10, where you will see how CARP contributes to gestalt principles. For now, just think of each of these actions as working together to create a better image, in which the whole of the image ends up being greater than the sum of its parts.

CONTRAST

You create **contrast** by making a difference between elements in a visual. How much of a difference do you need to create? Create more than you think you need. Most people, especially educators, are way too timid. As Robin William (1994) advises, make things *really* different. Look quickly at Figure 7-5. Try not to read the words, but do try to determine which image, *A, B,* or *C,* has the optimal contrast. Images *B* and *C* have enough contrast to make you notice the heading; however, image *C* is the best.

The Book Icon for Contrast

Figure 7-6 shows contrast using dark and wide letters adjacent to light and thin letters. It is fairly easy to do this when you have a typeface that is packaged with variety of heavy and thin fonts. The icon in Figure 7-6 uses Futura Heavy with Futura Condensed Light. Futura also has fonts that are called Black (not as bold as Heavy), Black Italics, Book (a reading weight), and others. I think it is a good idea to have at least one serif and sans serif typeface in a variety of weights because it is a quick and effective way to create contrast.

Sylvia's Use of Contrast

Look over Sylvia's redesign (Figure 7-4) again to see if you can identify where contrast was employed. Notice how Sylvia used contrast with type and space:

- in the title
- in the headings
- between the body text and the headings
- between the text chunks

Faux Painting Materials

Paint is the primary ingredient in all of the faux techniques. The most important thing to consider when dealing with paint is the color. Use either complementary or contrasting colors to achieve your desired look.

Glaze is used to create translucent effects in many techniques including color washing, sponging, ragging, etc. If you are using a latex glaze, mix it with a colored paint, 4 parts glaze to one part paint. If you are glazing over that, next use 8 parts glaze to one part paint.

Brushes are especially important in the color wash painting techniques. If you are color washing, first cover wall with a coat of paint. Then, dip your brush in glaze and randomly brush in crisscross strokes across your wall.

Rollers are necessary for many techniques that need a base color before applying the technique. However, they can also be used to create effects. To create a faux technique with rollers, roll different colors in horizontal stripes vertically on your wall. Let the different colors "bleed" into each other at the edges.

Sponging is one of the most common paint techniques. It is also one of the easiest for the novice to achieve. First, have a base coat on your wall. Then, dip sponge in another paint color or glaze mixture and distress wall.

Ragging is used to achieve a variety of effects depending on the fabric used in the technique. Either bunch rag up or twist into roll. Dip in paint and either distress or roll across your wall.

FIGURE 7–4   Redesigned brochure
Source: Used with permission of Erin Hunt.

A and B don't have enough contrast. If you want to make an effective contrast, make the difference REALLY different, as in C.

A

This heading has contrast
but it is kind of wimpy. There isn't that much of a difference in the heading and this body text.

B

This heading has more
contrast. The typeface in the heading is bigger than this body text. The contrast here is adequate.

C

This heading has the
most contrast. Not only is the typeface bolder than this body text, but the typeface is from a different type family as well.

FIGURE 7–5   The more contrast, the better

FIGURE 7–6   Book icon for contrast

Another Example of Contrast

Look over the three sets of instructions for creating whisky barrel flower arrangements (Figures 7-7 through 7-9.) Which do you think has the optimum contrast for helping someone perform the task of potting a plant? (Hint, think of the task—potting plants.)

You might choose Figure 7-8 because the title contrasts strongly with the image and it has a pleasing look. The instructional part of this image, however, doesn't have enough contrast. You mostly see a big gray block of text. Imagine yourself trying to follow the instructions. You'd perform one of the steps, and when the step was completed you'd probably have to read through everything again just to find where you left off. Figure 7-9 does a better job because it breaks all of the instruction up into smaller instructional chunks. The white space between the text chunks creates contrast between the gray masses of text. Figure 7-7 does the best job because it calls attention to three overall steps, which might help people potting the plants keep track of where they are in the process.

FIGURE 7–7 Contrast in instructional materials, example 1

Whiskey Barrel Flowers

1 Fill the whisky barrel or plastic insert with potting soil. If you are working with old dirt, dig through it until the large clumps are broken.

2 Place your plants in the pot so they are just sitting on the top of your soil. Work from the middle of the whisky barrel to the outside edges, putting your tallest plants in the middle and your shortest plants on the edges. Be sure to place any flowers or plants that droop on the edges too, since these will look nice draping over the edges of the whisky barrel. Use tall grass, fern and ivy as fillers.

3 Dig a hole about the width and length of each flower. Before putting the flower in, sprinkle a few beads of fertilizer into the hole. Pack the dirt around the flower. When finished lightly sprinkle the beaded fertilizer over the top surface. Water liberally.

FIGURE 7–8 Contrast in instructional materials, example 2

Whiskey Barrel Flowers

Fill the whisky barrel or plastic insert with potting soil. If you are working with old dirt, dig through it until the large clumps are broken. Place your plants in the pot so they are just sitting on the top of your soil. Work from the middle of the whisky barrel to the outside edges, putting your tallest plants in the middle and your shortest plants on the edges. Be sure to place any flowers or plants that droop on the edges too, since these will look nice draping over the edges of the whisky barrel. Use tall grass, fern and ivy as fillers.Dig a hole about the width and length of each flower. Before putting the flower in, sprinkle a few beads of fertilizer into the hole. Pack the dirt around the flower. When finished lightly sprinkle the beaded fertilizer over the top surface. Water liberally.

FIGURE 7–9 Contrast in instructional materials, example 3

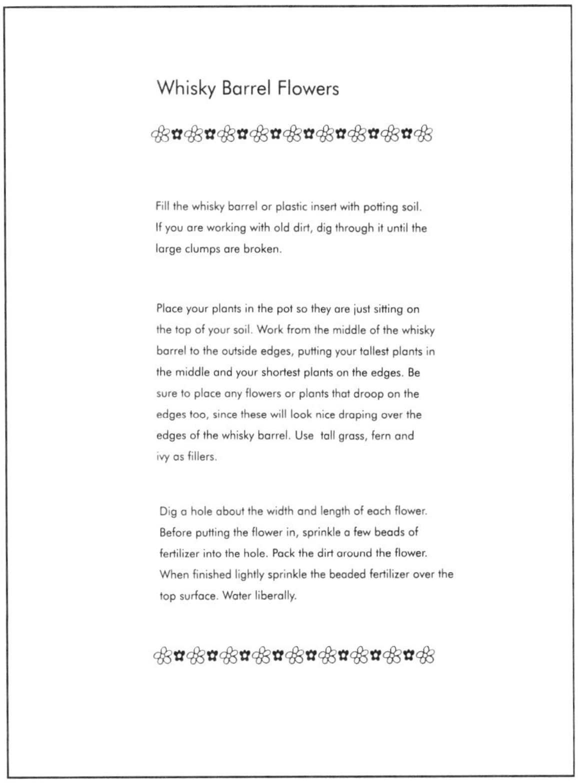

Whisky Barrel Flowers

Fill the whisky barrel or plastic insert with potting soil.
If you are working with old dirt, dig through it until the
large clumps are broken.

Place your plants in the pot so they are just sitting on
the top of your soil. Work from the middle of the whisky
barrel to the outside edges, putting your tallest plants in
the middle and your shortest plants on the edges. Be
sure to place any flowers or plants that droop on the
edges too, since these will look nice draping over the
edges of the whisky barrel. Use tall grass, fern and
ivy as fillers.

Dig a hole about the width and length of each flower.
Before putting the flower in, sprinkle a few beads of
fertilizer into the hole. Pack the dirt around the flower.
When finished lightly sprinkle the beaded fertilizer over the
top surface. Water liberally.

ALIGNMENT

When you line things up along an edge or some type of imaginary line or path, you are **aligning.** You can create horizontal alignment, vertical alignment, and shape alignment (as in aligning to the shape of a page or image, including centered, right, top, bottom, or left edge alignment).

Horizontal, left, right, and centered alignment (see Figure 7-10) can convey subtle messages. For example, centered alignment (top right image) is often considered more formal than the other types of alignment. Left alignment (the middle example) is fairly common since it is used extensively in textbooks and is considered easiest to read. Right alignment (the bottom example) is less common and because of this can often be used to create interest or convey novelty. Shape-inspired alignment (the large swirl) is often used to create interest while communicating a message.

The Book Icon for Alignment

The book alignment icon (Figure 7-11) shows the word *alignment* curving around the top half of a circle. It is easier to create alignments like this one in Draw programs like Adobe Illustrator. In Adobe Illustrator you create the shape (for example, the half circle), then click on the edges of the shape with a Text Alignment icon, and type. As you type, you see the letters align themselves to the shape.

Sylvia's Use of Alignment

Look over Sylvia's redesign and see if you can identify all of the places where certain types of alignment were used. Notice in Figure 7-12 how Sylvia used alignment with type and shape.

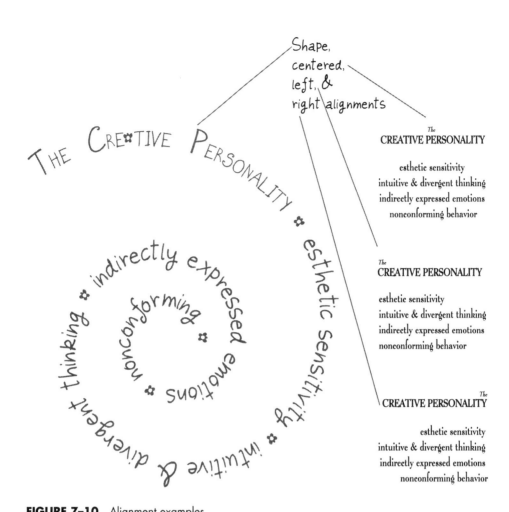

Shape, centered, left, & right alignments

THE CREATIVE PERSONALITY ❀ esthetic sensitivity ❀ intuitive & divergent thinking ❀ nonconforming ❀ indirectly expressed emotions

The
CREATIVE PERSONALITY

esthetic sensitivity
intuitive & divergent thinking
indirectly expressed emotions
nonconforming behavior

The
CREATIVE PERSONALITY

esthetic sensitivity
intuitive & divergent thinking
indirectly expressed emotions
nonconforming behavior

CREATIVE PERSONALITY The

esthetic sensitivity
intuitive & divergent thinking
indirectly expressed emotions
nonconforming behavior

FIGURE 7-10 Alignment examples

Alignment

FIGURE 7-11
Book icon for
alignment

Heading is center aligned

Faux Painting Materials

Information is centered on page

The top of the text is aligned with the rule on this side of the page

Circles, rules, and text blocks are left aligned

Text is aligned to the graphic shape

The bottom of the text is aligned with the rule on this side of the page

Circles on this side are right aligned

Paint is the primary ingredient in all of the faux techniques. The most important thing to consider when dealing with paint is the color. Use either complementary or contrasting colors to achieve your desired look.

Brush

Brushes are especially important in the color wash painting techniques. If you are color washing, first cover wall with a coat of paint. Then, dip your brush in glaze and randomly brush in crisscross strokes across your wall.

Sponge

Sponging is one of the most common paint techniques. It is also one of the easiest for the novice to achieve. First, have a base coat on your wall. Then, dip sponge in another paint color or glaze mixture and distress wall.

Glaze is used to create translucent effects in many techniques including color washing, sponging, ragging, etc. If you are using a latex glaze, mix it with a colored paint. 4 parts glaze to one part paint. If you are glazing over that, next use 8 parts glaze to one part paint.

Rollers are necessary for many techniques that need a base color before applying the technique. However, they can also be used to create effects. To create a faux technique with rollers, roll different colors in horizontal stripes vertically on your wall. Let the different colors "bleed" into each other at the edges.

Roller

Ragging is used to achieve a variety of effects depending on the fabric used in the technique. Either bunch rag up or twist into roll. Dip in paint and either distress or roll across your wall.

FIGURE 7-12 Using alignment in the faux painting example

FIGURE 7-13   Giving equal treatment with alignment

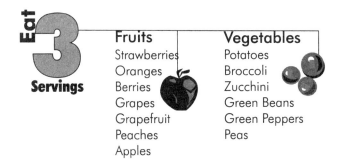

Another Example of Alignment

How would you organize the following information using alignment?

> Three servings a day are recommended for fruits and vegetables. Among fruits are apples, oranges, berries, and grapes. Among vegetables are potatoes, broccoli, zucchini, and green beans.

Figure 7-13 shows how alignment is used to structure this information. Because the fruit and vegetable heading are aligned along the top horizontal plane, they are more likely perceived as having equal importance. If fruits were placed above vegetables, many people would perceive fruits as more important.

REPETITION

When you employ **repetition,** you take some element of a visual and use it again. Repetition can create a sense of harmony and unity. When you repeat similar colors in a display, or similar typefaces, you make things seem related. One of the reasons why too many typefaces in a document are distracting is that each typeface creates a slightly different message. With too many messages going on, things can get confusing.

The Book Icon for Repetition

Figure 7-14 shows the letter *n* repeated many times. You'll find that repetition is one of the easiest actions to perform because you just have to copy something, or some aspect of something. For example, the book icon could just as easily have been the word repetition duplicated three or four times. Notice how all of the book's icons repeat something? They each show their meaning by using words only. This repetition makes them seem related, and at the same time it simplifies the overall message.

FIGURE 7-14
Book icon for repetition

Sylvia's Use of Alignment

Look over Sylvia's redesign and see if you can identify all of the places where repetition is used. Notice in Figure 7-15 how Sylvia repeated the tools typefaces, color, shape, and space.

Another Example of Repetition

Figures 7-16 features examples of a computer based training on clouds. Which example do you think uses repetition most effectively? Can you identify any repetition problems in any of the figures?

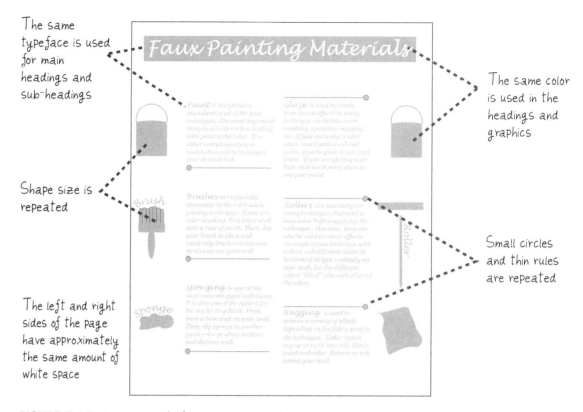

The same typeface is used for main headings and sub-headings

Shape size is repeated

The left and right sides of the page have approximately the same amount of white space

The same color is used in the headings and graphics

Small circles and thin rules are repeated

FIGURE 7–15   Repetition in the faux painting example

Parts A and B of Figure 7-16 use repetition more effectively than Part C. In Part A, the lines of the typeface match those of the clouds and the border. In Part B, the cloud covering the letter "o" in the title repeats the cloud theme. The blocky appearance of the square buttons, however, gives a heavy look to the screen that isn't as effective as the light and cloud-like buttons in Part A, unless you like the contrast the dark letters create. Part C is the least effective because it uses conflicting types of cloud images for buttons. The cartoon cloud does not work effectively with the photograph images of clouds, and the cloud inside the pointing finger isn't even visible.

PROXIMITY

Working with **proximity** involves moving things close together or far apart. When elements are close together, they seem related; when they are far apart, they seem unrelated. Notice in Part A of Figure 7-17 how the duck is separated from the other ducks. This positioning makes the duck seem independent or isolated. Part B shows the opposite effect with all of ducks positioned close to one another and seeming to be part of a larger family.

The Book Icon for Proximity

Doesn't the letter "y" in Figure 7-18 look a little bit like that independent duck? And don't the other letters look like the duck family? As you can see, just moving things close or apart can make a big difference.

A

The typeface
matches the
cloud shapes.
The buttons are
also cloud
shapes.

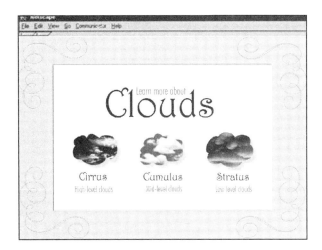

B

The "O" in
"Cloud" repeats
the other cloud
graphics.

C

A cloud theme
is repeated,
but overall
the shapes
and styles
are too
different
(cartoon and
realistic images
are mixed).

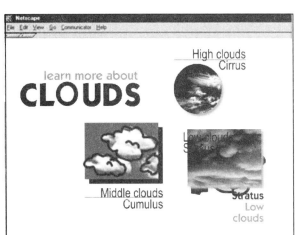

FIGURE 7–16 Using repetition effectively

Proximity is used here two ways. The grouping of ducks far apart or close together contributes to the message of either being part of something or independent. Typography also contributes to this message. In A, the word "Independence" is in proximity with only one duck and looks disassociated with the other ducks. In B, the word Teamwork centered over the ducks strengthens the message of unity/togetherness.

A.   B.

FIGURE 7–17   Emphasizing meaning with proximity
Source: Clip art © 1997 RomTech.

FIGURE 7–18   Book icon for proximity

Proximit   y

It's time for a break in reading. You have two Web assignments to complete. First, check out the chapter website for Microsoft Word and Adobe Illustrator instructions for working with CARP tools. Go to the book website (Chapter 7 > More information).

Next, create icons for the concepts of contrast, alignment, repetition, and proximity. To see similar solutions to this problem, go to the book website (Chapter 7 > Web activity).

Sylvia's Use of Proximity

Look over Sylvia's redesign and see if you can identify all of the places where proximity is used. Notice in Figure 7-19 how Sylvia grouped information by placing type and shape in close proximity.

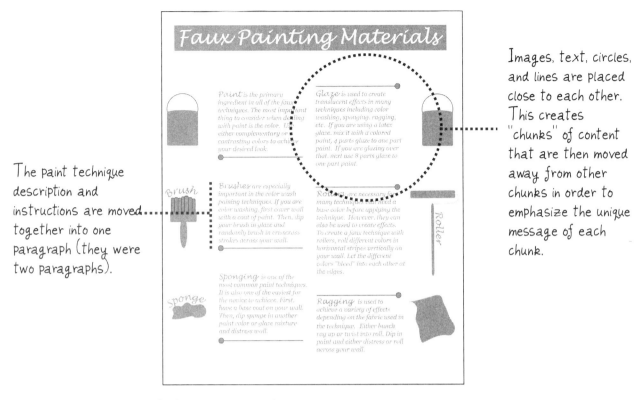

The paint technique description and instructions are moved together into one paragraph (they were two paragraphs).

Images, text, circles, and lines are placed close to each other. This creates "chunks" of content that are then moved away from other chunks in order to emphasize the unique message of each chunk.

FIGURE 7-19 Proximity in the faux painting example

If you look back to the original image (Figure 7-3), you'll notice two columns of information were used to describe each paint technique. Sylvia strengthened the connection between the two columns by combining them. She also moved the heading closer to the text and made the two seem more related. White space was used as well, as seen in the chunks of information that make up each paint technique. The white space surrounding the information helps create the chunk. Each of these chunks is moved far enough away from the other techniques to set them apart. In these examples, moving elements close together made them seem more related (as in the title and text) and moving elements apart (as in the individual chunks of information) made them seem more distinct.

Another Example of Proximity

I've often noticed a proximity problem with the math worksheets my daughter brings home from school (see Figure 7–20). Worksheet 1 shows 3 math problems, numbered 1, 2, and 3. These numbers, however, are positioned too closely to the first equation number. The learner is likely to read the first equation as 12 + _____ = 20, not as 2 + _____ = 20. This may seem far-fetched, but just this year I have seen several math worksheets with this very problem.

Worksheet 2 is better because the numbers are positioned further apart. Worksheet 3 is even better because the heavily bolded problem number look very different (good contrast) from the equation numbers. Worksheet 4 is the best because it uses letters for the different math problems, eliminating the problem of mixing numbers (a solution that wouldn't work as well for algebraic equations).

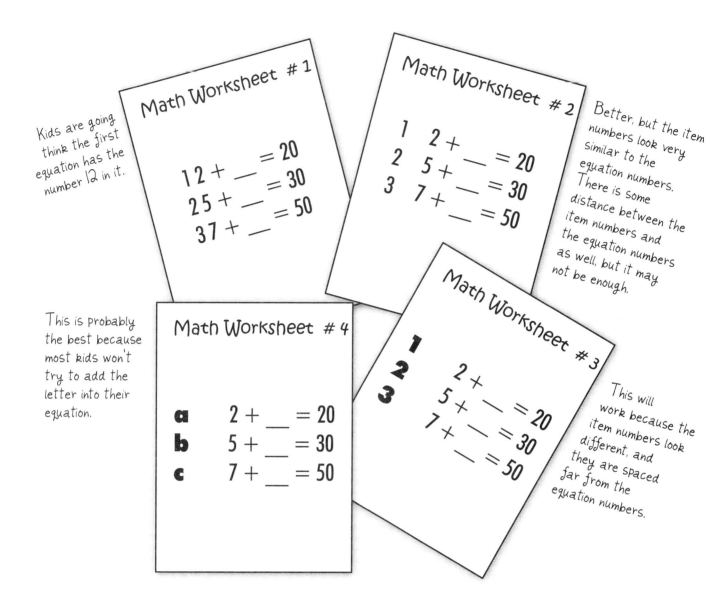

Kids are going think the first equation has the number 12 in it.

Math Worksheet # 1

$$12 + \underline{\quad} = 20$$
$$25 + \underline{\quad} = 30$$
$$37 + \underline{\quad} = 50$$

Math Worksheet # 2

1   $2 + \underline{\quad} = 20$
2   $5 + \underline{\quad} = 30$
3   $7 + \underline{\quad} = 50$

Better, but the item numbers look very similar to the equation numbers. There is some distance between the item numbers and the equation numbers as well, but it may not be enough.

This is probably the best because most kids won't try to add the letter into their equation.

Math Worksheet # 4

a $2 + \underline{\quad} = 20$
b $5 + \underline{\quad} = 30$
c $7 + \underline{\quad} = 50$

Math Worksheet # 3

1
2
3

$$2 + \underline{\quad} = 20$$
$$5 + \underline{\quad} = 30$$
$$7 + \underline{\quad} = 50$$

This will work because the item numbers look different, and they are spaced far from the equation numbers.

FIGURE 7–20 Problems with math worksheets

SUMMARY

In previous chapters you've learned about type, shape, color, depth, and space. This chapter helps you work with these tools using contrast, alignment, repetition, and proximity. While simple, these actions can make the difference between something that is and isn't instructionally useful. Contrast, alignment, repetition, and proximity are all called design *actions* because they describe something that you *do* with type, shape, color, dimension, and space.

When you work with contrast, you create strong differences in typefaces, shapes, and colors. You resize images or give them shadowing or text to make them appear to come forward or fall backward. Contrast is the action that helps learners see the main point; thus, it is important for enhancing the figure/ground (you'll learn more about this in the next chapter) in an image.

When you align type, shapes, and even space, you help establish unity among different elements and establish hierarchies of information. Unity helps the learner sense a connection between elements of an image, and hierarchy contributes to the organization of an image. You will learn more about hierarchy in Chapter 9 and unity in Chapter 10.

When you repeat type, shapes, color, size, and spatial arrangements, you likewise help the learner make connections. Color coding is an example of assigning a color to similar items to show their relationship. Consider shopping mall maps that show store levels and codes using the same color.

When you move items close together to make them seem to be part of the same message or when you move things apart to make them seem to be different messages, you are working with the power of proximity. Moving headings closer to the subordinate content often improves learners' understanding of the information.

Altogether contrast, alignment, repetition, and proximity are powerful actions because they influence learner perception. You will manipulate contrast, alignment, repetition, and proximity in endless ways to improve your instructional message. You'll use contrast to help your learners see what is most important, as you'll see in Chapter 8. You'll use alignment, repetition, and proximity to help learners identify layers of information in Chapter 9.

You'll use alignment, repetition, and proximity to help learners make connections with the "bigger picture," which you'll learn more about in Chapter 10.

FOR MORE CHALLENGE

Visit Chapter 7's *Challenge* section on the book's website. There you'll find several instructional problems that require your visual solutions. Compare your solutions to those of others.

DISCUSSION FOR DISTANCE LEARNING

Visit the book's website (Chapter 7 > Discussion) for discussion or chat questions.

REFERENCES

Williams, R. (1994). *The non-designer's design book: Design and typographic principle for the visual novice.* Berkeley, CA: Peachpit Press.

Williams, R. & Tollett, J. (1998). *The non-designer's web book: An easy guide to creating, designing, and posting your own web site.* Berkeley, CA: Peachpit Press.

CHAPTER 8

Figure/Ground Perceptions

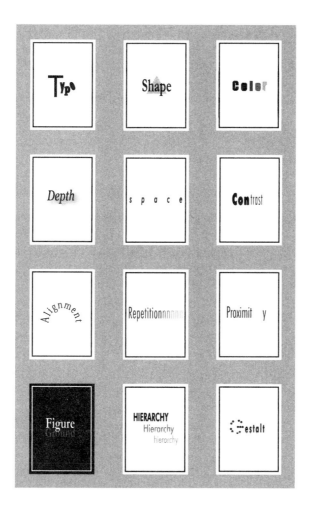

"The interior decoration of graphics generates a lot of ink that does not tell the viewer anything new. The purpose of decoration varies—to make the graphic appear more scientific and precise, to enliven the display, to give the designer an opportunity to exercise skills. Regardless of its cause, it is all non-data ink or redundant data ink, and it is often chartjunk."

Edward Tufte

NOTES ABOUT THE OPENING VISUAL

The cover graphic was designed in part to emphasize figure/ground. By making the chapter topic black and leaving all the other chapter topics white, viewers tend to focus on the black. Since the black topic catches attention, it is considered the figure. Everything else is the ground.

I considered using a novel image (Figure 8–1) because the topic of figure/ground deals with what seizes our interest. For example, Figure 8–1 was designed to illustrate the concept of figure/ground by showing the moon moving toward us over time, evoking a sense of mystery. When what we see conflicts with what we expect, we become interested.

I collect images I find interesting and file them away for an occasion where they might be appropriate. Figure 8–2 Part A comes from the Dover publication *Curious and Fantastic Creatures*, which contains a collection of drawings created in 1565. Figure 8–2 Part B is one I noticed in a clip art collection that could be used as stimulus for discussion about food industry standards. Figure 8–2 Part C is an image I use in my instructional design classes to show how most people view training—something you just pour into a passive brain.

You may be asking how these images are related to figure/ground. I consider them related because these images are unusual and their novelty makes people notice them. In other words, they stand out. They become the figure out of the ground.

FOCUS QUESTIONS

- What is figure/ground?
- What kinds of instructional problems relate to figure/ground?
- How do you improve figure/ground perception for instructional information?

KEY TERMS

1 + 1 = 3   the phenomenon that two images combined may create a third; sometimes the third image helps make the overall image easier to understand, other times the third image makes the overall image more difficult to understand

The moon in this image demonstrates figure/ground. You see the moon advancing forward in time (becoming the figure out of the ground), and the moon's bright white color makes it advance out of the black background.

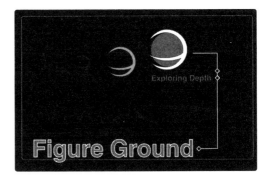

FIGURE 8–1   Alternative opening visual

Source: Created by Don Klumker. Used with permission.

The novelty of these images make you notice them. They grab your attention; thus they become the figure.

A.

Dress for success

C.

B. FRESH DAIRY

FIGURE 8-2 Grabbing attention with novel images
Source: (A) clip art © Dover Images; (B) clip art © 1997 RomTech.

FIGURE/GROUND   the perception principle that describes the mind's tendency to seek figure and ground distinctions; as a visual designer the figure is typically the information you want to stand out, and the ground is the information you want to recede or support the figure

GENERATIVE STRATEGIES   instructional methods (outlining, concept mapping, drawing, charting, note taking) that require learners to contribute to and construct their own understanding

INTRODUCTION

Sylvia is helping a mountain bike manufacturer create better repair instructions. Figure 8-3 Part A is a wall poster to accompany printed instructions that refer to the bike parts displayed on the poster. The repair employees refer to the poster to locate the bike parts they need to adjust. Sylvia has these questions as she considers the redesign of the poster:

- What is the most important information for the repair employees?
- How do I make that information grab the employee's eye?
- How do I make that information easy to refer to when fixing a bike?
- Is a photograph the best way to do the image or would a line drawing be better?
- Is there a way to make several elements seem part of the same focal point to help focus information?

Figure 8-3 Part B and C show two possible solutions. Part B uses labels against a plain background while Part C focuses attention on the front wheel with a light gray background and a simplified line drawing of the wheel. Which is better? When Sylvia informally tested these

This poster has too much ground: the gray background the little bikes, the ghosted label, and the text over the image. These images compete with the bike part labels for attention.

A.

These images are better. The bike part labels and the actual bike parts are easier to see.

B.

C.

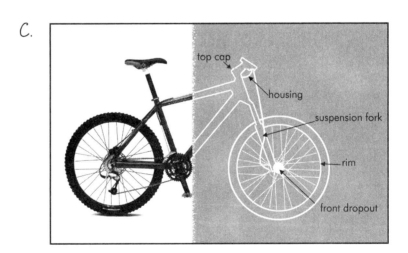

FIGURE 8-3 Revising the bike repair poster

two images with nine people, seven preferred the line drawing (Part C), stating that it clarified the information, especially if it were used to go along with instructions about front wheel repair.

Sylvia's question "Which is better, a line drawing or a realistic image?" has been asked and researched for a long time. During the 1940s and 1950s realistic instructional images, such as photographs, were favored by research. During the 1960s, however, many researchers agreed that realistic visuals often provided extraneous stimuli that detracted from learning. Simple line drawings were favored because they provided only the essential cues (McIntyre, 1983).

Today the question remains. As with all of the information in this book, the effectiveness of one approach over another often depends on the instructional context (the "It Depends" rule again). In areas such as medical education and engineering, realistic images are considered more effective because the external stimuli in the images are part of the real-life experience. To know if Part B or Part C is more appropriate, Sylvia needs to seek the opinions of bike repair employees—or better yet observe them while they are repairing the bike with the poster.

The purpose of the bike image is not to discuss line versus realistic drawings so much as to introduce the importance of figure/ground considerations when creating visuals. In working with Part A, Sylvia was attending to the importance of figure/ground in training or support materials. She asked the questions, "What information do learners need most?" "What is the best way to show that information to help them do their task?"

As you learned in Chapter 2, instructional images should help people *select, organize,* and *integrate* information in meaningful ways. We try to facilitate the selection task when we focus on improving figure/ground. As a designer you must decide if providing realism is the best way for learners to identify and extract the information or if the provision of simple line drawings is the best approach.

This chapter shows you how to use the perception principle of figure/ground to make instruction easier to understand. The **figure/ground** principle explains how the limited information processing capacity of the human mind forces people to focus on one stimulus at a time rather than several. Figure/ground essentially names the two types of attention, that which the learner is paying attention to (the figure) and that which the learner is not paying attention to (the ground). Implementing figure/ground to improve instruction is simply the act of making the most important information stand out from the rest of the information. When you do this, you help the learner focus on what is critical. By eliminating some of the information that learners immediately pay attention to, you reduce their cognitive load, or the demands placed on their short-term memory. This makes your instruction seem easier and more efficient to the learners.

The Danish psychologist Edgar Rubin made figure/ground experiences notable with the now famous vase/profile illusion (Figure 8–4). Look over this image. What do you see? Do you see two human profiles or do you see a flower vase? When you look at this image, your mind seeks to identify contours that will form into either figure or ground status. Notice in Figure 8–5 how a line can be associated with either a vase shape or a profile shape. Since you've seen both flower vases and human profiles, your mind easily associates the contours with those two images.

FIGURE 8–4   A vase/profile illusion

Source: Based on Rubin's Goblet from Archives of the History of American Psychology. Used with permission.

Do you see the vase or the profiles?

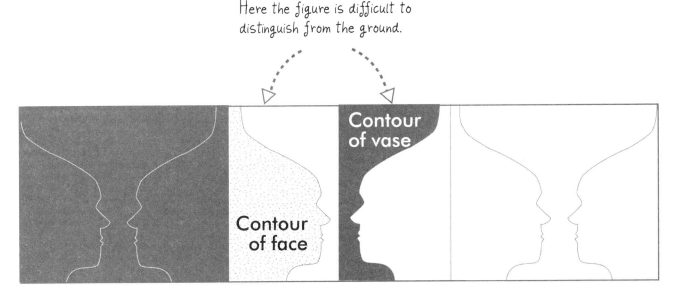

FIGURE 8–5   Different depictions of the vase/profile image

Source: Based on Rubin's Goblet from Archives of the History of American Psychology. Used with permission.

FIGURE/GROUND IN EVERYDAY LIFE

The importance of figure/ground is everywhere. Signs are used all over the world to help people perform particular tasks, such as making a phone call in a busy airport. The black and white telephone sign (Figure 8-6 Part A) means a telephone is nearby. The black receiver is considered the figure, and the white background is considered the ground.

Now, consider instead seeing the sign in Part B of Figure 8-6 the figure isn't clear and neither is the sign's message. This can cause problems since airport travelers are usually in a hurry and don't want to spend unnecessary time interpreting the sign; they want the sign to convey its message loud and clear in the simplest way possible. Good designs support the tasks of the users. In this case, the busy airport traveler is the user, and the task is to quickly find a telephone and make a call.

HOW IS FIGURE/GROUND RELATED TO INSTRUCTION?

Here is a widely recognized example of figure/ground that can be interpreted from somewhat of an instructional perspective. Imagine now that you are presenting information about characteristics of elderly women and display Figure 8-7 Part A to your learners. Some of your learners will see an old woman (Part B), while others will see a young woman (Part C). They are both seeing correctly. Take a minute and try to see both the young woman and the old woman. Most likely your mind will go back and forth. At some moments you will be focusing on the young woman, who becomes the figure, and at other times you'll be focusing on the old woman, who then becomes the figure. While you are switching back and forth between the young and the old woman, your mind is at work creating those figure/ground distinctions. (If you are wondering why this young woman/old woman image wouldn't be considered an example of gestalt, your questioning is on track! It is. As mentioned early in the book, figure/ground is a type of gestalt.)

To help you see the old lady and the young lady, I adjusted the images. To make the old lady more visible, I made the big nose more prominent by completely removing the young

FIGURE 8–6 Clear vs. cluttered image

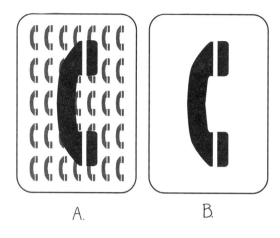

A.   B.

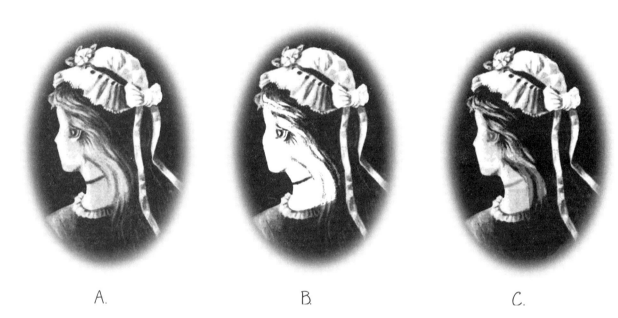

A.   B.   C.

FIGURE 8–7 Example of figure/ground distinctions

Source: A New Ambiguous Figure, by E.G. Boring, from American Journal of Psychology. *Copyright 1930 by the Board of Trustees of the University of Illinois. Used by permission of the University of Illinois Press.*

woman's nose. I made the face brighter all over so it would stand out more. These adjustments were done in Adobe PhotoShop with an eraser and a tool that allows you to make a section of an image either darker or lighter. This type of image manipulation takes practice since your goal is to create or adjust images to influence learner perception, and you must be careful that you are not altering copyrighted material without the copyright holder's approval.

While the young lady/old lady is an entertaining visual and effectively illustrates the concept of figure/ground, for most instruction you don't want the learner's mind switching back and forth between figure and ground because it takes too much mental energy. You want the learner to focus easily and quickly on your key message, the figure. Your design goal is to create a clear figure supported by, but not competing with, the ground.

Look at the Figure 8–8 Part A, paper-based instruction related to career choice. You can quickly identify the instructional topic and key characteristics. The topic is clearly visible since the title is bold, large, and emphasized by surrounding white space. Figure 8–8 Part A has a good figure/ground relationship. Because this relationship is good, you can distinguish the critical from the less critical information. Contrast Part A with Part B. In Part B, nothing

The figure/ground in Figure A is much better than the figure/ground in Figure B. Figure A is better for three reasons: (1) the title stands out and is written in a way that would be meaningful to the reader; (2) the page uses chunking to make the different career categories stand out; and (3) there is a clear contrast between the text and the background.

Finding a Career for YOU!

Finding a career that you are happy with isn't always an easy task. John Holland has a theory of six different types of workplace jobs:

1. **Realistic jobs** are for those with athletic or mechanical ability.

2. **Investigative jobs** are for those who like to observe and analyze.

3. **Artistic jobs** are for those who have innovative and intuitional abilities.

13

Career Choice

Finding a career that you are happy with isn't always an easy task. John Holland has a theory of six different types of careers, called the RIASEC theory.

According to RIASEC theory Realistic jobs are for those who have athletic or mechanical ability. Investigative jobs are for those who like to observe and analyze. Artistic jobs are for those who have innovative and intuitional abilities. Social jobs are for people who like to work with people. Enterprising

13

A.   B.

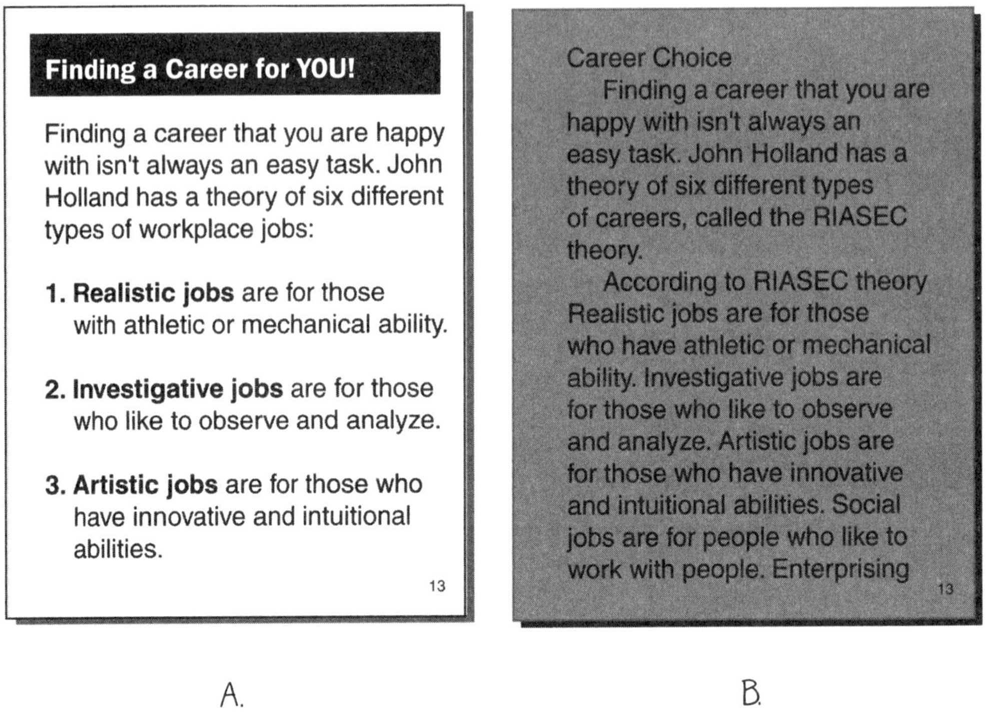

FIGURE 8–8   Capitalizing on figure/ground

really stands out. You'd have to read through the whole page to get a sense of what it is about. The gray text on the gray background creates an overall gray and bland page. It is also difficult to read the information because there isn't that much contrast between the text and the background. Figure 8-8 Part B doesn't have a good figure/ground relationship because nothing stands out.

Examine Figure 8-9A. This is an image showing a residential heating system. What do you think of the figure/ground relationship in this image? At first glance you might notice a lot of information in the basement area. Figure 8-9B focuses attention only on the critical information. Notice how the lines defining the house and many of the heating elements are less obvious in Figure 8-9B than are the lines and labels in Figure 8-9A.

Tufte (1983) writes about the importance of conserving data ink for important rather than extraneous information. Data ink is "the non-erasable core of a graphic" (Tufte, 1983, p. 93). I think of data ink as anything that isn't white space. Good use of data ink enhances figure/ground. Notice how there is less data ink in Figure 8-9B. Because the designer saves the ink for the most important information, the learner is not distracted from the critical information.

WHAT ARE THREE TYPES OF FIGURE/GROUND PROBLEMS?

Three types of figure/ground combinations or relationships covered in this chapter seem to interfere with instruction:

1. an instructional image where the figure and the ground compete
2. an instructional image where the figure should be the ground and the ground should be the figure
3. an instructional image where the figure and ground create an optical illusion

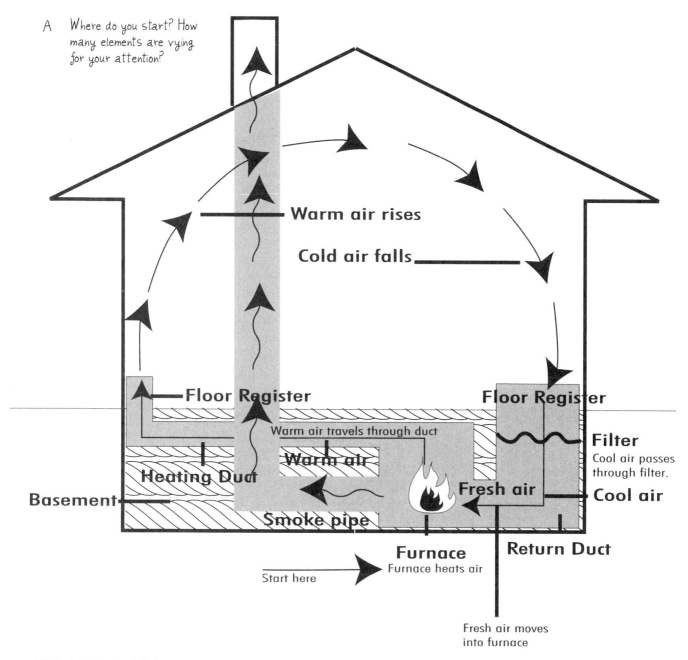

FIGURE 8–9A   Dueling labels competing for attention

Source: Adapted From Reader's Digest Complete Do-It Yourself Manual (1973), Pleasantville, NY: Readers Digest Association, p. 279.

Figure and Ground Compete

This example comes from an experience that I observed when attending my daughter's second grade field day. The class met outside with another second grade class to plant tulips. The activity took the place of the regular science and math class. Second graders were supposed to mark a Popsicle stick four inches from its end (the math part) and plant it in the ground the right way up (the science part). Since the students were outside near a noisy street, many did not hear the teacher's verbal instructions so they picked up the instructions in Figure 8–10a to figure out what to do. If you look and read closely, you'll see that Figure 8–10 Part A

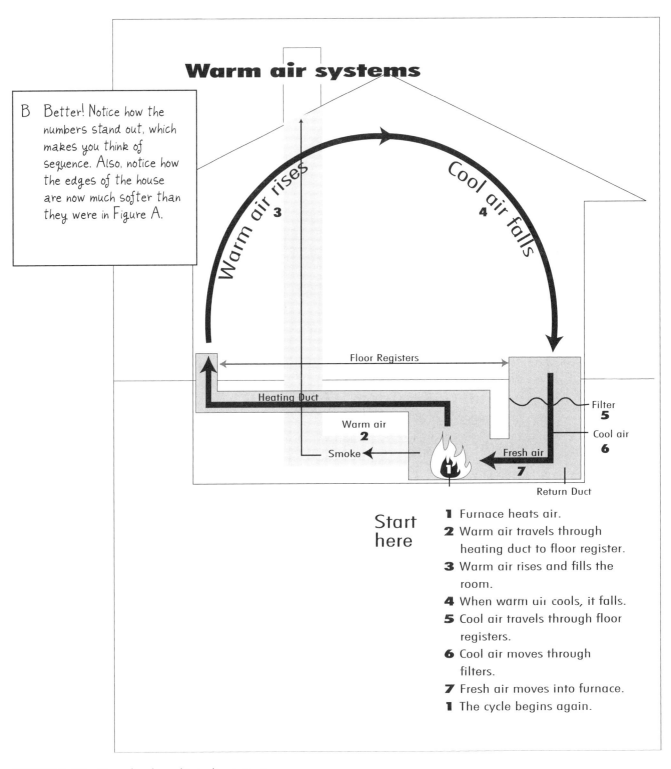

Warm air systems

B Better! Notice how the numbers stand out, which makes you think of sequence. Also, notice how the edges of the house are now much softer than they were in Figure A.

Warm air rises **3**

Cool air falls **4**

Floor Registers

Heating Duct

Warm air **2**

Smoke

Filter **5**

Cool air **6**

Fresh air **7**

Return Duct

Start here

1 Furnace heats air.
2 Warm air travels through heating duct to floor register.
3 Warm air rises and fills the room.
4 When warm air cools, it falls.
5 Cool air travels through floor registers.
6 Cool air moves through filters.
7 Fresh air moves into furnace.
1 The cycle begins again.

FIGURE 8–9B Streamlined graphic to direct attention

Source: Adapted from Reader's Digest Complete Do-It Yourself Manual *(1973), Pleasantville, NY: Reader's Digest Association, p. 279.*

What is the student supposed to look at in Figure A? What are they supposed to do? Figure B is much clearer, and the graphics serve an instructional purpose.

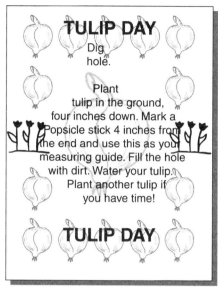

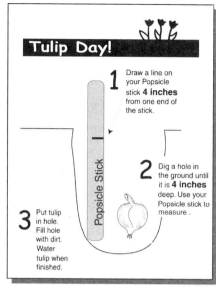

A.   B.

FIGURE 8-10   Correcting a figure/ground problem

has a figure/ground problem: Both the figure and the ground are equally competing for attention. What happened was predictable. Many of the second graders watched what others were doing and tried to copy them. I noticed that more than half of the students that day didn't get their tulips planted. The math and science lesson was lost in the confusion. I think if the second graders had used the instructions in Figure 8-10 Part B, there might have been much less confusion. Notice how attention to figure/ground did not stop with a redesign of the graphic elements alone. The writing and sequencing (a hierarchy principle covered in Chapter 9) of the instruction was changed to emphasize the most important information in an organized manner.

Figure and Ground Are Reversed

Images where the figure should be the ground and the ground should be the figure are common in instruction. Of all the figure/ground faux paux, this reversed figure/ground is the most common among novice designers who "play" with fonts, colors, borders, and clip art. What happens is that these "fun" features often take over visually, making the instruction hard to access. Edward Tufte, in his classic books on information and quantitative design, shows many examples of information or data that is difficult to understand because its display is junked up with graphical embellishment.

An image where the figure should be the ground and the ground should be the figure is one where an image's emphasis is in the wrong place. The computer-based training screens on time management in Figure 8-11 show this type of problem. The clock in Part A takes up a lot of space, and the title of the unit is hard to read since it curves around the clock. The text is in a soft gray as well, which is harder to read than black. In Part A, the visual focus is on the clock, not the content. Part B, on the other hand, is a redesign that makes the title of the instructional unit and the instructional text clear. By dimming the clock graphic, the clock becomes the ground and the learner is more likely to focus on the instructional content. The gray color for the text is replaced by black, making the text easier to read.

What is supposed to stand out? The clock or the content? Compare the placement of the title "Time Management" in figures A and B.

A.

B.

FIGURE 8-11   Focusing on the instructional content

Figure and Ground Create an Optical Illusion

You've already seen an example of figure/ground combinations that create optical illusions when you looked at the vase example and the old woman/young woman example. Another interesting type of optical illusion to watch for is the **1 + 1 = 3** phenomenon. This phenomenon states that two figures may combine to form a third, often unanticipated image. Look at Figure 8-12. You first see a black and a gray bar added together. This is an example of 1 + 1 = 2. You see a total of two bars, the black one and the gray one. The next example shows you 1 + 1 = 3. In this example, notice how the space between the black and gray bar visually becomes a bar, too. Now there is a black bar, white bar, and gray bar.

This is the 1 + 1 = 3 phenomenon. When the gray and black bar are placed side by side, you see two bars. When the gray and black bar are separated, you see three bars. (The space becomes a bar, too—the third element.) Sometimes you'll put two elements together like this and unexpectedly get a third. It is OK if the third element doesn't detract from your message, but if it does, you may need to edit the image.

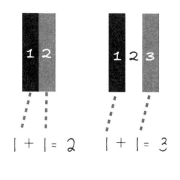

FIGURE 8-12   1 + 1 = 3 phenomenon

Figure 8-13 shows some entertaining examples of the 1 + 1 = 3 phenomenon. In Part A of Figure 8-13, compare the size of the centered white circle in each of the "flower" type arrangements. Which centered white circle is largest? The top circle or the bottom? (We'll come back to this shortly.)

Look now at Part B. Stare at the eye in the center of the gray circle. Stare long enough that your eye plays some tricks on you. What happens?

Now look at the Part C. Are those columns of black and white squares parallel with each other?

What do you read in Part D? Are you sure you read correctly? Read it again. Pay attention to each word.

Look at Part E. Try to count the black circles. What happens?

The 1 + 1 = 3 phenomenon takes place in all of these images. In section a, the two centered white circles are the same size. The top centered circle seems bigger because it is surrounded by smaller images. This shows that surrounding elements in a visual affect our perception. The two black dots at the very top of Figure 8-13 are copies of each centered white circle. As you can see, they are the same size. I just filled them with black to make their sizes easy to compare.

If you stared long enough at the eye in Part B, you probably saw the surrounding gray circle shrink. Again, your perceptions and the effect of other elements in the visual distort the size of the actual image.

The columns of Part C are parallel but it is pretty difficult to see. The placement of the squares distorts the image in our minds.

The statement "I love Paris in the Springtime" (Part D) is actually "I love Paris in *the the* Springtime." Notice the two "the" words? Again the surrounding elements in the visual may have made you unaware of what was actually there. Perhaps your mind was processing all the detail in the image: the sun, the different colors of gray, the decorative letters, and in the process dropped out one of the images (the word "the") that didn't agree with what it already knew.

The dancing black dots in Part E of Figure 8-13 are an example of the mind seeing elements that aren't there. There are no black dots in image at all, but if you stare at it long enough, your eye makes them up.

Of all these examples, I think the one that is easiest to relate back to instruction is the "I love Paris in *the the* Springtime" example. There are so many graphic embellishments in the simple sentence that the eye overlooks what is actually there and the mind does not process all of the information. Poorly designed multimedia instruction often does this by using too many signals: visual, auditory, and motion.

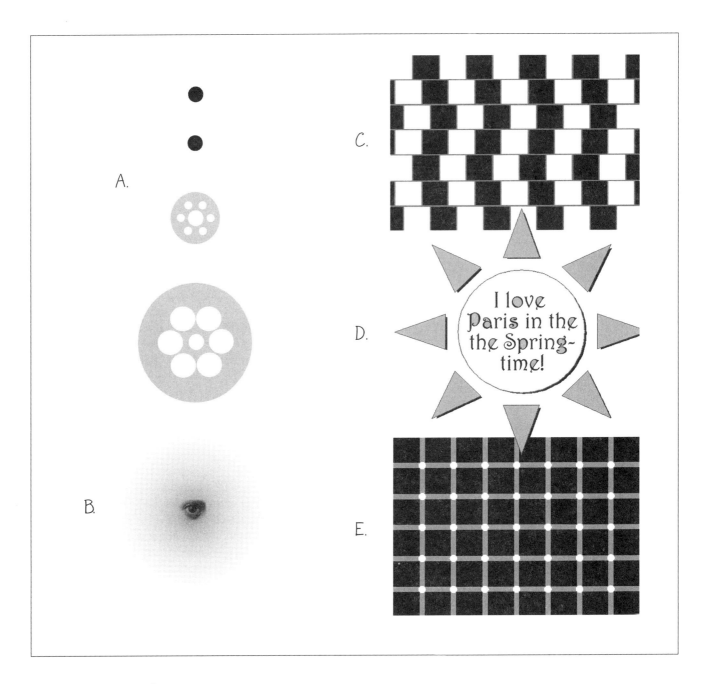

FIGURE 8–13   Examples of 1 + 1 = 3

The 1 + 1 = 3 rule takes place in a lot of poorly designed instruction and information. Rather than seeing the figure supported by the ground, a mixture of the two creates a completely different message than was intended. Tufte (1983, 1990) writes about problems with design that emphasizes the data container instead of the data. An example would be the chart in Part A of Figure 8-14. If you look at the chart your eyes are not really drawn to the data, because the data isn't emphasized. What is emphasized? The lines, or what Tufte would call the *data container*. More ink goes into the lines of the chart than into the actual data in the chart. This example is a subtle form of 1 + 1 = 3 because the visual result of this chart is a black and white texture. Try stepping back from the chart, perhaps squinting at it. You see more of a black and white pattern than you see data. Part B of Figure 8-14 takes care of

Do you notice
the lines or the
data?

A.

Quantum Numbers for Electrons in Atoms		
Name	Symbol	Values
Principal	n	1, 2, 3 ...
Orbital angular momentum	l	0, 1 ... n-1
Magnetic	ml	-1 ... 0 ... +1
Spin	ms	+1/2, -1/2

B.

Quantum Numbers for Electrons in Atoms

Name	Symbol	Values
Principal	n	1, 2, 3 ...
Orbital angular momentum	l	0, 1 ... n-1
Magnetic	ml	-1 ... 0 ... +1
Spin	ms	+1/2, -1/2

FIGURE 8-14   Focusing on the content

Source: Created by Christine Gaudinsky. Used with permission.

the figure/ground problem by making that data stand out, not the lines of the chart. Notice how the designer used a soft, less intrusive gray to separate the different rows of information? As a reader, you can see the data easier.

It's time for a break in reading. Check out the figure/ground instructional problem on the book website (Chapter 8 > Web activity). Create a solution to this problem and share your results with those of others.

HOW DO YOU WORK WITH FIGURE/GROUND?

As a designer of instructional visuals, your task is to create an optimal figure/ground balance. To do this you need to create a clear distinction between the figure and the ground and help learners by doing some of their brainwork for them. When a learner sees an image, the brain is working in ways that the learner isn't even aware of, sorting information into figure (important) and ground (supportive) categories. Your job as a designer is to do some of that organizing up front, so the learner doesn't have to bother with it. By doing so, you make it easier for the learner to access and identify critical information. Wouldn't you rather have the learner expending mental energy on processing or thinking about the content rather than just trying to access and figure out what the content is? The goal of most performance support environments is to help the learner perform a task, not figure out what the task is.

Later in this chapter we'll look at some situations in which requiring the learner to sort information into figure/ground categories themselves *is* a good instructional practice. In some situations, requiring learners to consciously organize the information into figure and ground categories actually helps them process the information more deeply and learn more thoroughly. While this may be true in some cases, many more situations benefit from optimal design of figure/ground to facilitate the learning process simply by making access to instructional information easier.

Tools and Actions

As you can see in the previous examples, creating the optimal balance of figure/ground is challenging. There are no simple rules for achieving optimal figure/ground, but you will find that the tools and actions in the previous chapters will help you.

You'll mainly use contrast as a way to make important information stand out. Tools that create contrast include type, color, space, shape, and dimension. Type can be used to create contrast in a variety of ways. It can be bigger or smaller, bolder or softer, closer or far away. Shape can be used to draw the eye, since simple shapes provide easy contours for perceptual recognition. Color can make elements of a visual more noticeable. Images that are larger or seem to advance use dimension to catch the viewer's attention. White space can direct your eye to what is important. You can even create a mental contrast by using images that contrast with your expectations.

Take a minute to look over the information on viruses (Figure 8-15). Part A could use more contrast to help the learner immediately grasp the important information. Part B uses tools and actions to make the figure stand out from the ground more clearly.

- White space surrounding the title makes the title/main theme stand out from the text.
- Size and dimension are used in the title and in key points (bolded) of the text.
- Shape is used in the ebola virus image.
- Typography is used to repeat the "look" of the virus. (The title letters are similar in appearance to the shape of the virus. Both have a hollow appearance created by parallel lines.) The word "virus" repeats itself to play upon the replication theme. This is also a use of repetition.

Figure/ground distinctions are enhanced using contrast (see Figure 8-16). Contrast is achieved when two elements are different. In Figure 8-16 the top set of words does not have as much contrast as the bottom and consequently does not look as good together as do the bottom words. Williams (1994) describes effective contrast as elements that are very different:

> If the two elements are sort of different, but not really, then you don't have contrast, you have conflict. That's the key—the principle of contrast states that if two items are not exactly the same, then make them different. Really different. (p. 55)

The following are examples of figure/ground makeovers for computer-based training, Web-based training, slides, job aids, and instructional documentation. These examples are presented in the categories of picture functions identified by Levin (1981) discussed in Chapter 2.

Decorative Instructional Visuals

Web-based training/computer-based training   Part A of Figure 8-17 shows a Web-based training menu for the topic of candle making. One good rule of thumb for Web or computer-based training is to use photographs to add dimension and interest to your training. Although the computer screen does cut down on the resolution and sharpness of a photographed image, photographs as a whole tend to add instant decorative appeal. Part A, however, has a figure/ground problem since the details in the photography interfere with seeing the training topics clearly. Part B is an improvement.

A

What is a Virus?

A virus is made of membranes, proteins, and one or more DNA or RNA strands. These strands allow the virus to replicate. A virus is "compact, hard, logical, totally selfish, and dedicated to making copies of itself" (Preston, 1994, p. 83). Viruses are parasites; to replicate they must be attached to something else. When a cell comes along, the virus will attach itself to the cell, making the cell its host. When this happens, the cell wraps itself around the virus, drawing it into its system. Once inside the virus begins its work using the cells structure and energy to duplicate itself with incredible speed.

B

virusvirusvirus

A virus is made of membranes, proteins, and one or more DNA or RNA strands. These strands allow the virus to replicate. A virus is "compact, hard, logical, totally selfish, and **dedicated to making copies of itself**" (Preston, 1994, p. 83).

Viruses are **parasites;** to replicate they must be attached to something else. When a cell comes along, the virus will attach itself to the cell, making the cell its host. When this happens, the cell wraps itself around the virus, drawing it into its system. Once inside, the virus begins its work using the cell's structure and energy to **duplicate itself with incredible speed.**

Ebola Virus

The difference in figure/ground is better in B. You instantly notice the topic of this passage since you see a representation of the Ebola virus and the title clearly stands out. Notice how the outlined letters in the title match the outlined edges of the Ebola virus? This repetition makes the image seem more connected to the topic, and together they work to create a stronger message. Notice too how key phrases are bolded, helping you focus on the most important words.

FIGURE 8-15 Figure/ground improvements

The lower set of words has a better figure/ground contrast since the word "Ground" is in a lighter shade of gray, making the word "Figure" stand out more.

FIGURE 8-16 Capitalizing on contrast

The words and the candles are hard to see here.

A.

Here the words and candles are easier to distinguish. The contrast between the candles, words, and background was increased to make this happen.

B.

Image by Erin Hunt

FIGURE 8–17 Figure/ground improvements for a website graphic

Source: Created by Erin Hunt. Used with permission.

Reducing the clarity of the background image has strengthened the contrast between figure and ground images. Notice how in Part A you can clearly see a net underneath the candles. Part B makes the net, as well as other images, less visible. Typography is less ornate in Part B as well. Altogether these changes improve the figure/ground relationship.

Erin Hunt, the artist who created this image, had to experiment with opacity options in Adobe PhotoShop. By reducing the opacity of the net and some of the other background images, she was able to make them drop into the background more. Adobe Illustrator has a similar Transparency function.

Slide Presentation

Part A of Figure 8-18 uses a photograph of an owl for a slide presentation. While this image looks perfectly fine on paper, it loses much of its clarity when projected. A good rule of thumb for projected displays is to use dark backgrounds rather than light ones. When the room is darkened, the dark backgrounds provide greater contrast and legibility, as in Part B.

Representational Visual

Book diagram   Part A of Figure 8-19 is used in training documentation to show where to type a Web address. While the information is correct, it is difficult to distinguish. Not only is the address small and slightly illegible, but it gets lost in all of the other information. Part B is an improvement because it focuses your eye on the important information using a visual magnification strategy. Size is used to create contrast and improve figure/ground distinction in this example.

Organizational Visual

Overhead transparency or book diagram   In Figure 8-20, Part A shows a career code based upon Holland's theory of occupational careers. The A, S, E stand for artistic skills, social skills, and entrepreneurial skills, respectively. Part A doesn't do as good of a job

A

Figure A looked washed out when projected in a dark room.

B

Increasing the contrast made this image project well in a darkened room.

FIGURE 8-18   Improving a slide presentation

Source: Clip art © 1997 RomTech.

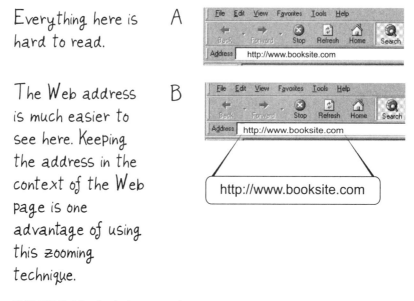

Everything here is hard to read.   A

The Web address is much easier to see here. Keeping the address in the context of the Web page is one advantage of using this zooming technique.   B

FIGURE 8-19   Book diagram enhancement

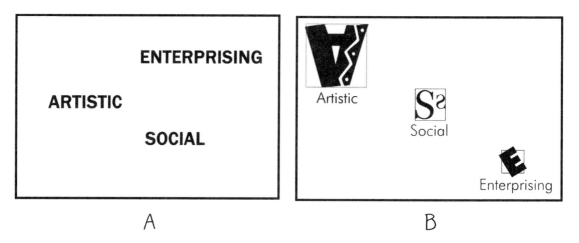

FIGURE 8-20   Using novelty, depth, and alignment to improve a visual

of presenting this information in a way that organizes it for the learner. The occupational code should be presented as a hierarchy to communicate that the first letter is the skill in the greatest demand for that career.

Part B of Figure 8-20 does a better job of showing the relative importance of the occupational codes using novelty, depth (size), and alignment. The initial letters are drawn to represent their meaning (novelty), different sizes represent different degrees of importance, and the stair step alignment represents declining importance.

Explanative Visual

Job aid   Part A of Figure 8-21 is an explanative graphic because it shows hand signals associated with alphabet characters. This figure suffers from Tufte's "chartjunk" because so much of the ink in the image is dedicated to the noninstructional data. Part B is an improvement because the chart lines are removed altogether. Each hand is filled with a gray color to help separate the letters. The combination of the gray fill and the white space serves to separate the elements in a way that is less visually intrusive than the line.

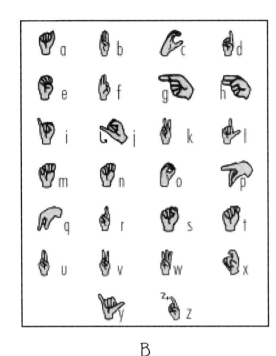

A   B

The borders and lines compete with the hands.   Removing the lines and filling the hands with gray improves the instructional quality.

FIGURE 8-21   Removing "chartjunk" from a job aid

Projected Visual (Slide or Overhead)

Part A of Figure 8-22 shows biker position for road and mountain bikes. While the angle of the back is easy to see in both bikes, the image could be improved even more. Part B creates greater contrast between the two images, making comparisons easier. First, the biker images are reduced to silhouettes because reducing the unneeded detail focuses attention on the critical information. The dark line emphasizes the position of the bikers' backs. Making the bikers face the same direction (repetition of direction) and placing them side-by-side (proximity) helps the learner see the distinction.

GENERATIVE STRATEGIES

Throughout this book you learn tools and actions that you can put to work to improve learner perception and understanding of instructional visuals. You are doing some of the work for learners by organizing information clearly up front, so their minds don't have to do the work.

At times, however, it might be better to make the learner do the organizing work. When your goal is *learning* oriented, it is time to consider generative strategies. **Generative strategies** are learning techniques that require learners to generate their own meaning. Generative strategies include outlining content, creating organizational charts, creating mental images and analogies, and summarizing information in one's own words (Whittrock, 1989). Using these strategies helps the learner think about the information more deeply and learn it more thoroughly.

A.

B.

It is easier to compare the positions when there are fewer distracting elements. The bikers are now facing the same way, and both images are silhouettes. The dark line showing the back position is the darkest, making it stand out the most. Placing images side by side helps people make comparisons, too.

FIGURE 8–22   Making comparison easier in a projected visual
Source: Clip art © 1997 RomTech.

FIGURE 8–23   Example of mental imagery

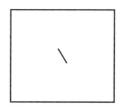

Manhattan

Generative strategies can be used to help students distinguish the critical information from the rest. When you use generative strategies, you are requiring the learner to make the figure/ground distinction. The following examples show you how the learner might generate his or her own figure/ground using mental imagery, adding graphic elements to an image, and selecting or creating an image that summarizes the key point of instruction.

Mental Imagery

The following passage from *The Hot Zone* (Preston, 1994) communicates the size and number of viruses present on our planet using mental imagery.

> Viruses are too small to be seen. Here is a way to imagine the size of a virus. Consider the island of Manhattan shrunk [to the size of the line you see in Figure 8–23.]
>
> This Manhattan could easily hold 9 million viruses. If you could magnify this Manhattan and it were full of viruses, you would see little figures clustered like the lunch crowd on Fifth Av-

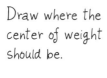

Draw where the center of weight should be.

FIGURE 8-24   Asking learners to complete the diagram

enue. A hundred million crystallized Polio viruses could cover the period at the end of this sentence. There could be two hundred and fifty Woodstock Festivals of viruses on that period—the combined populations of Great Britain and France, and you would never know it. (Preston, 1994, p. 85)

Adding Graphic Elements to a Diagram

If you were teaching snowboard weight shifts, you might ask students to draw where the center of weight falls for different snowboard positions. Part A of Figure 8-24 shows what the student would use. Part B shows what the student might draw.

Generating a Visual Representation

Have students generate an image to help them remember information. Parts A and B of Figure 8-25 show how one student created an image to help her remember to place a comma inside a parenthesis rather than outside the parenthesis in a computer programming class.

Creating a Conceptual Example

If you were teaching a unit on self-esteem, you'd most likely want the learner to understand what self-esteem means conceptually. One good way to teach a concept is to provide many

A.   B.

FIGURE 8-25   Learner's generation of a visual representation

examples of the concept, along with examples that do not represent the concept. Part A of Figure 8-26 is a cartoon bubble demonstrating a high-self esteem statement and a statement that doesn't reflect high self-esteem. This exercise requires the learner to generate similar statements. Part B shows how the learner might use this exercise.

SUMMARY

In previous chapters you've learned about visual tools (type, shape, color, depth, and space) and actions (contrast, alignment, repetition, and proximity) to improve instruction. In this chapter you get a chance to put tools and actions together to improve figure/ground. *Figure/ground* refers to the mind's tendency to pay attention to only one thing at a time. Whatever the mind is attending to is the figure, and whatever the mind isn't attending to is the ground.

That the mind seeks to find contours and images in visuals has fascinated psychologists for many years. If a contour is associated with more than one image, as in the case of the vase/profile image, the mind tends to perceive both images associated with the contour. What results is a switching back and forth between images, making the vase a figure at one moment and the profiles the figure in the next. This example is important for instruction. Because our goal is usually straightforward communication, we do not want to have the learner expend time trying to find out what the figure is. We want that message to be clear. To achieve this we then make the figure/ground distinction strong, mostly using the design action contrast, through implementing any of the tools. For instance, type can be made large, bright colors can be used for type or shape, and space and depth can draw the eye to what is important.

In the next chapter you learn how to apply tools and actions to improve hierarchy. Hierarchy is the second of the three principles of perception (figure/ground, hierarchy, and gestalt).

A. Make thoughts for each bubble

B. Make thoughts for each bubble

FIGURE 8–26 Creating a conceptual example

FOR MORE CHALLENGE

Visit Chapter 8's *Challenge* section on the book's website. There you'll find several instructional problems that require your visual solutions. Compare your solutions to those of others.

DISCUSSION FOR DISTANCE LEARNING

Visit the book's website (Chapter 8 > Discussion) for discussion or chat questions.

REFERENCES

Levin, J. R. (1981). On the functions of pictures in prose. *In* F. J. Pirozzolo & M. C. Wittrock (Eds.), *Neuropsychological and cognitive processes in reading* (pp. 203–228). San Diego: Academic Press.

McIntyre, W. A. (1983). The psychology of visual perception and learning from line drawings: A survey of the research. (ERIC Document Reproduction Service No. ED230901)

Preston, R. (1994). *The hot zone.* New York: Anchor Books.

Tufte, E. (1983). *The visual display of quantitative information.* Cheshire, CT: Graphics Press.

Tufte, E. (1990). *Envisioning information.* Cheshire, CT: Graphics Press.

Whittrock, M. C. (1989). Generative processes of comprehension. *Educational Psychologist, 24,* 345–376.

Williams, R. (1994). *The non-designer's design book: Design and typographic principles for the visual novice.* Berkeley, CA: Addison-Wesley.

CHAPTER 9

Hierarchy Perceptions

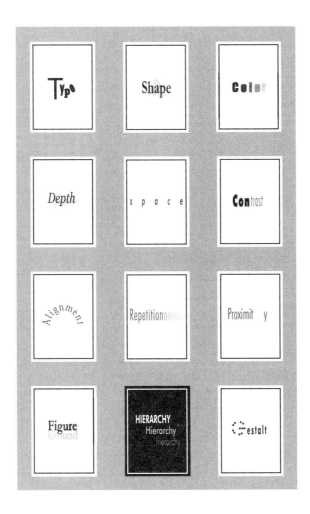

"People have no idea of the extent that information structures rule their lives."

Jenny Robbins

NOTES ABOUT THE OPENING VISUAL

I had a hierarchical dilemma with the image on the previous page, which is the graphic used on most of the chapters in this book. I had to choose between two looks (see Figure 9–1), and each of these looks had a good reason for why it should have been selected.

I ended up with the image on the right, which if you look closely starts out with Type, Shape, and Color and moves down to Figure/Ground, Hierarchy, and Gestalt. This sequence is the order in which the chapters are read.

I'm still not sure this is the best placement of icons though, since the left image in Figure 9–1 makes just as much sense. The last chapters are the most important and, according to rules of visual hierarchy, you place the most important images on the top. Additionally, all of the chapter topics and concepts explain the final chapter. They lead *up* to understanding the final chapters. Notice the word *up?* Even in our language we assign a visual order of importance to location. Things on the top are generally considered more important than things on the bottom. The same is true for left and right positioning (more about this later).

I had to make a choice. Do I match the chapter cover images to the overall meaning of the book, or do I match the chapter cover images to how I think the learner will most easily understand it? Since the goal is learner-friendly design, I chose the latter. I wanted to move the learner through the chapters from easy to difficult, a sequence recommended

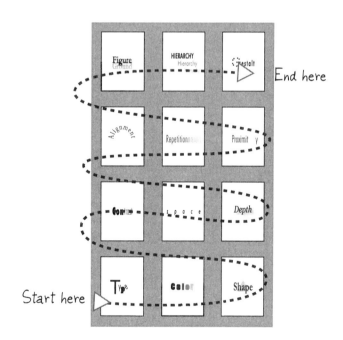

Figure/ground, hierarchy, and gestalt should be on the top because everything else leads up to them. But to leave them on the top means starting the reader on the bottom, which isn't intuitive.

This approach seemed easier for the learner initially.

FIGURE 9–1   Choosing the opening visual

in the instructional design literature (Morrison, Ross, & Kemp, 2001). Thus, I chose the order you now see. This remains to be user-tested, so I'll just have to see what most readers prefer.

This kind of dilemma is worth sharing, because it shows that there are no clear rules. So much of what you do involves decision making based on a number of factors. The questions I asked related to the chapter cover are fairly typical questions, and they are the types of hierarchical questions that this chapter addresses.

FOCUS QUESTIONS

- What is hierarchy?
- Do visuals have levels of importance?
- How do you use tools and actions to create visual hierarchy?

KEY TERMS

CHUNK   a unit of information
CHUNKING   the action of grouping information
CUES   visual signals that capture and direct attention
HIERARCHY   perception principle that deals with communicating the relative importance of elements in a display
LAYERS   different levels of information used for visually stratifying information
PLANES   imaginary or visible lines that form horizontally, vertically, or diagonally

INTRODUCTION

Sylvia and Zack are redesigning the interface of a parking ticket dispenser. To check out the design they drive to a parking lot that uses the faulty design. Like many automated environments, no "live" parking attendant is employed at the site; the dispenser and the person parking the car do all the work. When Sylvia and Zack encounter the machine, they are aware of three cars waiting behind them so they do not want to take too long to figure out how to get the ticket. Part A of Figure 9-2 is what they see. The large circle in the middle catches their attention first because of its highly visible words "Takes Bills Only." When searching through his wallet for the money, Zack realizes he only has quarters, no bills! "Is this the problem with the interface?" he questions. Upon closer observation he notices an obscure area showing where to insert quarters. Sylvia and Zack agree that many of the drivers probably think they can't use quarters and start to worry when they realize they do not have any bills.

As Sylvia and Zack analyze the interface they ask these questions:

- What is the user trying to do?
- What is the user's environment like?
- Do any environmental restrictions need to be considered?
- Is there a sequential order to information that you want the user to follow?
- How do you establish what the user should read first, second, and third?
- If there are items of equal importance, how do you communicate this status?

The parking meter redesign (see Part B) involved consideration of each question. Since purchasing a parking ticket was the key user task, the words "Pay in Advance Parking" were emphasized in large letters at the top of the display (where Western cultures tend to look first). Because waiting lines needed to be minimized, the information the driver must interact with must be minimal. Given that purchases would need to be made from the driver's side of the car, the display needed to be positioned at the correct height, with all typefaces large

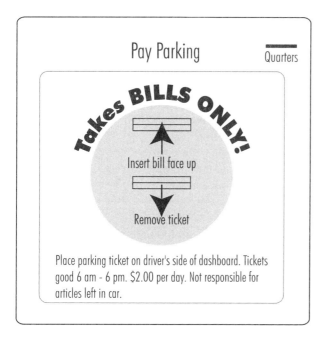

A

This seems pretty intuitive, but something is wrong. The machine does take quarters. The first impression you get is that it takes bills ONLY.

B

The option of bills or quarters is more evident here. Notice, too, how the shades of gray move from light to dark, implying a sequence of steps.

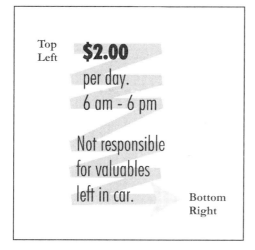

C

Eastern cultures read from the right top to the left bottom.

FIGURE 9-2 Making the parking lot meter more user-friendly

enough to be readable from the driver's seat. Numbering the steps 1 and 2 helps users identify the tasks they must perform. Since the parking ticket dispenser was designed for Western cultures, the steps could be displayed in a left-to-right, top-to-bottom organizational sequence (see Part C) that follows the Western culture reading order.

Considerations that Sylvia and Zack made about how the order in which a culture reads information and how sequence and order can best be communicated deal with hierarchy, the topic of this chapter. This chapter shows you how you can make most instruction easier to follow using hierarchy design principles.

Hierarchy deals with communicating relative importance between elements in a display. To quickly understand hierarchy, think of an outline for a written composition (see Figure 9–3). You have the top levels (see point a in Figure 9–3), subordinate levels (see point b), and coordinate levels (see point c). Visuals can be made with these same levels of importance. Instead of using numbers and letters, these levels are created using tools (type, shape, color, depth, and space) and actions (contrast, alignment, repetition, and proximity).

You'll see many applications of these tools and actions in this chapter.

When you create hierarchy, you are working through several issues:

- What do I want the user/learner to look at first, second, and third?
- Should I make this big and bold to make people look here first?
- If I make this smaller and less bold will people look here next?
- Will white space between these elements make them seem distinct and unrelated, while at the same time making the clustered elements seem related?
- What do I want the learner to compare?

By asking these types of questions, you create what artists and information designers (Mullet & Sano, 1995; Tufte, 1990) call *levels* or **layers** that provide *pathways* for people to navigate. In the parking ticket example, the designer of the original interface was probably not aware that the large, brightly colored section of the interface would attract the user's attention first and lead to the mistaken assumption that only bills were required. These dominant features of the interface (the brightly colored circle) created an entry level for reading the interface. Unfortunately, the user's eyes failed to wander, in part because little else caught the user's attention.

This outline has
three levels:
A, B, & C.

Validity and Reliability

a —I. Validity
b —A. Measures what it is supposed to measure
   B. Types of measures
c —1. face validity
   2. content validity
   3. predictive validity
   4. concurrent validity
   5. construct validity
a —II. Reliability
b —A. Produces consistent results whenever used
   B. Types of measures
c —1. test-retest
   2. parallel forms
   3. split-half
   4. internal consistency

FIGURE 9–3 Hierarchy in an outline

When you create hierarchy, you provide the learner or user with pathways through information. In doing this, you reduce the learner's cognitive load, or as described in previous chapters, you reduce the demands information is placing on the learner's short-term memory. In the parking ticket example, drivers don't need or want to think through how the information is organized hierarchically; they just want to do a simple task quickly. As with figure/ground, when you organize the information hierarchically up front, you save the learner from having to do the work themselves.

WHAT DOES THE RESEARCH SAY ABOUT HIERARCHY?

Creating hierarchy is the act of creating a series of **cues,** or signs to direct the eye toward certain information in a certain order. For purposes of this discussion, assume cues and sign mean the same thing; they are both signals that catch the learner's attention. These cues are created using the tools and actions covered in previous chapters of this book. Simple shapes such as lines and arrows, larger or bolded typeface, color, use of white space, and elements that create a visual texture or depth all act to direct attention (McIntyre, 1983). Contrast, alignment, and proximity are important actions for creating hierarchy, as you will see as you read through this chapter.

While reading this chapter, you may find yourself wondering why some of its content wouldn't be considered as figure/ground or even gestalt. If so, your thinking is on track! Some of this information could just as easily have been presented in the figure/ground chapter or the gestalt chapter. These principles are intertwined and difficult to separate. Figure/ground principles are part of hierarchy principles, and hierarchy principles are part of gestalt principles. Figure/ground is important to consider in hierarchy because what you notice first directs you to what you notice next. Figure/ground acts in a larger perspective as a means for providing direction, location, position, motion, and sequence—all hierarchical functions.

A number of researchers support the use of visual cueing (a form of hierarchy using arrows, headings, lines, and other devices) in instructional materials (Misanchuk, 1992; MacIntyre, 1983). These studies find that visual cueing facilitates learning for low-ability individuals, children, or learners in new situations (like the parking ticket example). Other researchers, however, find the usefulness of cues to be questionable. Kennedy (1971) found that students would overlook many signals, such as arrows and headings, that were provided in textbooks. Allen (1975) found that higher ability students might be handicapped by cues since these students could already focus their attention and the cues just distracted them.

I think cues are important, especially in performance environments where part of your goal is to help someone *at the moment of need.* Just imagine what driving would be like without clear traffic signs or signals. Or, think of being in a busy airport trying to catch a plane without visible or well-organized gate numbers or arrival and departure times. Perhaps you can even think of a recent experience in a distance learning environment where you wanted something as simple as instructions on how to get started. The increase of self-directed learning and performance environments, as in the parking ticket example, requires that information be especially clear and easy to follow. Use of cues to establish hierarchy can be crucial in making information easier to understand and use.

The use of the quote at the beginning of this chapter, "People have no idea of the extent that information structures rule their lives" (from a conversation with Jenny Robbins), emphasizes the importance of designing information with hierarchy in mind. People interact with hierarchically arranged information every day. Consider these examples:

- finding where pasta is in the grocery store by using the store index (information is organized alphabetically)
- filling your car with gas using the instructions on the pump (information is organized sequentially, step 1, step 2, etc.)
- getting money from the cash machine (information is organized sequentially, step 1, step 2, etc.)

- finding a comedy in your local video rental store (information is organized by emotional categories such as drama, new releases, and horror)
- registering for classes (information is organized by academic department)
- locating information on the Internet (information is organized by common search categories such as shopping, travel, and education—though some consider the Internet not organized at all)
- locating a particular type of store in a mall (information is organized by store type, such as department store, shoe store, home accessories stores)

Some of these categories and information structures involve sequence, such as steps in a process or alphabetical ordering, and are clearly hierarchical in nature. Other steps just involve placing things in a category, such as pasta in a grocery store. Pasta isn't more or less important than canned vegetables, so how could that be hierarchical? In this chapter, however, categorization is considered a part of hierarchy. It may seem a stretch, and we'll cover it more when we discuss chunking. For now think of it as hierarchical simply because it has to be positioned somewhere and that somewhere usually has a relative position.

Three steps for creating hierarchy are covered in this chapter: (1) chunking information, (2) providing entry points to instruction, and (3) using horizontal and vertical planes. These steps enhance the learner's perception of an image's hierarchy.

Enhancing hierarchy is similar to enhancing figure/ground. Just as the learner mind would automatically and unconsciously seek figure/ground distinctions, it seeks out hierarchical relationships as well. Fleming and Levie (1993) describe it this way:

> Early processing organizes perceptual units into groups and the groups into other groups in a hierarchical manner. The way the elements of a message are clustered by the designer may therefore have an important influence on perceptual organization. (p. 63)

As a designer, your job is to identify clusters of information and to arrange them hierarchically. You are likely to ask these three questions, directly corresponding to the three research-based steps mentioned previously:

1. How should I chunk (or cluster) the information?
2. Where do I want the learner to look first? Should I initially direct the learner's eye to the whole display or just part of the display?
3. Where do I position chunks to make the most sense and draw the eye to different parts of the visual?

HOW SHOULD YOU CHUNK INFORMATION?

Instructional designers call the step of clustering information into related groups **chunking. Chunks** are simply groups of related data, like sections of a grocery store for canned vegetables and pasta. A simple way to think of chunks is to think of the paragraphs on this page as chunks. Each paragraph consists of a group of related sentences. You could go a step further and consider each heading section in this chapter a chunk and each chapter in this book a chunk. As a designer, it is up to you how much chunking you want to do.

You might be wondering how chunks fall into the category of hierarchy. Think of chunks as part of a larger hierarchy. A chunk of information usually has some type of hierarchical status. For example, think again of the paragraphs in this page. Each paragraph is superordinate, subordinate, or coordinate (of equal status) to other paragraphs. As a designer you continually decide where to place each chunk. For example, if you were explaining how to make cookies, you might separate the instructions as follows:

> measuring all of the dry ingredients (flour, sugar, baking powder)
> measuring the wet ingredients (oil, eggs, milk)
> preheating the oven and greasing the pan.

Your dry ingredient instructions would be one chunk, your wet ingredient instructions would be another chunk, preheating the oven and greasing the pan another chunk. You'd probably arrange the chunks in a logical order, preheating the oven and greasing the pan being your first chunk, and measuring dry and wet ingredients the second and third chunks.

Your goal when chunking is to help the learner think about information in a meaningful or an efficient way. Information processing theory states that short-term memory can handle seven plus or minus two items at a time (Miller, 1956). Anything over that and the mind is likely to lose pieces of information. This is relevant in our cookie example because there are typically about 14 units of information in a typical cookie recipe, ranging from getting utensils ready to several steps each for measuring, mixing, preparing, and baking. Breaking those steps down into chunks helps the user think about the information without becoming overloaded.

Designers use the seven plus or minus two units of information as a rule of thumb for chunking. Keep in mind that chunk sizes can vary. There may be quite a bit of information in one chunk and very little information in the next. Many factors influence how many units of information a designer might put into a chunk. The information itself, the learning situation, or the expertise level of the learner all influence how you might chunk information. Take, for example, a simple recipe for spaghetti. This situation might call for three chunks: the sauce instructions, the pasta instructions, and the assembly and presentation instructions. In this example, the topic of learning influences the chunk size.

The expertise level of the learner influences chunking as well, with greater expertise on the part of the learner corresponding to a greater number of information units within a chunk. An advanced cook might need only two or three chunks in the recipe for spaghetti, where a beginning cook would likely need more chunks, beginning with a chunk of information on utensils needed and another chunk of information on the spices in the sauce. As a designer it is up to you to chunk information accordingly.

Here is an everyday example of chunking that you've experienced. How would you remember the numbers of the left side of Figure 9–4? If you shift your attention to the right side of Figure 9–4, you'll notice immediately that the first number is a phone number. Notice how the seven digits have been chunked into two groups? The chunked version seems easier to think about, doesn't it? The second number is a dummy social security number (the letter A is my way of keeping someone's number private), 35A-89-7280. Here nine numbers have been chunked into three groups. Chunking must work, or we wouldn't be using it so much.

To emphasize the need for chunking, try this simple exercise. Without looking at your telephone, try to recall which letters on the keypads are associated with which numbers. While you are at it, also try to remember where the #, the operator, and * keys are. If you can't remember, it's because it is too much information, altogether 26 units of information. You have 12 buttons, 24 letters (Q and Z are left off the keypad), 10 numbers, and 2 symbols.

FIGURE 9–4 Chunking numbers

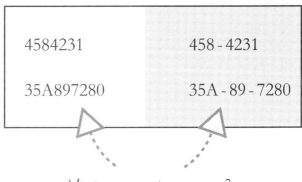

Which is easier to remember?

FIGURE 9–5   Telephone keypad, an example of chunking

If you picked up the phone, though, you'd notice that letters are chunked in groups of three. The letters ABC are positioned next to the number 2, DEF next to 3, and so on (see Figure 9-5). When looking for letters on the keypad, the user has an easier time because the alphabet is chunked into groups of three letters. Each row on a telephone keypad consists of three buttons. This is a good example of a performance versus training environment. There is no need to have people memorize which letters are associated with which numbers on a phone keypad. Since the goal isn't a learning goal (memorization), the information simply needs to be presented in a way that helps the person perform the task at the moment of need.

If you look throughout this book, you'll see many images that are divided up into information chunks. For example, Figure 9-6 was used in a previous chapter. Notice how this information was chunked to help the reader understand the different paint techniques.

Notice, too, how white space is used to emphasize chunks. In the telephone number and social security examples in Figure 9-4, a white space is used to separate numbers. In the paint techniques visual, white space is used between different techniques. Likewise, a line of white space separates paragraphs in text. Increasing the white space between elements makes the elements seem more distinct. Decreasing the white space makes the elements seem more similar. White space is an important tool for creating the appropriate distance (proximity) between information elements.

It is time for a break in reading. Assume that you've been given the following content for Web-based training on the universe. The topics include:

- the solar system
- earth and sun activities
- active galaxies
- quasars

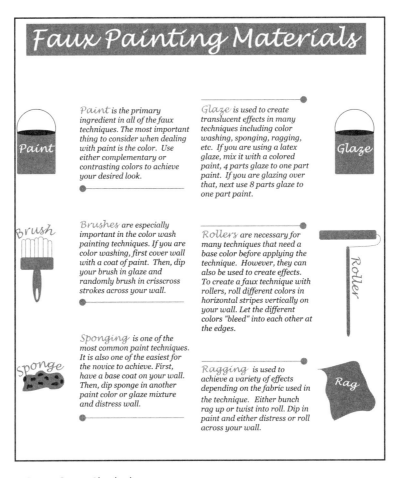

FIGURE 9–6   Chunked instructions

Source: Created by Erin Hunt. Used with permission.

- the sun
- matter
- activities like exploring and observing
- the Milky Way
- constellations

Create an interface (just a main menu and submenu) showing how you might provide the learner with pathways through this content. How would you set up an interface that would give them clear directions for navigating through the Web-based instruction? After you create this solution, visit the book website (Chapter 9 > Web activity) to compare your solution to those of others.

In whatever you design—whether it is an instructional handout, a document, a Web-based instructional unit, or an electronic presentation—you'll find yourself chunking information and then arranging those chunks in ways you think will make sense to your learner. This arrangement is usually based on some type of hierarchy. Your chunks might be part of something sequential, they may be part of a natural order (you chunk things based on the way they appear in real life), or the chunks might simply be arranged alphabetically. As you arrange the chunks, you must decide where you want the learner to begin, the next step in enhancing the hierarchy of instructional information.

WHERE DO YOU WANT THE LEARNER TO LOOK FIRST?

The overall arrangement of information chunks influences how a visual is initially perceived. What does a learner look at first in a picture? The whole picture or just part of it? Fleming and Levie's (1993) principle 1.5b suggests that seeing the "big picture" or the "details in the picture" first depends on the relative size of the image to the space that image takes up in the visual field. Thinking of the visual field as the white space that surrounds an image may help you see the distinction (see Figure 9-7). When the visual field is small and the image is large, the learner may be more likely to notice the detail. When the visual field is large and the image is small, the learner may be more likely to notice the big picture. Fleming and Levie (1993) suggest that

> typically neither global (big picture) nor local (detail) precedence dominates, but rather that people enter the image at a level of detail that is somewhere between the two extremes. (p. 64)

This suggests that you manipulate the white space in an image to create an equal perception of the big picture and detail. Likewise, Tufte (1990) recommends that you "create simplicity in the underlying design and complexity in the details." Perhaps the best way to think of this is to turn to another writing analogy. An outline with levels I, II, III, A, B, C provides both a big picture and detail at the same time. The outline, because it is brief and displays

Here you are likely to notice the whole image first (the big heart).

Here you are likely to notice parts of the image first (the individual hearts).

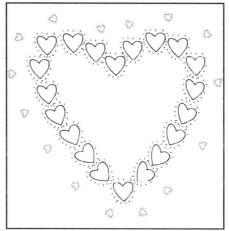

FIGURE 9–7   Seeing the big picture and the details

the key topics, lets you see the big picture. Each line of the outline lets you see the detail. The heart images (Figure 9–7) also show you both the big picture and the detail. In both images you see the large heart and the details that make it up (the small hearts).

Providing detail is important since people are attracted to and often motivated by it (Fleming & Levie, 1993; Tufte, 1990). People have been found to choose to study displays that have many rather than few elements and asymmetrical or irregular arrangements (Fleming & Levie, 1978). Advice to keep things simple and sayings such as "less is more" are often misinterpreted as advice to keep out some of the necessary detail. Tufte (1990) describes the unfortunate consequence of such activity as "dummying down" the data.

To help the learner enter a visual depends in part on how you've dealt with figure/ground. The information in the figure/ground chapter (providing contrast, emphasizing important information using size, color, and type) can help you make certain areas of a visual be noticed first.

HOW DO YOU DRAW THE EYE TO DIFFERENT PARTS OF THE VISUAL?

You've chunked and created a good figure/ground balance to help people enter a visual. Now you need to think about helping the learner move through the visual. You need to create paths or layers through which learners can travel. Creating paths isn't difficult when you control the sequence in which information is displayed. For example, when you use electronic presentations, movies, and books, the sequence of information is presented very clearly. The learner might be presented with step 1 on the first page or screen, step 2 on the second page or screen, and step 3 on the third page or screen. When this is the case, the type of media you use will control the order and sequence of the information and you don't need to worry about how the learner will perceive the pathways through the information, or where their eyes move to next.

When this ordering is not controlled, as in some hypertext environments, visual charts, tables, graphs, and diagrams, then you *do* need to be concerned about how the learner will travel through the information. As is the case with charts and graphs, learners must read information that falls at the intersection of rows and columns. In hypertext settings learners must move through a series of nonlinear links, keeping track of where they've been.

Several attention-drawing principles of design using devices such as "lines, arrows, and the message's composition" (Fleming & Levie 1993, p. 69) can help you control where you direct the learner's attention. You can use these devices to facilitate the mind's natural tendency to:

- organize information on vertical, horizontal, and diagonal planes.
- respond to different degrees of contrast.
- perceive relationships based on proximity.

It is interesting to note that these three tendencies rely on three actions: alignment, contrast, and proximity.

How Do You Use Vertical, Horizontal, and Diagonal Alignment to Improve the Hierarchical Organization of Your Message?

Without thinking, the learner's mind will seek out lines and contours, as we noted in Chapter 8. By placing important information onto either horizontal or vertical alignments, it is more likely to be noticed.

Vertical Alignment

Horton (1994) suggests people see items placed on the top part of a vertical **plane** as being: high, powerful, lightweight, light color, spiritual, valuable, rare, primary. Low positions are seen to have these properties: heavy, dark, earthy, common, secondary.

In general, items on the top are assigned a status of more importance. Consider the two passages that follow. Which is easier to understand?

> Stephanie is taller than Jackson. Jackson is taller than Nick. Nick is shorter than both Stephanie and Jackson.

> Stephanie is taller than Jackson.
> Jackson is taller than Nick.
> Nick is shorter than Jackson and Stephanie.

If you think the second example is easier to understand, it's probably because of the arrangement of information. It seems easier to understand that Stephanie is the tallest when her position is also the highest.

Horizontal Alignment

According to Horton, elements on the left side of the plane have the status of before, cause, primary, problem, crude. Images on the right have the status of after, effect, secondary, solution, refined.

Fleming and Levie (1993) make a number of research-based suggestions to show relationships between elements using lines and arrows. They suggest that lines between elements show cause and effect. This perception can be strengthened when the causal element is placed to the left of the element that is affected. Thicker lines between the elements suggest a stronger connection or relationship than do thin lines, and arrows imply an even stronger relationship (Fleming, 1968).

Studies by Winn (1980a, 1980b, 1981, 1982a, 1982b, 1982c, 1983, 1986, 1987) and Winn and Holliday (1985) show how graphics act as strategies that activate learners' cognitive processes along both vertical and horizontal planes. Winn (1985) compared learning of evolutionary sequence using two flow diagrams. One diagram showed evolution of dinosaurs from left to right across the page, and the other showed evolution right to left. Students using the left-to-right diagram learned the category names and numbers better, theoretically because left to right followed the reading sequence where left is first (the oldest) and right is the latest (or youngest).

Figure 9–8 Parts A and B show evolution in a similar way. Take a moment to study Parts A and B. Which part would help you recall the sequence of evolution most easily? If you preferred the left-to-right sequence (Part B), it might be because you "read" this diagram just as you read most information (in Western cultures). Compare Figure 9–9 Parts A and B as well. Which of these diagrams would help you understand the concept of evolution best? If you choose Part A, it might be because you attribute a cause-effect relationship in a left-to-right sequence.

Winn (1981) also conducted a study to teach students the classification of insects at different stages of metamorphosis. Winn suggested that student memory structures (schemas) were activated by a matrix of rows and columns that helped students identify classification categories. Compare Figure 9–10 Part A with Part B. Which helps you understand the classification system of wild cats better? If you chose Part B, the row and column structure may match your schema for organizing information. The rows and columns provide an organizational structure that adapts easily to how your memory is organized. Part A doesn't help with organization at all. The circle is used to group the wild cat family but doesn't help as much as Part B. The families filinae and pantherinare *are* listed in Part A, but they are more difficult for the learner to group initially.

Diagonal Alignment

The use of a diagonal alignment to increase perception has not been mentioned frequently in the research literature. Horton (1996) associates information on the diagonal plane near the top of an image with adventure, far, later, unknown, and secondary. Images at the bottom of a diagonal plane have the status of near, now or soon, familiar, primary, intrusion, and involvement. Many graphic designers recommend that diagonal lines be used to generate excitement and energy in images (Nelson, 1989).

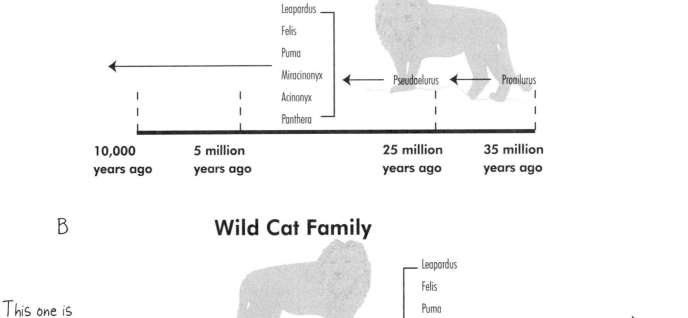

This one is easier for Western cultures to interpret.

FIGURE 9–8   Reading sequence example

Reading Order

According to Fleming and Levie (1993), if none of the vertical, horizontal, or diagonal strategies are used, learners will probably resort to their reading order. To tap into this tendency you need to place the most important items on the top left of a display, the next most important items to the immediate right, eventually working toward a lower position on the page, likely starting on the left again. While this left-to-right, top-to-bottom sequencing strategy is an easy way to establish hierarchy, the increase in international audiences will likely make this a less-than-ideal solution, since international audiences may read from right to left or start at the bottom of a page (or display) and move up. Therefore, it is important to find other ways to establish hierarchy.

How Do Different Degrees of Contrast Convey Hierarchical Information?

Aside from using alignment, hierarchy is perceived based upon color and size. Images that are brighter or darker are often perceived as more important, dominant, or superordinate. Likewise images that are larger are perceived as more important, powerful, and superordinate to images that are smaller.

Shades of color can communicate sequence, time passing, and rates of change. Figure 9–11 shows how shades of gray are used to show the spread of AIDS in Africa.

Cause and effect is often understood in a left-to-right sequence (for Western cultures).

A

B

FIGURE 9–9   Improving comprehension of a sequence
Source: Created by Bea Doyle. Used with permission.

How Does Proximity Help Learners Perceive Hierarchical Relationships?

Images that are close together are perceived as related, while those that are far apart are perceived as unrelated. Consider this example:

Events that people worry about

Turning 40

Public speaking

Events people worry about
Turning 40
Public speaking

This image makes it hard to sort the Filinae family from the Pantherinare family.

A

Felidae
Wild Cats

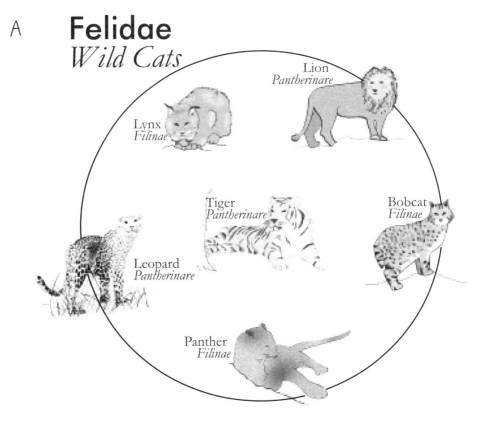

Lynx
Filinae

Lion
Pantherinare

Tiger
Pantherinare

Bobcat
Filinae

Leopard
Pantherinare

Panther
Filinae

B

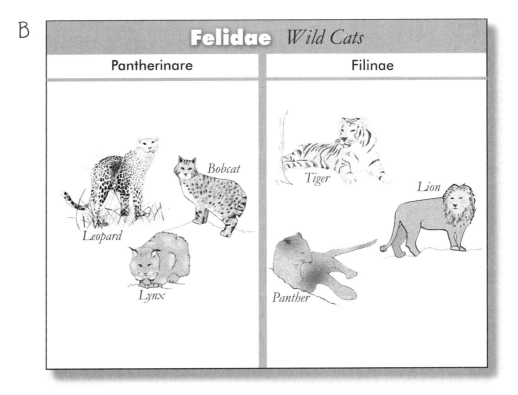

Felidae *Wild Cats*

Pantherinare

Filinae

Leopard

Bobcat

Lynx

Tiger

Panther

Lion

FIGURE 9–10 Organizing in columns

Spread of AIDS

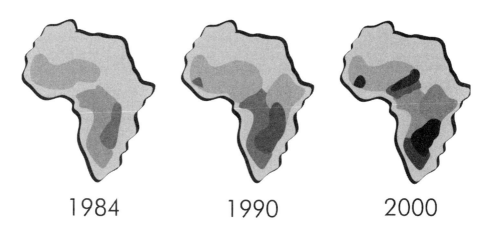

Shades of gray help you see the spread of AIDS in Africa from 1984 to 2000. This type of graphic is useful for conveying an overall message or for gaining attention.

FIGURE 9-11   Communicating with shades of color

In the first example, *Turning 40* and *Public speaking* do not appear related to *Events people worry about.* The second example, however, connects *Turning 40* and *Public speaking* to the label *Events people worry about.* The difference is that the phrases are closer together in the second example, making them seem related.

HOW DO YOU USE HIERARCHY TO DESIGN TABLES AND CHARTS?

All of these suggestions about hierarchy are especially helpful when you design tables and charts. Though easy to make and widely used, tables and charts are often misunderstood by young and old alike (Hartley, 1985; Misanchuk, 1992).

Tables and charts rely heavily on hierarchical principles to communicate trends, quantities, summaries, and relationships. This type of data usually involves making comparisons that are hierarchical in nature, such as greater than or less than, bigger or smaller, increased or decreased. Many people have problems with numbers, particularly when they need to locate a number at the intersection of a horizontal or vertical plane, which is the case when reading from tables and charts. This section covers a range of design suggestions to improve tables and charts.

Tables

Tables, often the quickest and easiest type of data display to produce, are used to make numerical information easier to understand and to present information when space is limited. Consider this passage and compare it to Figure 9-12.

In Maine, Rhode Island, and Connecticut, the average teaching salary is $45,800. The average salaries for these eastern states are $43,800, $43,100, and $50,000, respectively. Western salaries are lower, with an average of $40,800. Washington, Oregon, and California salaries are $37,900, $41,000, and $43,500, respectively.

Figure 9–12 shows east and west coast salaries side by side. This arrangement places east and west on a coordinate or equal level and makes comparisons easier.

Though tables may show the maximum amount of information in the minimum amount of space they are not always the best way to communicate information. Research shows that people find tables daunting and confusing; tables are perhaps best used with professional audiences when specific quantities are important (Misanchuk, 1992).

Several perceptually based recommendations are made to make tables easier for people to read. The actions of alignment and proximity play a role in making tables easier to understand. Several research-based recommendations for the design of tables follow.

Use Columns Instead of Rows When Making Comparisons

Ehrenberg (1977) suggests using the horizontal rather than the vertical plane when making comparisons. As we've already discussed, if you want to make it easier for the learner to compare data, put the data side by side. Look at Figure 9–13 Parts A and B. Which table makes it

West and East Coast Teaching Salaries

West				East			
WA	OR	CA	Average	ME	RI	CN	Average
$37,900	$41,000	$43,500	**$40,800**	$43,800	$43,100	$50,500	**$45,800**

Data is much easier to compare when numbers are side by side. Averages are included as well. Notice, too, how the West is located on the left as it is on most maps.

FIGURE 9–12   Displaying data in a table

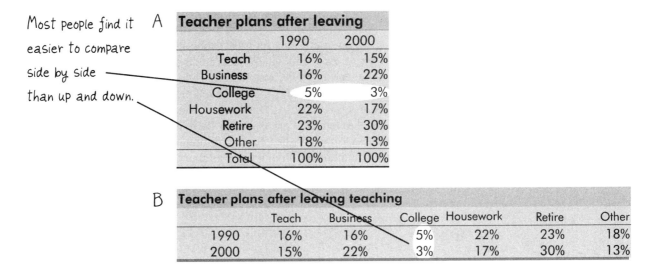

Most people find it easier to compare side by side than up and down.

A   **Teacher plans after leaving**

	1990	2000
Teach	16%	15%
Business	16%	22%
College	5%	3%
Housework	22%	17%
Retire	23%	30%
Other	18%	13%
Total	100%	100%

B   **Teacher plans after leaving teaching**

	Teach	Business	College	Housework	Retire	Other
1990	16%	16%	5%	22%	23%	18%
2000	15%	22%	3%	17%	30%	13%

FIGURE 9–13   Facilitating comparisons of data

The rounded numbers are easier to think about (unless you need the detail) than the numbers with decimal points.

Teacher plans after leaving		
	1990	2000
Teach	16%	15%
Business	16%	22%
College	6%	3%
Housework	22%	17%
Retire	23%	30%
Other	18%	12%

A

Teacher plans after leaving		
	1990	2000
Teach	15.6%	15.3%
Business	16.2%	22.1%
College	5.8%	3.1%
Housework	21.7%	16.7%
Retire	22.6%	30.6%
Other	18.1%	12.2%

B

FIGURE 9–14   Simplifying data by rounding off numbers

Including the average makes the numbers easier to comprehend.

East Coast Teaching Salaries

A

East			
ME	RI	CT	*Average*
$43,800	$43,100	$50,500	**$45,800**

B

East		
ME	RI	CT
$43,800	$43,100	$50,500

FIGURE 9–15   Including the average to improve comprehension

easier to compare teacher decisions between the years 1990 and 2000? Based on Ehrenberg's research, many people would find the data in Figure 9–13 easier to compare, perhaps because the side-by-side positioning implies a coordinate relationship.

Round Off Numbers

Ehrenberg (1977) also suggests that rounded numbers are easier for most people to comprehend. Figure 9–14 Part A shows rounded percentages. Compare the data in Part A with the data in Part B. Which is easier for you? Many people would find the rounded numbers in Part A easier to read and compare.

Include Averages

Averages should be used when possible to help readers summarize data (Ehrenberg, 1977). Figure 9–15 Part A shows a table with an average provided. Notice how the numbers in Part B are initially more difficult to compare without the average.

Place Words Before Numbers

Compare Parts A and B of Figure 9–16. Which do you find easier to follow? Many people prefer Part B because they want to know what they are comparing and prefer to begin reading a chart with words rather than numbers.

Figure B is easier to read because it starts with words.

Increase in online holiday shopping			Increase in online holiday shopping	
184%	Japan		Japan	184%
96%	Europe		Europe	96%
90%	Asia		Asia	90%
70%	N. America		N. America	70%
188%	Rest		Rest	188%
A			B	

FIGURE 9–16   Starting table rows with words

Increase in online holiday shopping			Increase in online holiday shopping	
Japan	184%		Japan	184%
Europe	96%		Europe	96%
Asia	90%		Asia	90%
N. America	70%		N. America	70%
Rest	188%		Rest	188%
A			B	

Too far for the eye to jump!

FIGURE 9–17   Using proximity in table design

Keep Words and Numbers a Readable Distance Apart

The words and numbers in a table should be kept a readable distance apart. This suggestion employs the proximity action, important for optimizing hierarchy. Elements that are closer together are considered related, whereas elements that are further apart are not. Compare Parts A and B of Figure 9-17. The numbers are closer to their descriptors in Part A. The eye must travel a greater distance in Part B. Designs like Part B are often created because the width of the heading determines where numbers are placed. The heading in Part A uses two lines of text to avoid a wide spread between the country name and its percentage.

Create Chunks in Data to Make It Easier to Read and Retrieve Information

Which table in Figure 9-18 is easiest to scan, Part A or Part B? Because Part A groups information into meaningful categories, most would say that Part A is the easiest. Shading, as in Figure 9-19, can also create chunks. Notice how different types of comparisons are facilitated by the horizontal or vertical direction of the shading.

Charts

Charts and graphs include many different type of data displays: bar charts, pie charts, and line graphs (or charts), to name a few. Like tables, bar charts and graphs can be difficult for people to understand; therefore, it is best to keep their design as simple as possible.

Tufte's (1990) advice related to "chartjunk" is important to consider in this era when people like to play with all the bells and whistles that come with their statistical computer programs. Chartjunk is Tufte's name for overly embellished statistical information. Think of the 3-D charts in bright colors you regularly see in some of the newspapers, or charts that

Figure A is easier to scan because the chunking is meaningful. For this task, the alphabetical sequence used in Figure B isn't very efficient.

Regional Teaching Interest (%)

		1990	1994	1997	2000
Far West	AZ	41	39	35	25
	CA	33	29	25	27
	ID	49	44	37	27
	OR	40	39	35	38
	WA	48	54	48	38
West	CO	43	38	33	23
	MT	45	41	34	24
	NE	45	50	44	34
	NV	45	43	35	23
	UT	44	40	35	25
Midwest	KS	26	30	33	23
	ND	52	49	42	32
	OK	30	35	30	20
	SD	48	45	40	30
	IA	35	37	32	22
	MN	45	49	42	33
	MO	22	27	23	14
	WI	44	47	42	44
South	AR	46	49	41	33
	LA	49	56	49	37
	NM	35	29	24	18
	TX	30	37	32	23

A

Regional Teaching Interest (%)

	1990	1994	1997	2000
AR	46	49	41	33
AZ	41	39	35	25
CA	33	29	25	27
CO	43	38	33	23
ID	48	54	48	38
IA	35	37	32	22
KS	26	30	33	23
LA	49	56	49	37
MN	45	49	42	33
MO	22	27	23	14
MT	45	41	34	24
NE	45	50	44	34
ND	52	49	42	32
NM	35	29	24	18
NV	45	43	35	23
OK	30	35	30	20
OR	40	39	35	38
SD	48	45	40	30
TX	30	37	32	23
UT	44	40	35	25
WA	49	44	37	27
WI	44	47	42	44

B

FIGURE 9-18 Chunking to improve understanding of table data

use little pictures, or weather reports that are accompanied by charts with a lot of graphical information in the charts in addition to numbers. Tufte focuses on making the data stand out, not the data container. The *data container* is considered anything that isn't data. For example, some of the elements of Part A in Figure 9-20 could be considered chartjunk: the chart lines aren't needed, the background shading doesn't add any information, and the dog and cat icons aren't really needed (though many readers liked them). In Part B, the focus is on the data, not everything surrounding the data. However, Part B might speed up recognition for some and would be more appropriate for young learners.

When there is too much chartjunk, it becomes difficult to determine hierarchy. Consider the visual weight of the different elements in Parts A and B. What seems to be the most important? The data to compare, dogs versus cats, is hard to separate from the background lines and shading. You can see the hierarchy (defined in this example as "greater than") better in Part B.

Fleming and Levie's principle 5.4 (1993) states that

The perception and interpretation of diagrams and charts can be influenced by a variety of graphic techniques that serve to clarify and emphasize the nature of relationships among elements. (p. 100)

Highlighting every other column/row helps.

Regional Teaching Interest (%)

	1990	1994	1997	2000
AR	46	49	41	33
AZ	41	39	35	25
CA	33	29	25	27
CO	43	38	33	23
ID	48	54	48	38
IA	35	37	32	22
KS	26	30	33	23
LA	49	56	49	37
MN	45	49	42	33
MO	22	27	23	14
MT	45	41	34	24
NE	45	50	44	34
ND	52	49	42	32
NM	35	29	24	18
NV	45	43	35	23
OK	30	35	30	20
OR	40	39	35	38
SD	48	45	40	30
TX	30	37	32	23
UT	44	40	35	25
WA	49	44	37	27
WI	44	47	42	44

Regional Teaching Interest (%)

	1990	1994	1997	2000
AR	46	49	41	33
AZ	41	39	35	25
CA	33	29	25	27
CO	43	38	33	23
ID	48	54	48	38
IA	35	37	32	22
KS	26	30	33	23
LA	49	56	49	37
MN	45	49	42	33
MO	22	27	23	14
MT	45	41	34	24
NE	45	50	44	34
ND	52	49	42	32
NM	35	29	24	18
NV	45	43	35	23
OK	30	35	30	20
OR	40	39	35	38
SD	48	45	40	30
TX	30	37	32	23
UT	44	40	35	25
WA	49	44	37	27
WI	44	47	42	44

FIGURE 9–19   Highlighting table data to direct attention

Figure A has drop shadows, a gray background, thick lines and borders, and images of a dog and cat. Figure B minimizes embellishment.

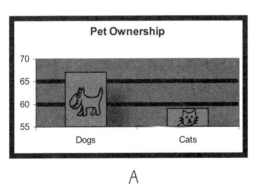

A

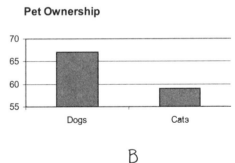

B

FIGURE 9–20   Eliminating 'chartjunk'

The following examples describe a number of strategies to help make data relationships in charts and graphs easier for learners to follow. Techniques to make bar charts, pie charts, and line graphs easier to understand are covered in this section.

Bar Charts

Bar charts display values across categories. They are used when comparisons between two or more variables need to be made or when trends need to be communicated. Both vertical (also called a column chart) and horizontal bar charts (see Figure 9–21) are used with generally equal results. Bar charts are favored over pie and line charts (Macdonald-Ross in Misanchuk, p. 225) because they allow the reader to see quantitative differences more clearly.

Vertical and horizontal bar charts tend to be equally effective.

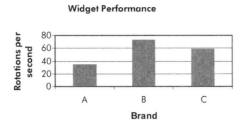 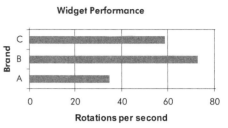

FIGURE 9–21   Bar charts

Numbers are provided here.

FIGURE 9–22   Labeling vs. not labeling bars in a chart

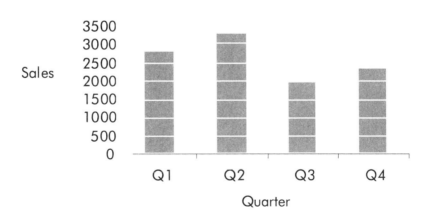

FIGURE 9–23   Keeping the visual focus on the data

The effectiveness of placing values on the individual bar is debatable. To some, directly labeling the bars (as in Part A of Figure 9–22) in a bar chart is the best approach; others prefer keeping the data as simple as possible (as in Part B). In line with all of Tufte's recommendations for the design of information, the data itself needs to be the visual focus, not the data container. To that end, Figure 9–23 is designed to follow Tufte's recommendations. Notice how grid lines are used only when necessary.

Isotope or picture graphs take a lot of time to produce and are often an inaccurate representation of data.

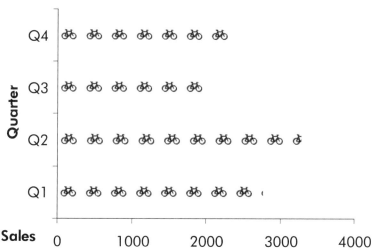

FIGURE 9–24   Picture graph

FIGURE 9–25   3-D Chart

3-D charts are discouraged since more work is required to figure out data. Your eye has to work with several edges. Is Brand A 28 or 29?

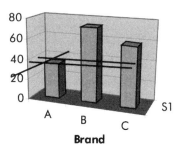

Tufte offers practical advice for creating bar charts. Figure 9–23 displays his suggestions to remove:

a. surrounding borders,
b. the *y*-axis (but keep the vertical lines), and
c. the *x*-axis (or make it a very thin rule).

What about picture bar charts or isotope charts like the ones you see in newspapers and magazines (see Figure 9–24)? While these graphs are often clever, more often than not they are amateurish, may detract from the data, take a lot of time to produce, and often misrepresent the actual data. For instructional materials the rule of thumb is to avoid them. As Tufte says, the use of pictorial data often dummies down the data and speaks down to the reader at the same time.

What about the effectiveness of three-dimensional bar charts (see Figure 9–25)? Do you think the third dimension puts the focus on the information? Although 3-D charts are easy enough to produce these days, they may not be as effective as the simple two-dimensional displays because exact quantities are more difficult to read when data is displayed in perspective.

Bubblegum is
what percentage?

FIGURE 9–26   Pie charts: trading precision for graphic depiction

What
percentage is
"All Others?"

FIGURE 9–27   Difficulty interpreting 3-D pie chart

Pie Charts

Pie charts show how much each value contributes to a total and are often used to show percentages. Pie charts are considered easy to understand and thus are widely used. However, using a pie chart presents some real disadvantages. Along these lines Tufte (1983) has strong opinions:

> A table is nearly always better than a dumb pie chart: the only worse design is a several of them, for then the viewer is asked to compare quantities located in spatial disarray both within and between pies. Given their low data-density and failure to order numbers along a visual dimension, pie charts should never be used. (p. 178)

Fleming and Levie (1993) are not quite so critical of pie charts, stating that pie charts can be useful where precision is not important.

Perhaps the biggest disadvantage of pie charts is that they are not effective for comparing data, especially if more than seven to nine segments of information and small quantities or differences in quantity are involved (see Figure 9–26). The pie shape just isn't an easy shape to compare because angles are involved. As with bar charts, the use of a three-dimensional pie chart makes information even more difficult to determine (see Figure 9–27).

When the goal is marketing a concept or teaching young children (see Figure 9–28), pie charts may be the most appropriate choice because they simplify information. For simple data, pie charts are often the most effective way to represent a concept. As with everything

Pie charts are effective in situations where data must be simplified. Young audiences and audiences introduced to a new topic may benefit from use of pie charts.

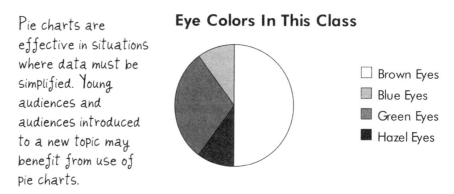

FIGURE 9-28   Benefits of pie charts

Line charts are good for showing trends over time.

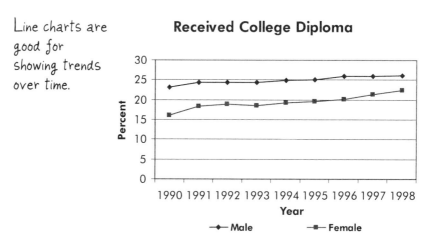

FIGURE 9-29   Line chart

else in this book, the "it depends" rule applies. If your audience is a dissertation committee, pie charts might not be specific enough. If your audience, however, is a business crowd, pie charts might be all that is needed to give an overview of a trend. Some household budgeting software programs effectively use pie charts to show how money is allocated, allowing family members to see quickly how they are spending their money.

Line Charts

If you need to show trends over time (see Figure 9-29), use a line chart. Licty (1989) recommends using a line chart for up to five lines of data.

Other Charts

Stacked area graphs   Like line charts, stacked area graphs show trends over time. Use of stacked area graphs is discouraged because they are easily misinterpreted. This is a perceptual issue since the quantity of the top value can be perceived to start where the bottom line ends. Relative quantity becomes difficult to determine (see Figure 9-30).

Picture charts   As expressed in the opening chapter, pictures can speak a thousand words, and this is true for pictures used in data display as well. Not all pictorial displays of quantitative information dummy down the information. Tufte's series of books on the subject is fascinating. Tufte has made Minard's map a classic example of the power of good information design. Minard's map (Figure 9-31) shows in one space how an army the size of

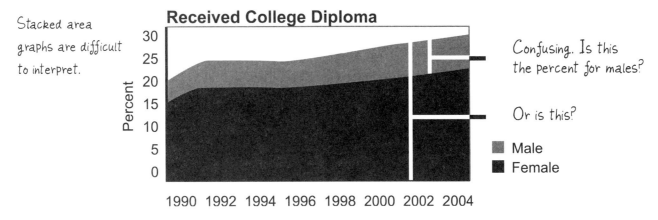

Stacked area graphs are difficult to interpret.

Confusing. Is this the percent for males?

Or is this?

FIGURE 9–30   Stacked area graph

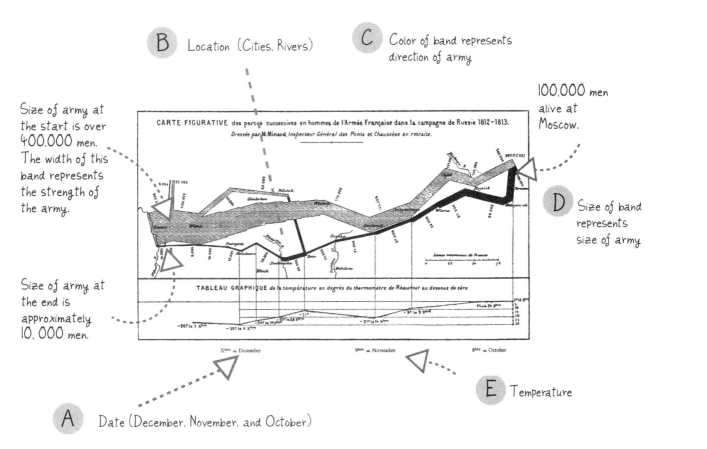

B   Location (Cities, Rivers)

C   Color of band represents direction of army

100,000 men alive at Moscow.

Size of army at the start is over 400,000 men. The width of this band represents the strength of the army.

D   Size of band represents size of army

Size of army at the end is approximately 10,000 men.

A   Date (December, November, and October)

E   Temperature

FIGURE 9–31   Minard's map (circa 1861)

400,000 dwindled to 10,000 during Napoleon's march to Moscow in 1812. On the map date (see A), location (see B), direction (see C), army size (see D), date and temperature (see E) are plotted, providing a powerful message about the tragedy of war.

Tell the Truth!

Much has been written to show how data displays can distort the truth. Perception plays a large role in this, as viewers often see the gestalt of information rather than the detail. Figure 9-32

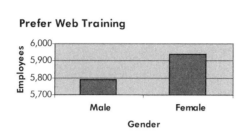

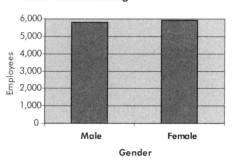

This chart makes it look like females strongly prefer Web-based training.

This chart tells it like it is: There really isn't that much difference.

FIGURE 9–32   Accurate depiction of data in charts

uses numbers to emphasize the difference in gender preferences for Web-based training. Because the y-axis starts at 5,700, the differences look much larger than they do when the y-axis starts 0 (see Figure 9-32). See Tufte's book *The Visual Display of Quantitative Information* (1983) for more information on this topic.

Hierarchy in Books, Electronic Presentations, and CBT/WBT

Many instructional visuals use a predefined format that has some degree of hierarchy already established. Figure 9–33 shows the hierarchy of a book chapter. In this graphic, higher levels (Level I, II, III) are assigned to the chapter cover and major topics or sections of the chapter. Lower levels (A, B, C) are assigned to subheadings.

Figure 9–34 shows the hierarchy of a set of electronic slides. You see different layers or levels of information in this display just as you saw them in the book example. When viewing an electronic slide presentation, however, learners have less control over the format. They cannot simply backtrack or flip through pages to reestablish their place. During a slide presentation learners may be able to see a heading topic, but they may have forgotten the relationship of that topic to other topics. A navigational structure built into the slide presentation and on the side of the slides (see the simple menu on the right side of Figure 9-35) can help learners keep track of where they are at in the total presentation.

Computer or Web-based training (CBT/WBT) typically uses a hierarchical organization scheme as well. Menus serve as the highest level (see part A of Figure 9-36), units of instruction represent the next level, and instructional content, practice activities, and feedback levels follow. Since CBT and WBT are typically learner controlled, it is important to help the learner see the hierarchical structure of the learning environment.

Can you see how an outline of chapter topics is represented visually? What traditionally would be the topic level in an outline (a Roman numeral, VII) is represented by the chapter cover layout. Each chapter in the book will look like this. What traditionally is an A, B, C in an outline is translated visually into headings, for example, Times 24 bold. What usually is a sub-section in an outline (numbers 1, 2, 3) are translated into sub-headings, such as Times 12 bold.

VII. The Solar System
  A. Introduction
    1. Planets
    2. Stars

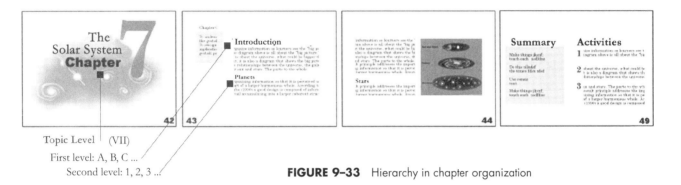

FIGURE 9–33 Hierarchy in chapter organization

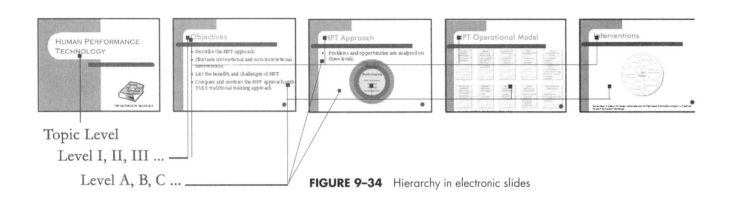

FIGURE 9–34 Hierarchy in electronic slides

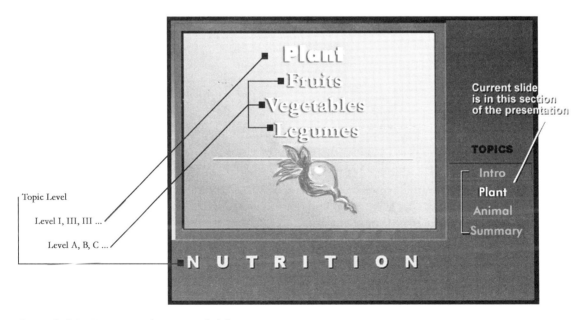

FIGURE 9–35 Navigational structure of slide presentation

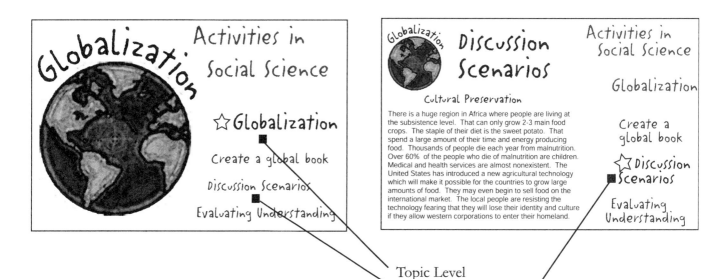

FIGURE 9–36   Menus at top of CBT/WBT hierarchy

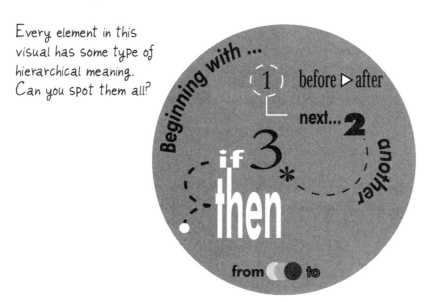

FIGURE 9–37   Words and images implying hierarchy

Techniques to Show Hierarchy

Figure 9-37 shows a number of words and images that imply hierarchy. Arrows, overlapping shapes, shapes that point, solid and dotted lines, implied lines, numbers, space, and signal words are used to convey hierarchical information. To increase the hierarchy in your images, try these strategies:

1. Using textual signals (see Figure 9-38). This strategy can use the type tool. Morrison, Ross, and Kemp (2001) suggest use of explicit signals to cue the structure of a message. By combining Armbruster's (1986) content structures with Meyer's (1986) signaling words, five strategies are suggested to show:

Lists	Comparisons	Temporal Sequence	Cause and Effect	Definition and Example
Use words like:	Use words like:	Use words like:	Use words like:	Use words like:
First	In comparison	In comparison	If	For example
Second	However	Beginning with	Then	See
Third	While	Then	The reason	Include
Subsequent	To distinguish	After	One explanation	Another
Another	To differentiate	Next		
		First		
		Second		

FIGURE 9–38   Verbal signs that show hierarchy

Source: Adapted from Morrison, Ross, & Kemp (2001). Designing Effective Instruction, 3rd edition. New York: John Wiley and Sons, Inc. pp. 150–151.

FIGURE 9–39   Using numbers to show sequence

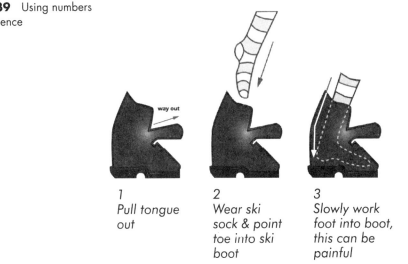

1
Pull tongue out

2
Wear ski sock & point toe into ski boot

3
Slowly work foot into boot, this can be painful

    a. a sequence or list using the words *first, second, third, subsequent, another.*

    b. contrast and comparisons using the words *but, in comparison, however, while, to differentiate, a distinguishing.*

    c. temporal sequence using the words *beginning with, after, next, first, second, etc.*

    d. cause and effect using words such as *consequently, as a result, if/then, the reason, one explanation.*

    e. definition and example using words such as *for example, include, another.*

    2. Using numbers or letters to show sequence (see Figure 9-39). This also uses the type tool.

Flowcharts show
hierarchical
relationships.

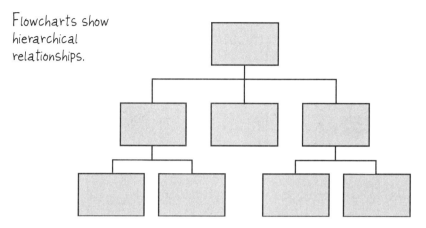

FIGURE 9-40   Using visual metaphors to show hierarchy

See how
first the line,
then the
bolded line,
and then the
arrow each
made the
relationship
appear
stronger?

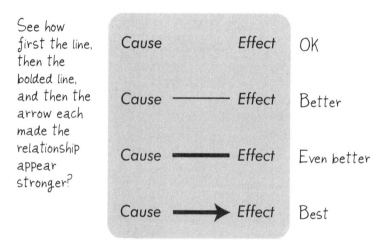

FIGURE 9-41   Using lines and arrows to strengthen relationships

3.   Using Horton's visual metaphors to show relationships (high = powerful, low = not powerful). Figure 9-40, a flowchart, uses the proximity action to show relationships.

4.   Using lines and arrows to strengthen relationships (see Figure 9-41). Thicker lines between elements suggest a stronger connection or relationship than do thin lines, and arrows imply an even stronger relationship (Fleming, 1968). This strategy uses the shape tool.

5.   Using lines, arrows, and shapes to imply speed (see Figure 9-42), and direct attention (see Figure 9-43). This uses the shape tool and the proximity action.

6.   Using ghost images, small multiples, and numbers or letters to show temporal events (see Figure 9-44). This uses the color tool.

7.   Using the size of common objects to make comparisons (see Figure 9-45). This uses the contrast action.

The tilt, size, and thicker lines make images appear to be moving faster

Fast	_Faster_	_Fastest_
→	→	→

FIGURE 9–42   Using lines, arrows, and shapes to direct attention

Look forward

Cats are noble pets, proud and independent. To keep your cat healthy, make sure it has plenty of water and both dry and wet food.

Look back

Cats are noble pets, proud and independent. To keep your cat healthy, make sure it has plenty of water and both dry and wet food.

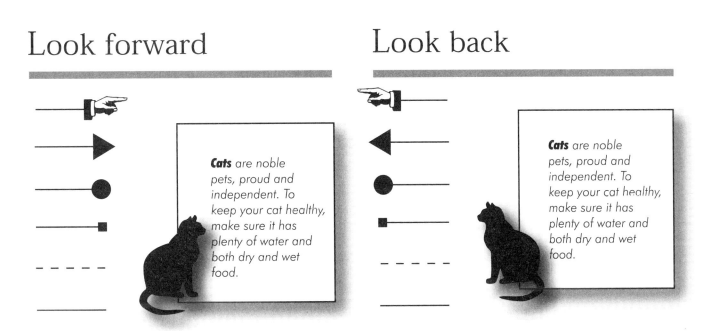

FIGURE 9–43   Additional use of lines, arrows, and shapes to direct attention

These images
show time
passing.

FIGURE 9-44   Using visuals to show temporal events

These show
relative size.

Baby Turtle Shell   Quarter

FIGURE 9-45   Using size to make comparisons

How Does Hierarchy Facilitate Different Picture Functions?

In Chapter 2 you learned about several types of instructional visuals (decorative, representative, explanative, transformational, and organizational). This section of the hierarchy chapter shows how principles of hierarchy have been used to improve visuals that represent these different categories.

Decoration

People and faces are often used in instruction. Figure 9-46 is used in print-based weight-lifting training. Notice how the image that faces the content (Part A) more effectively directs the eye than the image that faces away (Part B).

Representation

The purpose of representative pictures is to depict something. Representative pictures are particularly helpful when used in conjunction with text. Part A of Figure 9-47 is an image

This image
directs your eye
to the words.

This image
directs your eye
away from the
words.

FIGURE 9–46 Directing the eye with visuals

The ships in
Figure B may be
more effective
because they are
more interesting.

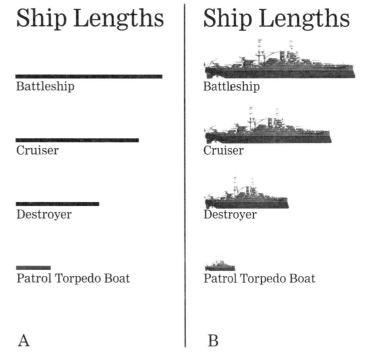

FIGURE 9–47 Using representational visuals

from computer-based training that shows the difference in the size of ships using lines only. Part B shows ship size using representative images, which are probably more motivational and interesting to look at during the CBT.

Organization

Organizational pictures are useful when temporal and spatial relationships need to be communicated. Figure 9-48a is a taco recipe without any hierarchical design. Figure 9-48b, with its title, chunking, numbering, and task orientation is vastly improved.

Figure 9-49 Part A is an electronic slide presentation that shows how the letter J is signed. Part B shows how the image is improved using ghosting.

Explanation

The purpose of explanative pictures is to explain often complex and difficult phenomena. Fleming and Levie (1993) recommend adding labels and stripping an image of all unnecessary detail. Figure 9-50 Part A is used to explain how the Hawaiian islands have developed over time and are slowly moving in the direction of Japan each year. Figure 9-50 Part B does a better job of showing the development of the islands by adding the labels "oldest island," and "youngest island," de-emphasizing the island names, and emphasizing the shift by placing the arrows in closer proximity to the island.

How Is Hierarchy Used to Facilitate Generative Strategies?

As stated in the previous chapter, when your goal is more *learning* oriented than *performance* oriented, it is time to consider generative strategies. To refresh your memory, generative strategies are learning techniques that require learners to generate their own meaning and include outlining content, creating organizational charts, creating mental images and analogies, and summarizing information in one's own words (Whittrock, 1989). The following examples show how learners might generate their own hierarchy using mental imagery, creating an outline that represents content structure, creating a flowchart that represents content structure, and creating an image that summarizes the key point of instruction.

Form Mental Images

To help a student gain a perspective on the size of earth in relationship to the sun, the following passage might be used:

> Imagine the earth as a little ball one-inch in diameter. On this same scale the moon would be a smaller ball, about a quarter of an inch in diameter, revolving around it at a distance of about thirty inches. The sun would be a sphere about nine feet in diameter approximately 969 feet (almost ⅕ mile) from this tiny earth and moon. Jupiter, the largest planet, would be a ball a little over 11 inches in diameter, revolving in an orbit of about 5036 feet (almost a mile). Pluto, the most distant planet known, would be a little object about 3/10 inch in diameter in an orbit about 7¼ miles from this same nine foot sun. (Eikleberry, 2000, p. 175)

Create an Outline

A student might be asked to create an outline (see Figure 9-51) based upon information related to the classification system for bats, insects, and birds. Concept mapping, flowcharting, and outlining tools, such as Inspiration, Mind Manager, and Smart Draw, can be used to help students organize and arrange ideas and information visually (see Figure 9-52).

Create a Flowchart

A student might be asked to create a flowchart (see Figure 9-53) tracking key players in a case study or story.

Recipe A would be hard to follow when making tacos because you would probably lose track of where you left off. Recipe B chunks information hierarchically, and creates superordinate headings for each chunk.

Terrific Tacos

Taco recipe

Brown one pound ground beef. Add one package of taco seasoning to water (about 1 cup), then add to browned ground beef. Cut up a tomato, shred lettuce and cheese (1 cup), and cook taco shells on a baking sheet in a 450 degree oven until brown, about 5 minutes. Cook ground beef in seasoning until most of the seasoning evaporates. Spoon ground beef filling into warm taco shells. Add cheese, lettuce, and taco sauce.

A

1 Gather ingredients and utensils

UTENSILS
1 cookie baking sheet
1 cheese grater
1 liquid measuring cup
Preheat oven 450 degrees

INGREDIENTS
1 lb ground beef
1 pkg taco seasoning
1 cup water
1 cup cheese
1 tomato
1 small head lettuce

2 Prepare ingredients

CHOPPING & GRATING
Chop tomatoes into squares
Chop lettuce into thin strips
Grate cheese

COOKING
Brown ground beef
Mix water & seasoning
Mix seasoning & grd. beef
Simmer until evaporates
Bake taco shells 5 minutes

3 Assemble

Spoon ground beef into taco shell. Top with lettuce, tomatoes, and cheese. Serve with favorite taco sauce.

B

FIGURE 9–48 Organizational visual

Figure A shows the original slide of how the letter J is signed. The arrow alone wasn't enough to show the sequence of hand movements. Ghosting made the movement order easier to see (Figure B).

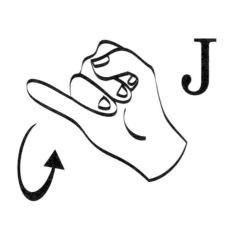

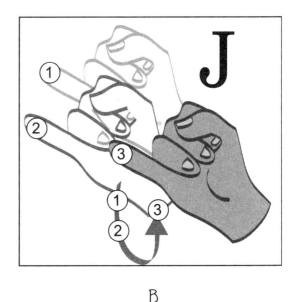

A

B

FIGURE 9–49 Improving an organizational visual

This is a difficult image because the movement seems counter-intuitive. Usually you think of younger to older moving left to right, but the North, South, East, West location of the islands and its representation on the page requires that the arrows point backwards. Try to create an improved representation.

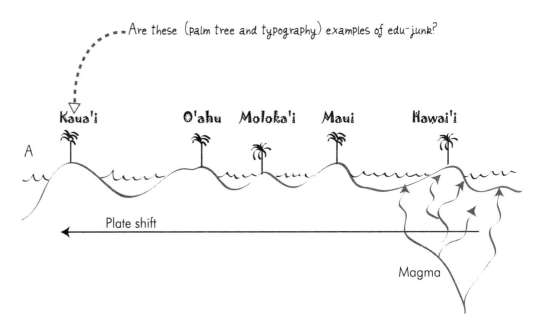

Are these (palm tree and typography) examples of edu-junk?

Kaua'i   O'ahu   Moloka'i   Maui   Hawai'i

A

Plate shift

Magma

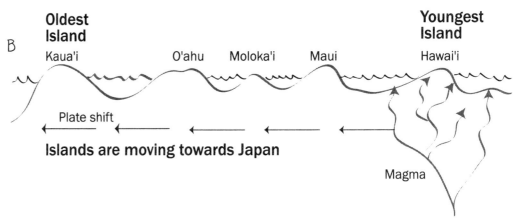

Oldest Island   **Youngest Island**

B   Kaua'i   O'ahu   Moloka'i   Maui   Hawai'i

Plate shift

Islands are moving towards Japan

Magma

Notice how the waves move from youngest to oldest in this image.

FIGURE 9–50 Explanative visual

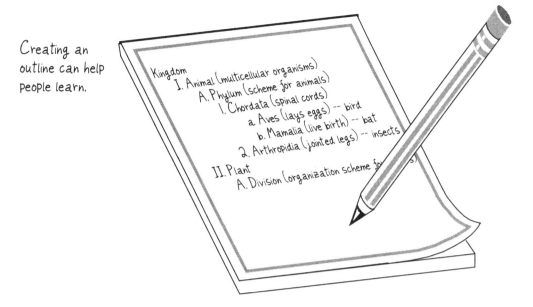

Creating an outline can help people learn.

FIGURE 9–51 Outlines as a generative strategy

FIGURE 9–52 Organizing ideas to enhance learning

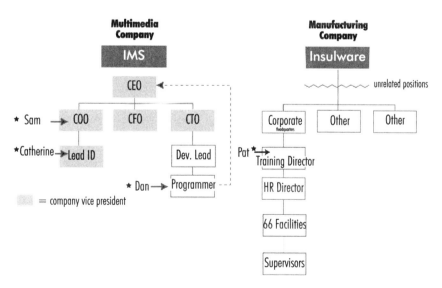

FIGURE 9–53 Learner-generated flowchart

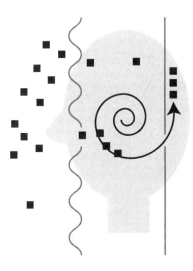

SELECTING   ORGANIZING   INTEGRATING
Sensory Memory   Short-Term   Long-Term Memory
                   Memory

FIGURE 9–54   Student-generated learning visual

Create an Image or Model

Students might be asked to create an image that helps them understand a concept or process. For example, Figure 9-54 might be a drawing created by someone trying to understand the following information:

> The information processing model shows information first perceived, then processed, then encoded into memory through sensory receptors, sensory registers, short-term memory, and long-term memory, respectively.

SUMMARY

In Chapter 8 on figure/ground you learned the importance of making the most important information stand out. This chapter took you a step further by explaining how to move to the *next* most important information, and then the next. The perception principle of hierarchy deals with helping learners move through information by providing them with clear pathways.

The hierarchy principle of perception covers the importance of organizing information into layers or levels of superordinate, subordinate, or coordinate status. The easiest way to think of hierarchy in an image is to compare it to a verbal outline with I, II, III, A, B, C levels of importance. Images typically have these same levels, though they are often communicated more subtly. The use of big and bold elements in an image usually implies that more importance is assigned to those elements than to the elements that are less big and bold. Thus, big and bold might be considered similar to level I in an outline, while less big and bold represents level A in an outline. The same logic is true for position. An image placed at the top is often considered more important (level I) than an image at the bottom (level A) of a page.

Much research has focused on hierarchy. People tend to focus on detail and complexity, making it important to master the skill of showing detail without overwhelming the learner and obscuring the critical message. Chunking information, using spatial analogies, and natural reading order are all hierarchical techniques to help people navigate through complex information. Information that is grouped into no more than seven to nine chunks is more likely to be remembered or efficiently used than information that is not. Making use of spatial analogies (images on the top are considered light, images on the bottom are considered heavy) also helps. Charts and graphs are uniquely complex displays that often involve several hierarchical design considerations, especially since by nature they depict hierarchical concepts.

Several tools and techniques are used to create hierarchical cues. Lines, arrows, depth, shape, and space can all be manipulated. For example, lines between items make the items seem related. Arrows strengthen that association. Bold and thick lines make the connected elements seem more related than do thin lines. White space allows similar elements to be grouped together, creating information chunks that are important to the hierarchical concept.

The actions of contrast, alignment, and proximity play an important role in creating hierarchy. Contrast usually provides an entry point into an image. Varying the degree of contrast between elements helps the eye move from most dominant to least dominant element. Alignment plays a big role in hierarchy, as the mind tends to seek items along horizontal and vertical planes. Furthermore, unique meanings are often assigned to positions along those planes that can be used to facilitate a message. Proximity, or the degree of distance between elements, is critical for creating not only information chunks, but messages about the relationship between chunks.

Chapter 10, Gestalt, employs both figure/ground and hierarchy perception principles. As you read about gestalt, you will learn how hierarchy is very similar to the gestalt continuity principle.

FOR MORE CHALLENGE

Visit the *Challenge* section for Chapter 9 on the book's website. There you'll find several instructional problems that require your visual solutions. Compare your solutions to those of others.

DISCUSSION FOR DISTANCE LEARNING

Visit the book's website (Chapter 9 > Discussion) for discussion or chat questions.

REFERENCES

Allen, W. H. (1975). Intellectual abilities and instructional media design. *AV Communication Review, 23,* 139–170.

Armbruster, B. B. (1986). Schema theory and the design of content-area textbooks. *Educational Psychology, 21,* 253–267.

Ehrenberg, A. S. (1977). Rudiments of numeracy. *Journal of Royal Statistical Society A, 140,* 227–297.

Fleming, M. L. (1968). Message design: The temporal dimension of message structure. USOE Final Report, NEDA Title VII Project 1401.

Fleming, M., & Levie, H. (1978). *Instructional message design.* Englewood Cliffs, NJ: Educational Technology Publications.

Fleming, M., & Levie, H. (1993). *Instructional message design.* Englewood Cliffs, NJ: Educational Technology Publications.

Hartley, J. (1985). *Designing instructional text.* New York: Nichols.

Horton, W. K. (1994). *The icon book: Visual symbols for computer systems and documentation.* New York: Wiley & Sons.

Kemp, J. E., Morrison, G. R., & Ross, S. M. (1998). *Designing effective instruction.* Upper Saddle River, NJ: Prentice Hall.

Kennedy, L. D. (1971). Textbook usage in the intermediate-upper grades. *The Reading Teacher, 24,* 723-729.

Lichty, T. (1989). *Design principles for desktop publishers.* Glenview, IL: Scot, Foresman.

Macdonald-Ross, M. (1977). How numbers are shown: A review of research on the presentation of quantitative data in texts. *AV Communication Review, 25,* 40-41.

McIntyre, W. A. (1983). The psychology of visual perception and learning from line drawings: A survey of the research literature. Eric Document Reproduction Service No. ED 230 901.

Meyer, B. J. (1985). Signaling the structure of text. In D. J. Jonassen (Ed.), *The technology of text* (Vol. 2, pp. 64-89). Englewood Cliffs, NJ: Educational Technology Publications.

Miller, G. A. (1956). The magic number seven, plus or minus two: Some limits on our capacity for processing information. *Psychological Review, 63,* 81-97.

Misanchuk, E. R. (1992). *Preparing instructional text: Document design using desktop publishing.* Englewood Cliffs, NJ: Educational Technology Publications.

Morrison, G. R., Ross, S. M., & Kemp, J. E. (2001). *Designing effective instruction.* (3rd ed.). New York: John Wiley & Sons, Inc.

Mullet, K., & Sano, D. (1995). *Designing visual interfaces: Communication oriented techniques.* Englewood Cliffs, NJ: Sunsoft Press.

Nelson, R. P. (1989). *The design of advertising.* Dubuque, IA: Wm. C. Brown.

Tufte, E. (1983). *The visual display of quantitative information.* Cheshire, CT: Graphics Press.

Tufte, E. R. (1990). *Envisioning information.* Cheshire, CT: Graphics Press.

Winn, W. D. (1980a). The effect of block-word diagrams on the structuring of concepts as a function of general ability. *Journal of Research in Science Teaching, 17,* 201-211.

Winn, W. D. (1980b). Visual information processing: A pragmatic approach to the imagery question. *Educational Communication and Technology Journal, 28*(2), 120-133.

Winn, W. D. (1981). The effect of attribute highlighting and spatial organization on identification and classification. *Journal of Research in Science Teaching, 17,* 201-211.

Winn, W. D. (1982a). The role of diagrammatic representation in learning sequences, identification and classification as a function of verbal and spatial ability. *Journal of Research in Science Teaching, 19,* 79-89.

Winn, W. D. (1982b, May). *Status and trends in information processing.* Paper presented at the Annual Meeting of the Association for Educational Communications and Technology, Research and Theory Division, Dallas, TX. (Eric Document Reproduction Service No. ED223236)

Winn, W. D. (1982c). Visualization in learning and instruction: A cognitive approach. *Educational Communication and Technology Journal, 30*(1), 3-25.

Winn, W. D. (1983, April). Processing and interpreting spatial information represented graphically. Paper presented at the Annual Conference of the American Educational Research Association, Montreal. (Eric Document Reproduction Service No. ED223236)

Winn, W. D., & Holliday, W. (1985). Design principles for diagrams and charts. In D. H. Jonassen (Ed.), *The technology of text* (Vol. 2, pp. 277-299). Englewood Cliffs, NJ: Educational Technology Publications.

Winn, W. D. (1986, April). *Simultaneous and successive processing of circuit diagrams having different amounts of detail.* Paper presented at the Annual Conference of the American Educational Research Association, San Francisco. (ERIC Document Reproduction Service No. ED270305)

Winn, W. D. (1987, April). *Graphic design as instructional design: Towards a syntax for computer graphics.* Paper presented at the Annual Conference of the American Educational Research Association, Washington, DC.

Wittrock, M. C. (1989). Generative processes of comprehension, *Educational Psychologists, 24,* 345-376.

CHAPTER 10

Gestalt Perceptions

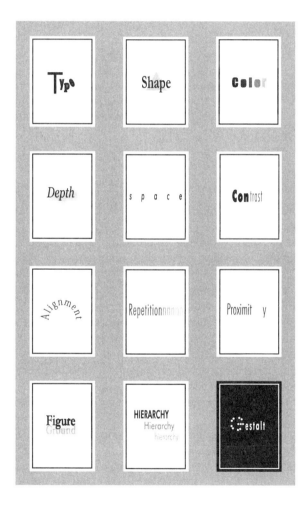

"Simplicity in the underlying message, complexity in the details."

Edward Tufte

NOTES ABOUT THE OPENING VISUAL

The graphic used for this chapter (and all the previous chapters since Type) employs the gestalt principle of design to enhance perception. Gestalt, commonly known as the whole being greater than the sum of its parts (*Gestalt Psychology*, 2000), is expressed using the large rectangle (the whole) filled with all the book icons (the parts). As a whole, this graphic conveys a larger message. Everything works together with a certain order or sequence to the different tools, actions, and perceptions.

I used this graphic because I wanted to build a sense of connection from chapter to chapter. Since this book covers five tools, four actions, and three perception principles (a total of 12 concepts), I needed a way to show that they are related. By keeping them all together in one image and focusing on only the relevant part of that image per chapter, I hoped to create that sense of connection.

FOCUS QUESTIONS

- Why are figure/ground and hierarchy considered gestalt principles?
- What is gestalt?
- How does improving the gestalt of an instructional message help the learner?
- How do you enhance gestalt?

KEY TERMS

ASYMMETRY   form that does not have balanced proportions

BALANCE   an even and aesthetically pleasing distribution of elements

CLOSURE   refers to the mind's tendency to seek completion

CONTIGUITY   refers to the mind's tendency to seek a direction to follow and continue to follow based on directional cues

GESTALT   the principle of perception that states the whole is greater than the sum of its parts; effective instructional visuals depend on creating gestalt, a total learning or performance environment (the whole) based upon the successful design and integration of all visual and instructional elements (the parts)

PREVIOUS EXPERIENCE   listed as a rule of gestalt, the law of previous experience explains the importance of helping the learner relate new information to previous knowledge and experience

PROXIMITY   refers to the mind's tendency to group elements based on their closeness to each other

SIMILARITY   refers to the mind's tendency to group items based on likeness; the action of repetition facilitates this grouping

SYMMETRY   beauty of form arising from balanced proportions

INTRODUCTION

A big, brightly colored poster of the writer's wheel (Figure 10–1) is prominently posted in the classroom of Antonio, the teacher you met in Chapter 1. This wheel is used to teach the process approach to writing to students in his school. The five key stages of the writing process—brainstorming, writing, conferencing, editing, and revising—are represented by color-coded, pie-shaped wedges. Each student has a folder with the writer's wheel on the cover. A movable pointer tells Antonio which stage of the writing process the student is taking part in (see Figure 10–2).

Here you see the big picture (the gestalt) of the writing process.

FIGURE 10–1 Writer's wheel

FIGURE 10–2 Student's writing folder

This writer's wheel is an example of effectively using the gestalt principle, the topic of this chapter. The wheel shows the big picture of writing. The circular shape makes it immediately apparent that writing is a cyclical process. The pie-shaped wedges show the individual components that make up writing. Students view writing as the sum of individual steps.

When creating the writer's wheel, Antonio asked these questions:

- How can I show the underlying structure of writing?
- How can I show the elements of writing in context of the underlying structure?
- How do I make the image simple, yet instructional?
- How do I make this look approachable, even fun?

These questions address gestalt. **Gestalt** involves the psychology of perception, a branch of psychology started by Max Wertheimer (1880–1943) around 1910. The underlying belief of gestalt is that individuals are predisposed to organize information in particular ways. Mullet and Sano (1995) consider the rules derived from the gestalt studies to provide useful insight into what makes images work effectively, a belief in harmony with the message of this book.

That gestalt is the final perception principle covered in this book is no accident. It is last because gestalt is the all-encompassing principle of perception. Every tool, action, and principle covered in this book can be applied to improving or enhancing gestalt. Even though Figure/Ground and hierarchy were treated as separate perception principles, they are actually considered gestalt principles. They were treated separately only because of their importance to the design of instructional materials.

The gestalt branch of psychology proposes that individuals construct representations that do not always reflect reality, an idea that should seem familiar. As you learned in Chapter 8, Figure/Ground, the mind unconsciously separates elements into figure and ground categories and assigns a status of importance to elements perceived as the figure. As a designer you can take advantage of this phenomenon by making the elements you want to emphasize stand out from other elements, thereby increasing the odds that your audience will see the central message. Likewise, in Chapter 9, Hierarchy, you learned that the mind tends to categorize and create hierarchies of information, especially grouping together elements that fall on horizontal or vertical planes. When you want certain items to be associated, you place them along a similar plane (this explains why alignment is considered an important design action).

Other ideas related to gestalt include the phi phenomenon, the law of Pragnanz (Koffka, 1935), and the importance of context. Wertheimer discovered the *phi phenomenon* using an experiment in which two blinking lights, switching on and off at a particular rate, were perceived as one. The *law of Pragnanz,* which emphasizes precision or simplicity (Ormrod, 1990), explains how individuals may see one thing (such as imperfect circles, squares, and lines) yet remember another (circles with perfect symmetry, squares with 90 degree angles, and straight lines).

Gestaltists also believed in the importance of presenting information within its natural context as opposed to isolated from its context. Antonio's writer's wheel is a good example of how information can be presented within the context of the whole. Rather than teaching individual elements of the writing process, Antonio focuses on the whole process of writing.

The meaning of gestalt, in fact, relates to the importance of context, since gestalt stands for whole, shape, form, configuration, and even essence. Gestalt psychologists noted that early in the perception process individual elements in an image were often perceived as a group or a form rather than as individual elements (Wertheimer, 1958).

I like to think of gestalt as the relationship of parts to whole. As you may already have gleaned from this overview, when you optimize gestalt in instruction, you are essentially helping learners to see the big picture without overloading their short-term memory. An easy way to think of designing for gestalt is to think of a map. City maps show the relationship of parts (symbols for streets, blocks, buildings) to the whole (the layout of the city). Shopping mall maps show the relationship of individual stores, restaurants, and restrooms to the layout of the mall. Airport maps (see Figure 10–3) show the relationship of terminals, concourses, and gates to the layout of the airport.

Maps show parts
(terminals) to whole
(concourse).

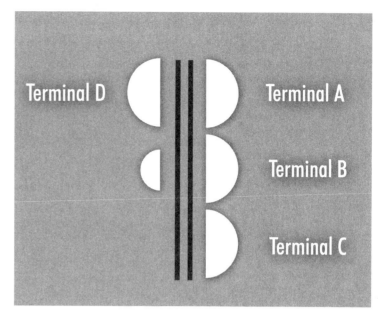

FIGURE 10-3   Airport map

This chapter covers five gestalt principles important to the design of instructional information: (1) closure, (2) contiguity, (3) proximity, (4) similarity, and (5) experience. The first four are widely recognized principles, and we have already discussed proximity and similarity (what this book refers to as repetition). The fifth rule, experience (Ormrod, 1990; Pettersson, 1993), has been added because it is critical for creating a big picture understanding of effective instructional visuals. This fifth principle contributes most to the task of helping the learner integrate information in a meaningful way. As you learned in Chapter 2, instructional images should help people select, organize, and integrate information. *It is the integration task that we try to facilitate when we focus on improving or optimizing gestalt.*

CLOSURE

The **closure** rule describes how the mind seeks completion. In Figure 10-4 you see four examples of this phenomenon. First, look at the closure title. Notice how the letter *o* isn't a complete circle? Your mind automatically filled that circle in and interpreted it as an o. Do you see a triangle in the left image? Do you see a square formed by the four dots? Does the letter *s* stand out? In all of these cases, there are no lines to define the shapes. Your mind filled in the lines. Your mind wanted those big pictures.

Closure relates to the need for the mind to have a general understanding. According to Luchins and Luchins (1959), closure is a key factor in cognitive organization. Extracting meaning and deriving conclusions is the function of closure. As learners we often walk away from a learning situation with an overall impression or feeling but lack awareness of the details. This phenomenon is related to closure, the mind's unconscious and continual effort to create meaning.

For as a designer of instructional visuals, this phenomenon suggests some basic directions. First, you can simplify your designs since you do not always need to include a complete image. Figure 10-5 shows a string with a ball attached to it dangling from a finger. The image doesn't need to show the entire body of the person. The arm and hand are enough to communicate. This simplification helps the mind summarize the critical attributes of a message.

Your mind seeks wholes. You notice the WHOLE (the triangle, the square, and the (S) before you notice the PARTS (the circles).

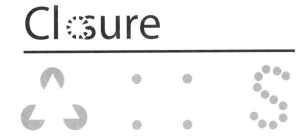

FIGURE 10–4   How the mind seeks closure

You see a PART (the arm), but your mind tells you that the part belongs to a WHOLE (the person).

FIGURE 10–5   Designing with closure in mind

Second, when you include some gaps in your design, you allow learners to fill in their own information. For example, if Figure 10–5 is a step you need to follow, the incomplete image might help you to imagine yourself performing the step.

CONTIGUITY

The **contiguity** rule is also called the theory of direction, which was covered in the previous chapter. The contiguity law states that the mind will seek a direction to follow and will continue to follow directional cues. You learned the role of contiguity in the hierarchy chapter, when the directive effects of arrows, lines, and shapes were used to establish order and hierarchy. When you have a strong line or plane in an image, the eye will follow that line. The eye also wants to continue following that line. If you look at Figure 10–6, you'll probably notice that your eye tends to travel on one of the diagonal lines, and when it gets to the halfway

Your mind seeks to follow a path, even if it is broken.

FIGURE 10–6   The contiguity rule

Your eye will follow an implied path. Here the arm of the statue directs your eye to the words.

FIGURE 10–7   Putting contiguity to work
Source: Click art © 1997 RomTech.

point of the image, the eye seems to prefer to continue traveling on that line. Notice how Figure 10-6 is really two arrows facing each other. Your mind doesn't seem to see the arrow shapes distinctly as it sees the long diagonal lines formed by the two images together.

When you create instructional images you can use the law of contiguity to direct your eye as in Figure 10-7. The hierarchy chapter covered in detail how direction can be established using lines and shapes.

SIMILARITY

The **similarity** rule is similar to the design action of repetition. When similarity is addressed in gestalt, it refers to the mind's tendency to group items based on similarity. In Figure 10-8 the first

FIGURE 10–8 The similarity rule

Your mind seeks to find patterns. How many pattern sets do you see in this image?

Rulers and guidelines keep layouts consistent, improving the gestalt of your training documents.

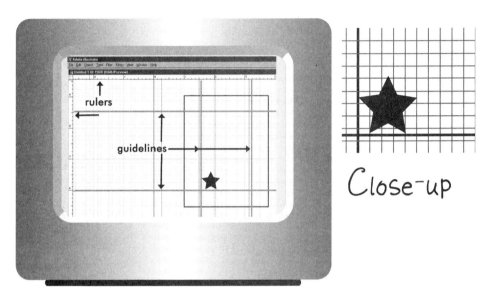

FIGURE 10–9 Using rulers and guidelines to ensure consistency

image shows 12 dots, but your eye is more likely to see a group of gray dots and a group of black dots. The middle image shows six dots and six squares, but your mind is more likely to see a group of circles and a group of squares. The final image shows six small dots and three large dots, but your mind is more likely to see a group of small dots and a group of large dots. In these examples elements in the image were grouped based on the similarity of color, shape, and size. By grouping elements, the mind is automatically reducing the cognitive load placed on memory.

Similarity is an important element in instructional development, particularly in hypermedia environments such as electronic displays, computer-based training, and Web-based training. In hypermedia environments a learner moves between screens of information, often in a nonlinear order. Marking one's position in these environments is difficult to do. Disorientation and a feeling of being lost are frequent complaints about these experiences. Books are easy to thumb through and establish one's position, but this is not always the case in hypermedia environments. It then becomes important to establish a "lay of the land" (Kristof & Satran, 1995) for learners.

Creating a lay of the land is often accomplished through a grid system used throughout the learning environment. A grid system is an underlying structure that is used to provide consistency throughout instruction. When you create a grid, you create a specific place for specific items. These places are repeated from page to page or from screen to screen. This repetition makes a grid fall under the category of similarity.

Grids are easy to create since most software programs allow you to turn a grid background on or off. Most computer programs have rulers and guidelines to help you establish horizontal and vertical placement lines (see Figure 10-9) that can be used to create consistency throughout an instructional document or environment.

This CBT has a grid system for learner orientation (topic heading), navigation, and instruction, and strategies (instructional content, practice, and feedback).

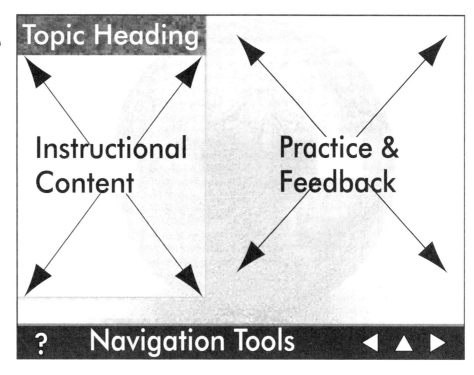

FIGURE 10–10   CBT grid system

You may be wondering if a template is a grid system. Think of a template as a format for documents, presentations, and Web pages that establishes a grid system in addition to other design conventions such as size and style of typeface, color of typeface, and color of background. Templates relate more to the total design of an instructional environment whereas a grid mostly defines horizontal and vertical borders for text and images.

Figure 10–10 is a grid system for computer-based training (CBT). Notice how the layout specifically defines where headings, instructional content, practice, feedback, and navigational tools are to be placed. Books (see Figure 10–11), Web-based training environments (see Figure 10–12), and electronic presentations use grid systems as well.

Sano and Mullet (1995) consider grid-based design essential to any large-scale information system:

> . . . By structuring each presentation along similar lines, the grid ensures that users will benefit from experience with the system as they learn to predict where a particular piece of information will be found. (p. 134)

It is the predictive value of a grid that has merit for design of instructional materials. When you provide a consistent layout, you theoretically reduce cognitive load. Users don't have to relearn the layout when they move from screen to screen or page to page. They know where to find specific information, and they can make distinctions between types of informational content. For example, if the right-hand column of a Web-based training environment is designated for outside links, the learner reading for only the most critical information will learn to skip the information in that column. Learners who want additional detail, however, may find themselves looking in the right-hand column.

Grids do not need to be followed all the time. Earl Misanchuk (1992) gives refreshing advice on the use of grids by emphasizing that grids be allowed to vary. At times, following a grid just doesn't work for the instructional content. Many designers find themselves

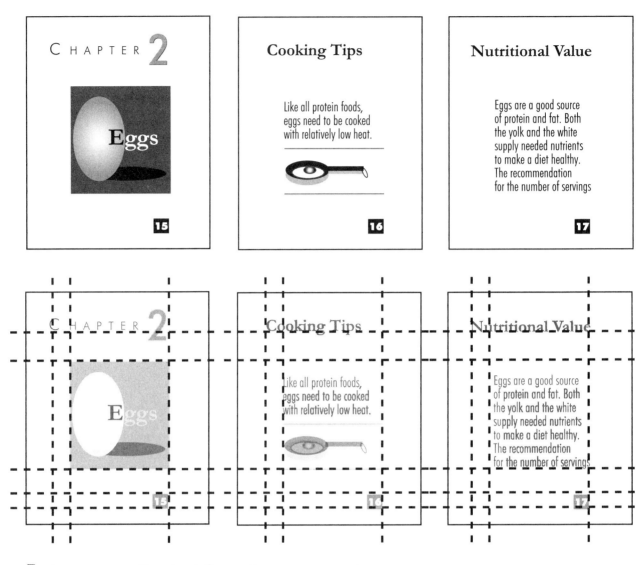

Each page looks different but follows the underlying grid.

FIGURE 10–11   Book grid system

changing content to accommodate a grid. This can done easily in some situations, but when it cannot be done easily, it is probably time to consider changing the grid.

Figure 10–13 shows a grid system that has been varied to accommodate content. The right-hand layout in Figure 10–13 shows a modified grid that allows for a lengthy text passage to be part of instruction.

Most document design and computer development programs allow you to create your own grid or use a template where the grid is provided (see Figure 10–14) for you.

It is time for a break in reading! Represent the meaning of *order* and *tension* using squares. Focus on the *similarity* principle. How can you make the appearance of the squares similar to the words *order* and *tension*? Create a visual solution to this information. Then visit the book website (Chapter 10 > Web activity) to compare your solution to those of others.

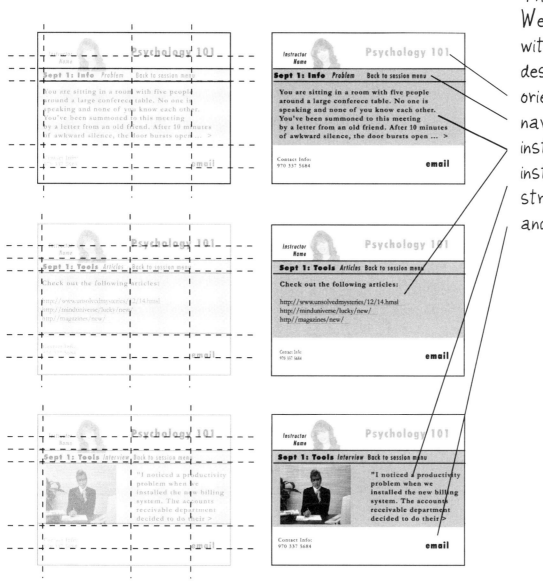

This is a grid for Web-based training, with these designated areas: orientation, navigation, instruction, instructional strategies, and feedback.

FIGURE 10–12 Grid system for electronic presentations

PROXIMITY

The rule of **proximity** states that the mind will group elements based on their closeness to each other. If you look at Figure 10–15, you see three groups of three dots rather than nine distinct dots. As with the other rules of gestalt, when the mind groups things, it reduces the load placed on short-term memory.

Using the proximity rule can help you make instructional information easier to understand. Part A of Figure 10–16 doesn't have the optimal proximity between the shaded area of the circle and the number of degrees. The pie-shaped area on the top left could be associated with either 90 degrees or 180 degrees. Part B shows an improved display, removing

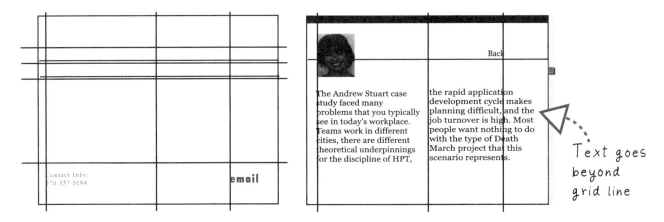

Notice how the right-hand screen deviates from the grid. The text passage here is lengthy, and consequently the margins have been increased. Also, the navigation bar that is part of the other screens has been removed since the only direction to go from this screen is back. It is OK to work outside of the grid once in a while, especially if your content demands it. When you continually change content to match a grid, however, you need to rethink the grid.

FIGURE 10–13 Working outside the grid

This electronic slide presentation has a fairly consistent grid.

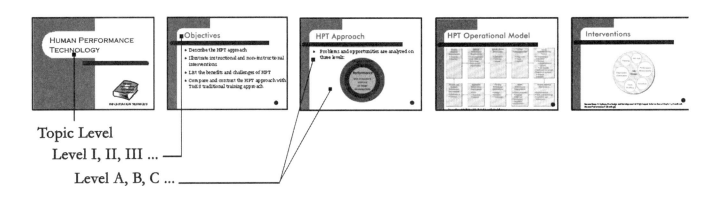

Topic Level

Level I, II, III ...

Level A, B, C ...

FIGURE 10–14 Maintaining consistency with a grid

Your mind seeks
to group elements
based upon how
near or far they
are from other
elements.

Proxim it   y

●●●   ●●●   ●●●

FIGURE 10–15   The role of proximity

By placing the
numbers close to
the pie shapes,
Figure B teaches
geometry more
effectively than
does Figure A.

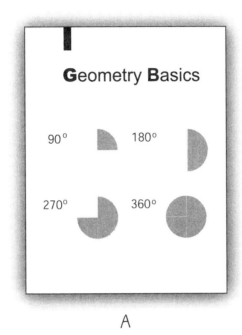

A

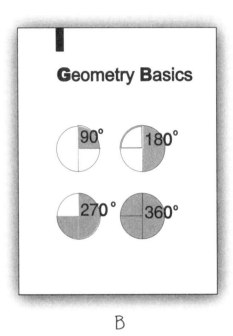

B

FIGURE 10–16   Improving design through proximity

all doubt about the number of degrees associated with the shaded areas. The closer the numbers are to the area, the easier it is to understand.

I had a dentist who cleverly used proximity to teach dental care. He met with each new patient and presented a short slide presentation on healthy gums and teeth. In this presentation he pointed out various features of strong teeth and gums using a photograph of a perfect set of teeth. He then showed a side-by-side display of the patient's x-ray next to the healthy gum image. He concluded his instruction by showing the healthy gums superimposed over the patient's x-ray. Having the healthy gums in such close proximity to the patient's x-ray made it easy for the patient to compare his or her teeth to ideal teeth.

The dentist example, though intuitive, isn't research-based. However, research supports the instructional benefit of proximity. Mayer and Sims (1994) find that inexperienced students gained from instruction where visual and verbal explanations were presented concurrently (in close proximity). They explain this finding using their dual coding theory of multimedia, which suggests that the concurrent presentation of visual and verbal descriptions increases the likelihood of internal connections (in the mind of the learner) between visual and verbal representations of those descriptions.

Mayer, Bove, Bryman, Mars, and Tapangco (1996) show that the best illustrations for summarizing scientific content are made up of a series of frames illustrating the major steps in

You see the steps
(PARTS) of the
process (WHOLE)
at the same time.

Add 3
egg whites
to bowl   x 3

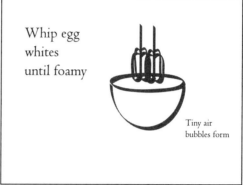

Whip egg
whites
until foamy

Tiny air
bubbles form

Stop when
peaks form

FIGURE 10–17   Illustrating the parts and the process

a process. The whole (the process) is in constant view of the parts (the individual steps). Figure 10-17 shows a series of frames teaching how to whip egg whites. Each frame shows the context (the bowl) and the changes that take place in the context of that bowl from step to step. The parts are in proximity of the whole.

EXPERIENCE

The **previous experience** rule states that new impressions are influenced by previous experiences or by the immediate context. How the learner analyzes and interprets new information depends in part on a range of learner experiences, emotions, and the prevailing situation (Pettersson, 1993).

This previous experience rule is explained by information processing theory, as described in Chapter 2. The ability to keep information alive in short-term memory is increased when learners can associate that information with what they already know. For example, if you are trying to teach the circulatory system, you might help learners compare the circulatory system with the plumbing system in their house. When learners can associate this new information about the circulatory system with old information about plumbing, they are able to remember it better, because their mind already has a schema set up for plumbing. This all depends, of course, on whether learners understand the plumbing in their house.

Recently a student was creating a lesson on downhill skiing and who has the right of way. The rule is that the skier higher on the hill must yield to the skier lower on the hill. She taught this rule using a driving analogy. When traveling on an interstate highway, the cars in the rear must yield to the cars in the front. Since most people drive on highways, this analogy was effective.

Metaphors and Symbols

Symbols and metaphors are widely used in instruction because of the power of the previous experience rule. Figure 10–18 includes some generally recognized symbols. The circle with a diagonal slash means *no* or *forbidden;* the cross and skull is a symbol of death; the smiley face is a symbol of friendliness or happiness. When people encounter the forbidden symbol, the cross and skull, and the smiley face, they quickly understand certain actions are discouraged, something might be poisonous, and goodwill or positive intent is present.

Metaphors and symbols are widely used in software applications, computer-based training, and Web-based training environments to help people learn new tasks or information. An eraser symbol means that information can be deleted, an envelope means you can send an e-mail message, a small disk means you can save a file on a floppy disk, and a check mark with letters above it means you can check your spelling (see Figure 10–19). Hourglasses, envelopes, file folders, and pages are fairly universal in appearance; thus, these icons are likely to be quickly understood. The spell check symbol with the letters ABC over a check mark, however, would not work in non–English-speaking cultures since the letters ABC are not part of their alphabet. While it might seem that pictures have a universal appeal, this really isn't the case, as many cultures interpret pictures differently.

People's interpretation of symbols and colors is highly dependent on their experiences, culture, and previous knowledge. If you are creating instruction for a specific audience and are familiar with their customs and culture, you can use your knowledge of their culture to help strengthen learning since you are tapping into what learners already know.

In China and other cultures a snake is a good thing (Miller & Brown, 2000), a symbol of birth and renewal. In Western cultures, however, snakes are likely to be associated with deception or evil (Horton, 1994).

Your mind seeks associations based upon past experience.

FIGURE 10–18   Common symbols as examples of the rule of previous experience

Non–English speaking cultures cannot be expected to understand the ABC symbol for spell checking. Previous experience helps with the interpretation of the WHOLE.
Metaphors are good ways to communicate WHOLES.

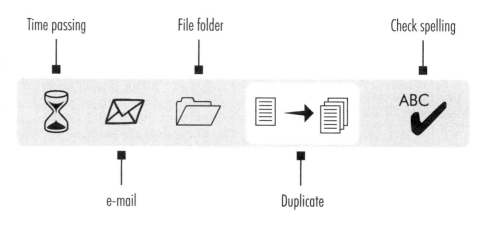

FIGURE 10–19   Communicating with visual metaphors

Depending on your culture (experience), these pointing fingers mean direction or dismemberment.

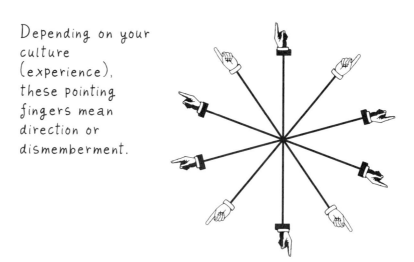

FIGURE 10–20   Cultural differences in decoding symbols

FIGURE 10–21   Same symbol, different meanings

Where a person from a Western culture would see a pointing finger (see Figure 10-20) as simply a directional device, a person in a different culture might interpret the pointing finger to mean dismemberment, since it is a body part. In general, use of body part icons or images with international audiences is considered risky. The hand symbol used for yes in the United States (see Figure 10-21) means zero or worthless in France and has even more insulting connotations in other cultures.

Figure 10-22 shows icons that tend to have universal recognition and some that have culturally specific meanings. This chart uses the five symbol categories of Miller, Brown, and Cullen (2000): animal, shape, gestures/language, man, and nature. The chart is not extensive as many symbol families range from professionally specific symbols (electrical circuitry) to symbols that have universal meaning (traffic signs). Consult the *Symbol Source Book: An Authoritative Guide to International Graphic Symbols*, by Henry Dreyfus or

These symbols tend to have

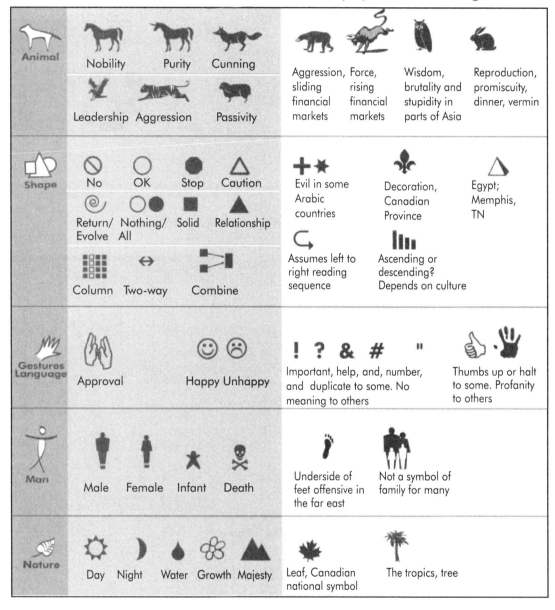

FIGURE 10–22 Common symbols and icons

Source: Adapted and constructed from the ideas of Miller, Brown, and Cullen (2000).

contact consulate offices in major cities around the world for more information about culture and customs.

Colors have different meanings across cultures as well. In Western cultures red often means danger; however in China, red means joy and festivity. White is often associated with purity and virtue in Western cultures, yet it means death and mourning in Eastern cultures (Horton, 1994). In general, it is important to test your design with a representative audience in order to identify any potential cultural sensitivity.

This is an outline interface. The menu lets you see PARTS (Intro, Art, Dance, Stories) to WHOLE (Early Childhood instructional content).

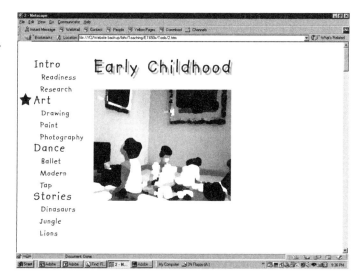

FIGURE 10–23   Outline instructional interface

This is a book metaphor. Previous experience with books helps you understand the relationships of PARTS (chapter topics) to WHOLES (books).

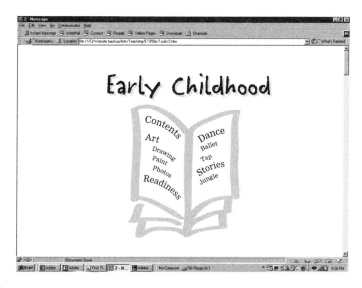

FIGURE 10–24   Book metaphor

Instructional Interfaces

With more and more instruction taking place in a distance format where a teacher may not be physically present, communicating clearly with visuals becomes more important than ever. When no one is available to provide directions, the instructional interface must do so.

An instructional interface can be considered to be all of the elements in an instructional environment that help the learner go about the task of learning (Lohr, 2000). For example, menus, buttons, navigational cues, and the like are typical components of an instructional interface.

Instructional interfaces rely heavily on previously presented learning gestalt principles. Some standard interface metaphors include the outline metaphor, the table of contents/book metaphor, the desktop metaphor, the file folder metaphor, and the syllabus metaphor.

The Outline and Table of Contents/Book Metaphors

Simple outlines, as in Figure 10–23, are frequently used to organize computer-based learning. Book metaphors with a table of contents (see Figure 10–24) and the display of instructional information against the backdrop of pages are common as well.

Previous experience
with desktops helps
you understand the
relationships of PARTS
(file folders) to
WHOLES (file cabinet
or collection).

FIGURE 10–25   Desktop metaphor

Familiarity with a
syllabus helps
organize all of the
elements (PARTS) of a
distance learning
environment (WHOLE).

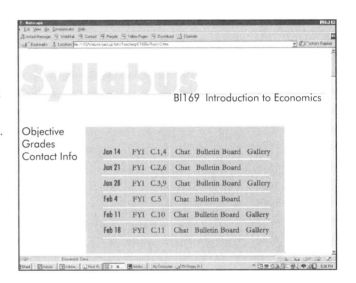

FIGURE 10–26   Syllabus metaphor

The Desktop Metaphor

The desktop metaphor (see Figure 10-25) organizes a learning environment around desktop elements. Important learning documents can be linked to images of file folders, computer screens, and desktop reference books. Many Web-based training settings make extensive use of file folder organization. The user simply clicks on file folder tabs to move to different content.

The Syllabus Metaphor

Distance learning environments are often organized around the familiar structure of a course syllabus. Objectives, grading policies, contact information, and other components of a course link from the syllabus page (see Figure 10-26).

Some of these metaphors are useful, but as with grid systems, a metaphor may not work optimally with the structure of the content. Another problem with metaphors is that people don't always have the previous experience required to interpret them.

Many templates are now available for interface design. These templates provide a pre-coded shell that allows the instructor simply to insert content into the appropriate section of the interface. Templates employ grid systems that designate where all types of content are to be placed. Many of these templates are fine; however, some reflect the mind-set of the programmer, making the interface technocentric and hard to follow.

Design Based on Student and Teacher Tasks

I've found that a good way to check the instructional effectiveness of a template or to design an instructional interface from scratch is to consider tasks of both teachers and learners and how these are made visual in the interface. When I consider the teaching role, I think more of a facilitator or someone who helps provide access to information but is not always the source of information.

An important question to ask is whether your interface is performing the many functions of a responsive teacher/facilitator. Does it anticipate the types of questions learners typically have when taking part in any type of training environment? For instance, does the interface answer questions like these: Am I being graded? What am I supposed to do? Am I doing things the right way? Lohr (2000, pp. 161–182) suggests that designers and usability experts do a quick run-through of an interface to see if it is addressing some of the most basic types of learner questions:

- Would the learner feel comfortable and welcome?
- Are there plenty of directions for the learner related to navigating through the environment?
- Is there support for the learning process?
- Is the interface giving the learner enough feedback?

To illustrate how these guiding questions might be used, think of a visual answer to each question.

Does the interface help the learner feel comfortable and welcome? Look for or create elements like:

- warm colors
- a "Welcome" page (see Figure 10–27)
- a picture of the instructor (see Figure 10–27)
- pictures of other students (see Figure 10–28)
- information that is chunked to reduce cognitive overload

Anything that makes a distance learning environment more personal will be appreciated by many learners. Here a welcome and a picture of the instructor make the environment seem approachable.

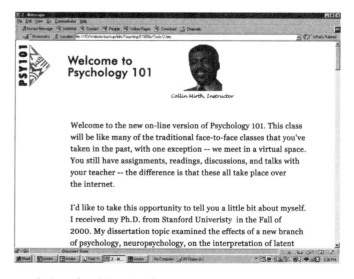

FIGURE 10–27 Making learners feel comfortable and welcome

Seeing other students in a class contributes to a sense of community.

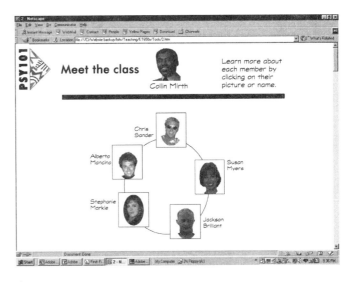

FIGURE 10-28   Welcoming learners

This is called "breadcrumbing" because learners leave a trail of where they have been. Here a learner went from the Typography section to the Research section, then to the Typographical Considerations section. If learners want to back out, all they need to do is click on these topic titles.

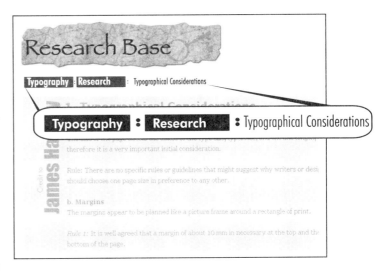

FIGURE 10-29   Providing direction to learners

Does the interface provide the learner with plenty of direction? Look for elements like:

- extra help
- ways to backtrack and exit (see Figure 10-29)
- assessment checklists
- link descriptions (see Figure 10-30)

Does the interface help the learning process? Look for elements like:

- visual overviews
- options to skip information or to go into greater detail (see Figures 10-29 and 10-30)
- opportunities for practice/rehearsal/application (see Figure 10-31)

This is an example of gestalt because you see detail (there is a lesson here about white space & layout), but you don't lose the context of the whole menu (the big picture).

Your cursor makes this pop up.

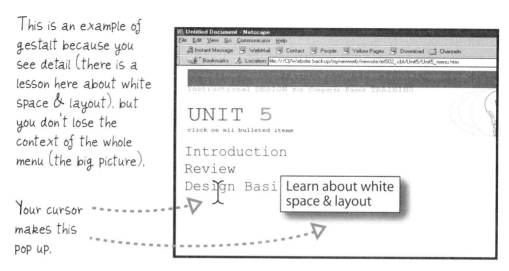

FIGURE 10–30 Link descriptions

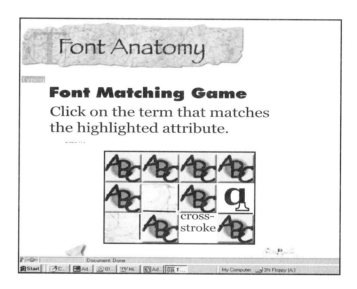

Completed game.

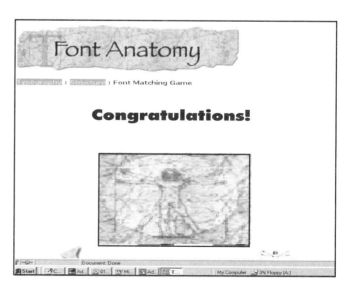

FIGURE 10–31 Providing opportunities for practice

- ■ case studies that provoke deeper thinking
- ■ collaborative learning activities such as chat sessions and threaded discussions

Does the interface give the learner feedback? Look for elements like:

- ■ progress report with current grade
- ■ hints to help learners focus (see Figure 10-32)
- ■ feedback from fellow students
- ■ sample projects

As you can see, the possibilities are endless. Designing the interface is a complex task when you consider all of the learning tasks that must be supported.

Figure 10-33 shows an interface for open-ended learning environments. Open-ended learning environments encompass a variety of self-directed learning approaches for ill-structured content, or content that you could consider to be more gray than black or white. For this particular unit, the learner is given a rather vague request for proposal and is asked to write a proposal response. The interface provides space for the learner to explore the history behind the request for proposal and some of the challenges in writing it. For these kinds of learning environments, there really isn't a clear solution to a problem. To address the unique tasks of learning in an open-ended environment, the interface is divided into Problem, Explore, Assess, and Tools sections.

The Problem section acts as an overview to the instructional problem. Since this is not your typical behavioristic approach, rather than listing objectives, this section describes the problem (see Part A of Figure 10-33).

The Explore section includes information that might help solve the problem or distracts from the solution, since the learner needs to learn to distinguish between important and nonimportant information. Part B of Figure 10-33 shows an interview transcript with one of the case study characters.

The Tools section provides access to resources and examples that might help the learner solve the problem. Part C shows a sample proposal to which the learner can refer.

The Assess section provides information that helps the learner assess the effectiveness of his or her response. See Part D.

The Course Info section (see Part E) provides access to the broader objectives of the course and to other case studies within the course.

Helping the learner focus is an important PART of the interface. Here the instructor is partly online. Chat session,s, threaded discussions, email, telephone calls, and face-to-face visits can be encouraged in the interface as well.

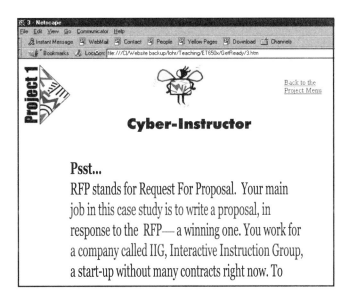

FIGURE 10-32   Hints to help learners focus

PARTS to WHOLE
view of an interface
for active learning

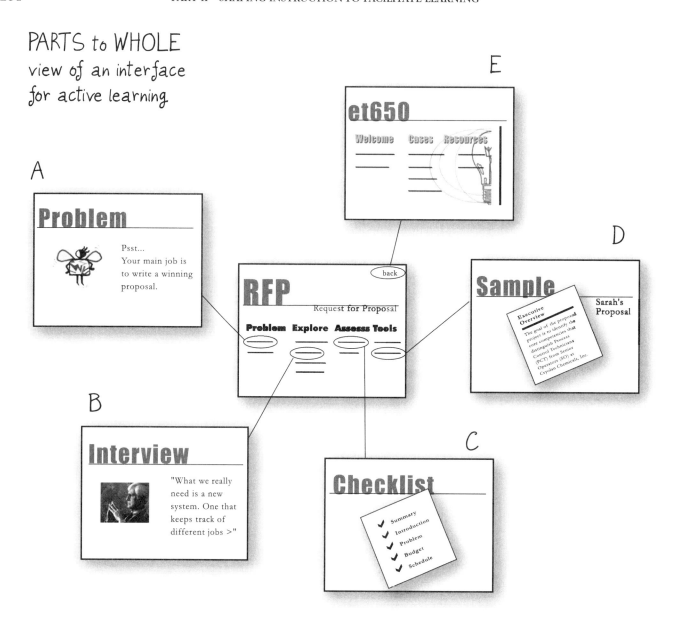

FIGURE 10–33   Open-ended learning environment

Interface Design Tips for the Web

Sometimes the interfaces you design are more information based than instructionally based, as is often the case in Web-based documents. Lynch and Horton (1999) suggest you put header and footer information on each page since you can never be sure how viewers found their way to your page. They may have come from your main menu, but then again, someone may have provided a link to a specific page. Therefore it is important to provide author name or institution, an informative title, creation/revision date, one link to the document's home page listing of links to the major menu pages.

Many of the steps for interface design for websites are similar to those covered previously. Lynch and Horton (1999) and Nielsen (2000) consider the following seven items important:

1. Know your users (are they advanced users or novices?).
2. Keep navigation clear (make sure users know where they are, where they came from, how to back out or exit if needed, and how to get back to a home page).

3. Provide one menu with many links rather than many menus and submenus of fewer links. Get people to the information as quickly as possible. Users would rather have one menu with many, many selections available than several menus with few selections.
4. Keep the time it takes to load your Web page to a minimum by using few graphics and animations/audio (users get frustrated when loading takes longer than 10 seconds).
5. Design for simplicity, using the same grid structures and layouts.
6. Make sure you give visual feedback to any actions users take (if they click to go somewhere new, make sure it looks new!).
7. Make sure you consider handicapped audiences (provide text-based description of your graphics).

How Do You Design for a Greater Sense of Gestalt?

As with figure/ground and hierarchy, your job is to do some of the organizational work up front in order to save the learner's mind from having to do unnecessary work. The human mind makes a continual effort to impose order and create meaning. The more you accelerate that process, the more you help the learner's mind. By thinking about the five gestalt rules presented in this chapter and by employing the tools and actions that follow, you are working to control the big picture that learner see but helping them keep track of the details as well.

Tools

Type

Typesetting and typefaces can be used to strengthen a message. In Figure 10–34 the words "Fit in" look like they are squeezed into the available space, emphasizing the message that creative people don't "fit in."

Shape and Proximity

A sense of gestalt is facilitated when images look balanced. One way to achieve quick balance is to use images that fit the display size and orientation. For example, the tall Egyptian figure in Part A of Figure 10–35 is particularly suitable for a display size that is taller than it is wide. If you were limited to a display that was wider than it was tall, you might use an image that is also wider than it is tall for that space (see Part B).

A visual metaphor helps you understand the overall (WHOLE) message.

FIGURE 10–34   Using type to strengthen the message

Although Figures A and B are different, both images are balanced. You have a sense of harmony — the WHOLE seems related to its PARTS.

A

Ancient Egypt

The ancient Egyptian culture started over five thousand years ago and survived for over three thousand years. Given that most cultures, with the exception of China, last at most hundreds of years, the longevity of the Egyptian culture is remarkable.

B

The ancient Egyptian culture started over five thousand years ago and survived for over three thousand years. Given that most cultures, with the exception of China, last at most hundreds of years, the longevity of the Egyptian culture is remarkable.

Ancient Egypt

FIGURE 10–35 Achieving balance in design

Mok (1996) identifies seven
information structures:

A. Linear
B. Web
C. Hierarchical
D. Spatial zoom
E. Matrix
F. Overlay
G. Parallel

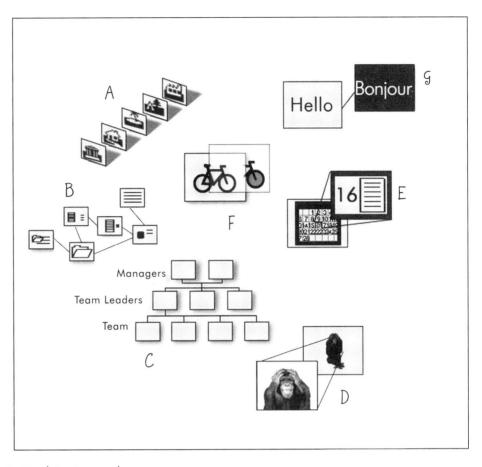

FIGURE 10–36 Data organizational structures or shapes

Source: Based on Mok's (1996) seven information structures.

Mok (1996) identifies seven universal data organizational structures or shapes, represented in Figure 10-36:

- linear (see section A)
- web (see section B)
- hierarchical (see section C)
- spatial zoom (see section D)
- matrix (see section E)
- overlay (see section F)
- parallel (see section G)

Notice how these structures consist of mostly lines and squares and how the closeness (proximity) of the elements increases a sense of relatedness.

Color and Repetition

Color coding is used to help people associate information. Figure 10-37 shows the Hawaiian Islands. The island of Kauai is shaded a light gray, as is a blowup diagram of Kauai. Since both elements in the display have the same color, the learner perceives them to be connected. This uses both color and repetition (similarity) to improve the learner's sense of gestalt.

The spatial zoom helps you see the gestalt. Kauai is the PART and the Hawaiian Islands are the WHOLE.

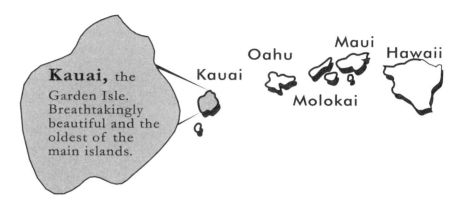

FIGURE 10–37   Using color and repetition to achieve gestalt

Photograph of grains draws attention to the Bread/Grain (PART) section of the food pyramid (WHOLE).

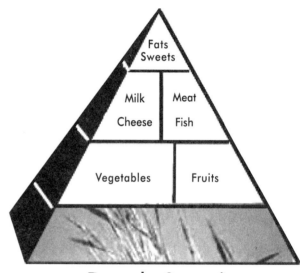

FIGURE 10–38   Using depth and contrast to achieve gestalt

Depth and Contrast

Photographs and dimension help people sense the gestalt of an image. Figure 10–38 shows a photograph of wheat placed in the background of the food pyramid. The opacity of the wheat photograph has been reduced to 40 percent so that the wheat image becomes a background element and doesn't compete with the pyramid text.

Many artists use this technique of blurring the background (reducing contrast) or using dull or cool colors because these actions create the illusion of depth. Next time you see a landscape painting, notice how the background consists of dull colors and the foreground consists of brighter colors and sharper images. Notice how depth is also created in Figure 10–38 by shading the left side of the triangle black.

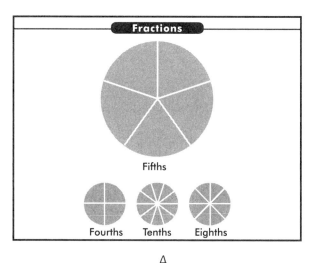

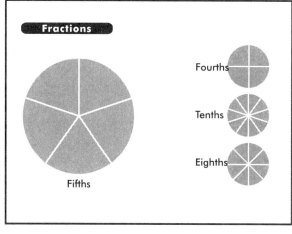

A

B

Symmetrical balance   Assymmetrical balance

FIGURE 10-39   Symmetrical vs. assymmetrical balance

Space

White space is a powerful tool for facilitating gestalt. As you learned in Chapter 6, Color, Depth, and Space, white space is considered a graphic element. White space is the background of an image. Even though it is called *white space,* it could be whatever color the background is, such as gray space, blue space, or orange space.

White space helps create a sense of balance. I define **balance** as the sense of harmony achieved when all of the elements in a display work together. By my definition, balance is a manifestation of gestalt. Two types of balance important for instruction are symmetrical balance and asymmetrical balance.

Symmetry is beauty of form arising from balanced proportion.

Symmetrical balance is achieved when all elements in a display are centered (as in Part A of Figure 10-39). If you aren't sure, imagine the image on a piece of paper and mentally fold the paper in half. Do you see the same image on both sides of the page? If so, you have symmetrical balance.

Symmetrical balance is considered formal, conventional, and calm. Consider *American Gothic,* the painting by Grant Wood that shows a farmer holding a pitchfork next to his wife or daughter. Both figures are centered in the painting (Peterson, 1996). Although the image would not be exactly the same if you were to fold it in half (the farmer is on one half and his wife on the other), it is still considered symmetrical because the weight of the visual elements is roughly equal.

Symmetrical balance is easy to create and works well in many instructional situations. Keep in mind, though, that symmetrical balance can become tedious if it is overdone.

Asymmetry is form that does not have balanced proportions.

Asymmetrical balance is achieved when all elements in a display are in harmony, but the elements are not in symmetry (as in Part B of Figure 10-39). If you imagine Part B on a piece of paper and mentally fold the paper in half, you would not see the same image on both sides of the page.

Asymmetrical balance is often used to create interest, excitement, and mystery. Consider the painting *Starry Night* by Vincent Van Gogh. Although this image is not symmetrical, the painting is balanced. The random shifts of emphasis all over the canvas create an interesting, energetic, and mysterious display.

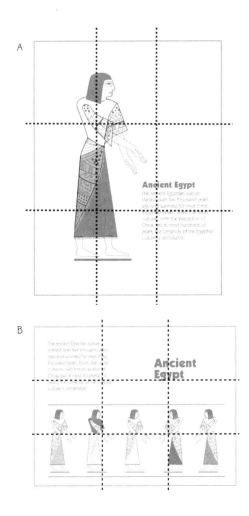

FIGURE 10–40   The rule of thirds

Unlike symmetrical balance, asymmetrical balance is more difficult to master. You'll find occasions that warrant the effort, though, particularly when an instructional message is unconventional or when you need visual interest or energy.

Following two useful rules can help you create effective balance: (1) the rule of thirds and (2) the golden rectangle. These are particularly helpful to employ when your goal is asymmetrical balance.

The rule of thirds   The rule of thirds suggests you divide your visual display into thirds as you scan across an image, down an image, or both ways. By placing visual elements along these imaginary lines you may find that your image seems more balanced (see Figure 10–40). Placing the focal point near the intersection of imaginary lines can be particularly effective. Notice how your eye is drawn to the intersections of Figure 10–40. The rule of thirds is a nice rule of thumb, but that doesn't mean you'll use it in all situations. You'll also find that you don't always want to place the elements of a display *exactly* on the lines or intersections. Perhaps you like something a little more to the right or left, or top or bottom. There is always a degree of judgment involved with all these rules. That is why we often call design rules *heuristics,* or rules of thumb that do not apply to all situations. The rule of thirds might best be called the *rule of approximately thirds,* given how it is applied and interpreted by designers. The rule of thirds, however, can be useful when you are assessing your layout.

The golden rectangle   Another helpful technique is to employ proportions of the golden rectangle (see Figure 10–41). A golden rectangle is any rectangle with sides that have

When the longer sides of a rectangle are 1.6 times the length of the other side, the rectangle tends to have a pleasing appearance.

You can also figure out this proportion by making two sides 8 units and the other sides 5 units.

This image shows several rectangles with these proportions. The 8 to 5 ratio can be any measure, inches, points, or centimeters, for example.

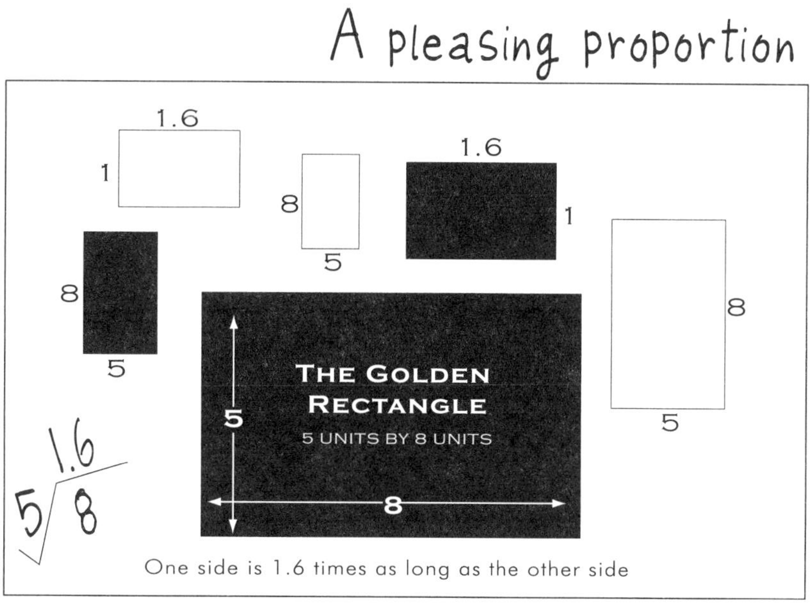

FIGURE 10–41   The golden rectangle

a ratio of 5 to 8. This ratio is believed to produce a balanced and pleasing (golden) image or to evoke from the viewer a sense of harmony. Another way to think of the 5 to 8 proportions is to use the ratio 1 to 1.6. That is, the long sides of a rectangle are 1.6 times as long as the shorter sides.

Like the rule of thirds, the golden rectangle won't work all of the time. To suggest that you specifically create rectangles with golden proportions in all of your work is impractical. Consider the standard page size of 8.5" × 11"; these dimensions do not have golden proportions. Golden proportions would 5" × 8", 8.5" × 13.6" (8.5 × 1.6 = 13.6), and other sizes. Given that it is impractical and costly to change paper size, you'd bypass the golden rectangle heuristic. It's useful to know that you *could* experiment with those proportions if needed, though.

HOW DOES GESTALT FACILITATE DIFFERENT PICTURE FUNCTIONS?

In Chapter 2 you learned about several types of instructional visuals (decorative, representative, explanative, transformational, and organizational). This section shows how principles of gestalt have been used to improve visuals that represent these different categories.

Decorative

Look over Figure 10–42 Parts A and B. Which figure has more harmony or unity? It's a tough call, but I think Part B is the better of the two and thus achieves a greater sense of gestalt. The box around Part A acts to separate the image from the content, making them seem less

In Figure A, the box separates elements (PARTS) of this image, making it look a little chopped up. The curved lines and the direction of the statue in Figure B make the image seem more unified (WHOLE).

A **Assignment**
Find a statue in the museum and make a pencil sketch. Focus on capturing depth and movement.

B

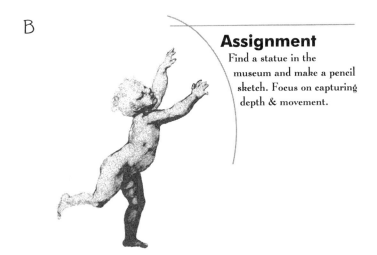

Assignment
Find a statue in the museum and make a pencil sketch. Focus on capturing depth & movement.

FIGURE 10–42   Achieving gestalt with a decorative image
Source: Click art ©1997 RomTech.

unified as a whole. I used this particular image for two reasons. First, I find that boxing images in, particularly when the image shows a whole body, whole building, or whole anything, isn't always a good idea, especially if you want to create a sense of relatedness or gestalt. Boxes often work better when you've used a section of an image. They act to visually define the edge if one isn't supplied. Since the angel is whole, there is no need to define edges.

Second, you'll see that the statue points to the edge of the display in Part A, making it seem even more disconnected from the words. Given that the statue is likely to grab your attention first (it is the biggest element), it becomes important that it directs you toward the content rather than off the edge of the display. You've seen examples like this in the hierarchy chapter. In this case, the hierarchy contributes to gestalt. The reader gets a better "big picture" when the elements of the display all work together.

Third, aligning text to an image creates gestalt. In Part B, the instructional text could have been aligned along the shape of the angel's belly, but this looked awkward. Creating a thin curved rule, aligning the text to the rule, and placing the text and rule in close prox-

A   Figure A allows you to see PARTS to WHOLE.

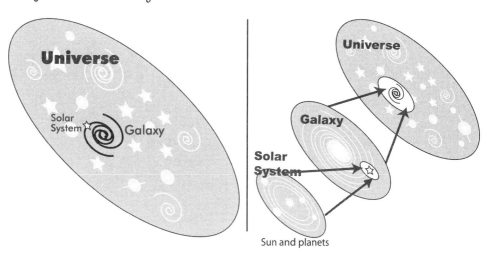

B   In Figure B you see mostly PARTS.

FIGURE 10–43 Achieving gestalt in a representative image

imity to the image helped the overall gestalt. Notice how design actions of contrast, alignment, proximity, shape, and type were used.

Representative

If your goal is to help people learn the general characteristics of the solar system, the galaxy, and the universe, as well as the relationship between these, would you use Part A or B of Figure 10-43? Most people would consider that Part A does a better job of representing the instructional content since it provides information about each entity (notice the sun and

In Figure B everything runs together: you don't see the important sections (PARTS) as clearly.

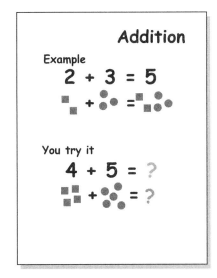

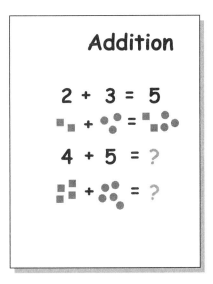

A   B

FIGURE 10-44 Achieving gestalt in an explanative visual

planets in the solar system) as well as their relationship to each other. Although the typeface size in Part B shows a hierarchical relationship (the word *Universe* is largest), each element is ill defined. You see the whole in Part B but do not get a clear picture of how the parts relate to the whole.

Explanative

Compare Parts A and B of Figure 10-44 and identify which one you think is best. Would grade schoolers have a better chance of interpreting the assignment correctly if they were given the worksheet in Part A or B?

Gestalt is a *parts* to *whole* relationship. Consider the *whole* in Part A and B as practicing addition. Consider the *parts* as the sections of the worksheet that help the learner practice. In which image do the parts do the best job of helping the learner practice addition?

From a gestalt perspective, Part A is better since it clearly identifies and separates the example section of the worksheet from the practice section. The *Example* and *You try it* headings make the student task clear. While Part B also provides practice, the expectation is less clear since the example and the practice sections are positioned so close together.

Notice how proximity is effectively used in Part A. By positioning the example and practice activities further apart, the learner can more easily distinguish the difference between the two. Figure/ground is used as well by providing the clear labels *You try it* and *Example*.

Organizational

Have you ever sat through an electronic presentation that seemed like a stream of unending bullets (see Figure 10-45)? During these presentations it is easy to stop paying attention.

Everything here is PARTS; you don't see the big picture (WHOLE).

FIGURE 10–45   An electronic presentation lacking gestalt

The problem is that when you do start paying attention again, you have no idea where you are because each screen looks the same. Orientation cues that mark the location of the displayed screen to the presentation overall are rare. You look at a particular slide or screen and think, where am I? What are we talking about now?

A greater sense of gestalt, or of understanding where you are in the larger context, is achieved in Figure 10-46. This presentation design employs a number of visual cues to mark your location. Notice the side panel that shows your location in the presentation. From any screen you see a representation of all future slides. You also have similar backgrounds for related topics (eye injuries are represented by an eye image). Treatment do's and don'ts are represented by a background no sign. All in all Figure 10-46 provides visual cues to help summarize, categorize, and keep content active in short-term memory. Keep in mind however, that these visual cues may not be needed, and may even detract, needed, when the subject is easy to understand and the presentation is short.

The outline on the left side, as well as the visual cues, help you stay connected to the WHOLE and understand the organization.

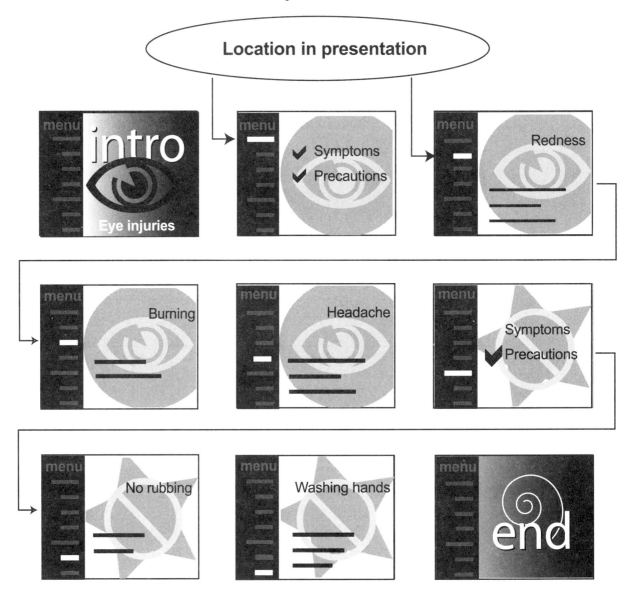

FIGURE 10–46 Achieving gestalt in an electronic presentation

How Do You Design Generative Strategies with Gestalt in Mind?

As in the past two chapters we'll shift direction and look at generative strategies that explore gestalt. As a reminder, when your goal is more oriented to *long-term learning,* it is time to consider generative strategies. Generative strategies are learning techniques that require learners to generate their own meaning. Generative strategies for integrating information in meaningful ways include using metaphors or analogies, outlining content, creating

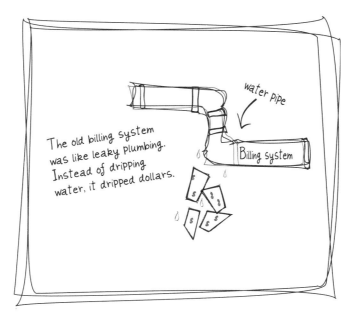

FIGURE 10–47   Using analogy

charts, creating mental images and analogies, summarizing information in one's own words, and telling stories (Wittrock, 1989). By doing these things, the learner thinks about the information more deeply and learns it more thoroughly.

Generative strategies can be used to help understand relationships between different elements. The following examples show you how learners might be able to use visuals to help them integrate information in meaningful ways and in ways that allow them to understand the big picture, or gestalt.

Analogy

Have the learner create a visual analogy of the overall instructional message (gestalt). The learner might be asked to draw an analogy of a topic. For instance, after a discussion of a faulty billing system, the learner might be asked to draw the problem. Figure 10–47 shows a drawing of a leaky pipe, but instead of the pipe leaking water, the pipe is leaking money. This image represents the learner's representation of a faulty billing system as something that over time wastes money.

Advance Organizer

Have learners create a diagram using any shapes they want to represent their thoughts on a topic and how they see parts fitting into a whole. Figure 10–48 shows the learner's initial ideas in preparing a presentation that covers the importance of needs assessment.

Summary

Everything in this book relates to this chapter, which is fitting since gestalt means whole. All of the information covered applies to gestalt. You need all of the tools, actions, and perceptions to create a sense of gestalt.

Drawing this type of diagram is a good way to help organize thoughts (PARTS) into a meaningful message (WHOLE).

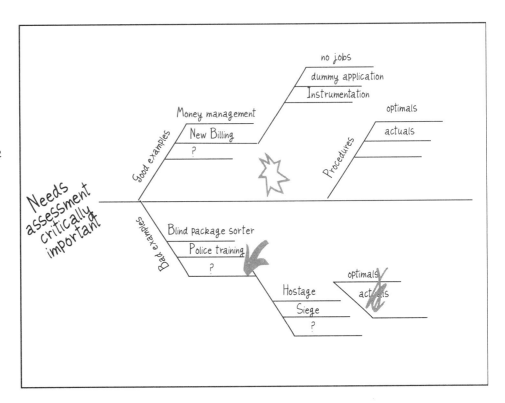

FIGURE 10–48   Using an advance organizer

This chapter reviews the importance of facilitating a learner's sense of gestalt through visual cues. *Gestalt* is a German word that roughly translates as "whole" or "form." Gestalt psychology is the study of how *the whole is greater than the sum of its parts.* When Edward Tufte (1990) describes good design as "simplicity in the underlying message, complexity in the detail," he is addressing gestalt. As designers, our goal is to help learners see the underlying message but to provide clear access to critical supportive information as well.

Five laws of gestalt were explained: closure, contiguity, similarity, proximity, and previous experience. Each of these laws describes how the mind, when presented with information, works to generate understanding. As designers, our job is to accelerate that process if possible.

The law of closure describes how the mind fills in gaps. For designers this means we may not need to supply all of the information. If we show part of an image rather than the whole image, the mind is likely to fill in the rest. By leaving out some of the information, we are reducing cognitive load, or the amount of information learners must process at any one time.

The law of contiguity tells us that the mind tries to follow a path or plane. Once it is started along that path, the mind wants to continue. As designers we want to take advantage of that momentum. By directing the eye along a path, we can control the sequence and ease in which information is processed. Chapter 9 covered the law of contiguity in detail.

The law of similarity explains how the mind groups information it perceives to be related. By using or repeating similar elements (colors, shapes, fonts), we can simplify data since the mind groups like elements, in turn reducing cognitive load. The action of repetition allows the mind to see these patterns and simplify information.

The law of proximity (one of the four actions covered in this book) explains how items that are placed close together are perceived as related and how items that are placed far apart are perceived as unrelated. By removing distance between elements, we can facilitate the mind's grouping of information into similar categories, making information easier to remember and understand. By increasing the distance between elements, we facilitate the perception of separate categories. Elements that are far apart are seen as distinct and unrelated.

The law of previous experience explains the importance of helping the learner relate new information to previous knowledge and experience. As designers we want to use colors and symbols that match the meaning of our content. For example, if we want to convey extreme danger, we could use a cross and skull image because it is universally the symbol of death. By using visual elements that already have meaning, we can reduce learners' cognitive load.

Computer-based training environments rely heavily upon effective use of gestalt principles, especially in the design of grid systems and interfaces. A grid system is an underlying structure used to provide consistency throughout instruction. Interfaces are the communication devices between a product and a system. An instructional interface consists of all the visual, verbal, and auditory cues that help learners go about the task of learning. Grids are typically built into interfaces. Gestalt is an important consideration in the design of grids and interfaces because this principle addresses reducing complexity and overload, an important consideration when dealing with the many functions of an instructional interface.

Many techniques facilitate gestalt. Tools and actions that contribute to figure/ground and hierarchy are all relevant. Consideration of white space and balance are especially important since they can be manipulated to create a sense of harmony and unity, both characteristics of gestalt.

FOR MORE CHALLENGE

Visit Chapter 10's *Challenge* section on the book's website. There you'll find several instructional problems that require your visual solutions. Compare your solutions to those of others.

DISCUSSION FOR DISTANCE LEARNING

Visit the book's website (Chapter 10 > Discussion) for discussion or chat questions.

REFERENCES

Dreyfus, H. (1984). *Symbol source book: An authoritative guide to international graphic symbols.* New York: Van Nostrand Reinhold.

Gestalt Psychology. (2000). Microsoft® Encartara® Online Encyclopedia. Retrieved from *http://encarta.msn.com.*

Horton, W. K. (1994). *The icon book: Visual symbols for computer systems and documentation.* New York: John Wiley & Sons.

Koffka, K. (1935). *Principles of gestalt psychology.* New York: Harcourt, Brace.

Kristof, R., & Satran, A. (1995). *Interactivity by design: Creating and communicating with new media.* Mountain View, CA: Adobe Press.

Lohr, L. (2000). Designing the instructional interface. *Computers in Human Behavior, 16*(2), 161–182.

Lohr, L., & Eikleberry, C. (2001). Learner-centered usability: Tools for creating a learner-friendly instructional environment. *Performance Improvement 40*(4), 24–28.

Luchins, A. S., & Luchins, E. H. (1959). *Rigidity of behavior—A variational approach to the effect of einstellung.* Eugene, Oregon: University of Oregon Books. Retrieved from *http://www.enabling.org/ia/gestalt/gerhards/closure.html*

Lynch, P. J., & Horton, S. (1999). *Web style guide: Basic design principles for creating web sites.* New Haven, CT: Yale University Press.

Mayer, R. E., Bove, W., Bryman, A., Mars, R., & Tapangco, L. (1996). When less is more: Meaningful learning from visual and verbal summaries of science textbook lessons. *Journal of Educational Psychology, 88*(1), 64–73.

Mayer, R. E., & Sims, V. K. (1994.) For whom is a picture worth a thousand words? Extension of a dual-coding theory of multimedia learning. *Journal of Educational Psychology, 86*(3), 389–401.

Miller, A. R., Brown, J. M., & Cullen, C. D. (2000). *Global graphics: Designing with symbols for an international market.* Gloucester, MA: Rockport Publishers.

Misanchuk, E. R. (1992). *Preparing instructional text: Document design using desktop publishing.* Englewood Cliffs, NJ: Educational Technology Publications.

Mok, C. (1996). *Designing business: Multiple media, multiple disciplines.* San Jose, CA: Adobe Press.

Mullet, K., & Sano, D. (1995). *Designing visual interfaces: Communication oriented techniques.* Englewood Cliffs, NJ: Prentice Hall.

Nielsen, J. (2000). *Designing web usability: The practice of simplicity.* Indianapolis, IN: New Riders Publishing.

Ormrod, J. (1990). *Human learning: Theories, principles, and educational applications.* Upper Saddle River, NJ: Merrill/Prentice Hall.

Peterson, B. L. (1996). *Using design basics to get creative results.* Cincinnati, OH: North Light Books.

Pettersson, R. (1993). *Visual information.* Englewood Cliffs, NJ: Educational Technology Publications.

Tufte, E. (1990). *Envisioning information.* Cheshire, CT: Graphics Press.

Wertheimer, M. (1959). Principles of perceptual organization, in D.C. Beardslee & M. Wertheimer (Eds.), *Readings in Perception* (pp. 115–135). Princeton, NJ: Van Nostrand.

Wittrock, M. C. (1989). Generative processes of comprehension. *Educational Psychologist, 24,* 345–376.

PART III

Putting It All Together

CHAPTER *11*

ACE It! Analyze, Create, Evaluate

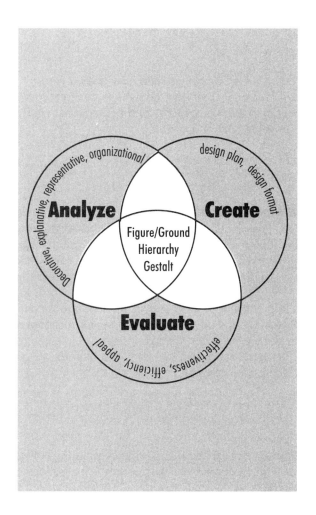

"Design is inherently a messy process. It's ironic that the end result is about creating order."

Tom Mecklen

NOTES ABOUT THE OPENING VISUAL

The cover image is a Venn diagram of the ACE (Analyze, Create, and Evaluate) design model that you'll learn about in this chapter. The model uses circles to represent the cyclical (ongoing and repetitive) and overlapping process of creating instructional visuals. How does this take place? Let's say you are designing a one-page set of instructions. You'd create the instructions, look them over, and probably would want to change something, perhaps the layout, the typography, or a few words. You ask yourself questions like, Does this look right? Does it read well? Do I need to make this easier to understand? Throughout this scenario, you are analyzing and changing, and sometimes analyzing, creating, and changing all at once. You tend to do this many times until all the tools and actions presented in this book seem to be in place.

FOCUS QUESTIONS

- What is the ACE process, and how does it work?
- How does one move from analysis to concrete form, from the invisible to the visible?
- In addition to tools, actions, and perceptions, what do you need to consider during the development of a visual?

KEY TERMS

ACE (ANALYZE, CREATE, EVALUATE)   model that explains how you create instructional visuals (see Figure 11–1). Analysis involves defining the objective of the visual, creation involves creating the visual, and evaluation involves testing and editing the visual. The ACE model is not my own; I've substituted one word of the Reigeluth and Nelson (1997) ASEC model (analyze, synthesize, evaluate, and change) because I think you'll remember and understand the word *create* better than *synthesize*. Also, the cyclic nature of ACE implies that change is continually taking place.

ADDIE MODEL   the acronym of a generic instructional design model that consists of these phases: analysis, design, development, implementation, and evaluation

INSTRUCTIONAL MESSAGE DESIGN   the plan for the physical form of instructional communication (Grabowski, 1995)

INTRODUCTION

Antonio (the teacher) and Latisha (the community college instructor) find themselves creating many instructional visuals, but they have no idea of how they are "supposed" to be doing them. Typically they "just do it." They don't even think about what they are doing. Sylvia (the instructional designer) and Zack (the graphic artist) both have training in design and, to some extent, have learned about the creative process. When it comes to creating instructional visuals, though, neither of them has thought much about a separate design process to facilitate learning. For Zack, creating an instructional visual is the same as creating any other type of visual. For Sylvia, the step where analysis takes on a concrete form has always seemed a little vague. She analyzes instructional needs and, poof! they take on a concrete form. The step between analysis and actual development has always seemed a little like magic. She's not really sure how she does it and has a hard time explaining the step to others.

This Venn diagram shows how everything in the book fits together.

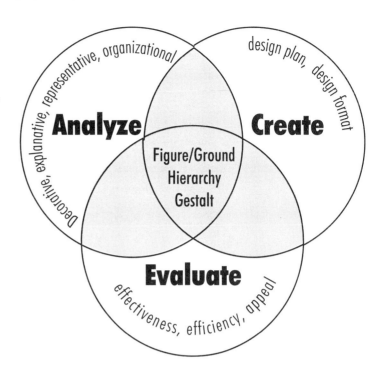

FIGURE 11-1 The ACE model

Source: From "Design and Development of an Instructional Interface," Journal of Visual Literacy. *Used with permission.*

Antonio, Latisha, Sylvia, and Zack have these questions:

- Do I start with analysis?
- Where does development of images take place in the larger design process?
- How do I know that the visual works the way I want it to work?

This chapter is written to answer these questions.

HOW DO YOU GET STARTED?

The ACE model has three cyclical components; analyze, create, and evaluate. Together they do a good job of explaining the design process for an instructional visual, but they don't really describe where you start or how you get started, often the toughest part of all. The best example I provide comes from the movie *Finding Forrester.* In this movie a famous (fictitious) author (Forrester) befriends a young writer to teach him how to write. When a typewriter is placed in front of the young writer, he freezes. "I need to think" he says. Forrester says something along these lines, "Don't think—write. If you can't think of anything to write, copy something already written. Type that, and keep typing until the words become your own. You save thinking for when you edit, and that is when you really need to think."

I purposefully saved this chapter (and the key perception chapters on figure/ground, hierarchy, and gestalt) for the end of the book because I wanted to get you to experiment with the tools and actions before having to think too much. I hoped you would experience the process and encounter this chapter with a mind more open and receptive to the ideas presented here.

WHAT ARE DESIGN MODELS?

A number of models are used to help create instruction, including, but not limited to, the Dick and Carey (1996) model, the Smith and Ragan (1993) model, and the Morrison, Ross, and Kemp (1999) model. These instructional design models help people visualize all the discreet and often invisible steps that take place when analyzing an instructional problem and delivering its intervention.

Each of the major instructional design models has its own strengths. The Dick and Carey model is widely used and has a long history of success in business and military projects. The Smith and Ragan model is known for its extensive focus on the development of instructional strategies based on information processing theories. The Morrison, Ross, and Kemp model is known for its application across business and academic settings and for its nonlinear approach. As you can see from Figure 11–2, covering all of these models in any depth is beyond the scope of this book. The figure shows how the Dick and Carey, Smith and Ragan, and Morrison, Ross, and Kemp models share an underlying structure called ADDIE, which can be described briefly.

ADDIE stands for the key stages of the instructional design process: analysis, design, development, implementation, and evaluation. These are described briefly to give you an idea of how instruction is likely to move through the ADDIE process.

	Dick and Carey (1996)	**Smith and Ragan** (2000)	**Morrison, Ross, and Kemp** (1999)
Analysis	■ Identifying an instructional goal ■ Conducting a goal analysis ■ Conducting a subordinate skills analysis ■ Identifying entry behaviors and characteristics	■ Analyzing learning context ■ Analyzing learners ■ Analyzing learning task	■ Identifying the need for instruction (needs assessment, goal analysis, performance assessment) ■ Conducting learner and contextual analysis ■ Task analysis
Design	■ Writing performance objectives ■ Developing criterion-referenced test items ■ Developing an instructional strategy based on content classification	■ Creating instructional strategies (organizational, supplantive, generative, macro, and elaboration strategies) ■ Developing an instructional strategy based on content classification)	■ Determining instructional objectives (based on content classification) ■ Designing the instruction (sequencing, strategies, message design, advance organizers)
Development	■ Developing instructional materials	■ Designing delivery and management strategies (media characteristics and selection) ■ Production of instruction (print, computer, video, teacher, time, and cost)	■ Developing instructional materials
Implementation	■ Planning and managing implementation	■ Designing delivery and management strategies	■ Planning for instructional implementation ■ CLER model (configuration, linkages, environment, and resources)
Evaluation	■ Formative evaluation ■ Revising instructional materials	■ Assessing learner performance ■ Formative and summative evaluation	■ Formative evaluation ■ Summative evaluation ■ Confirmative evaluation

FIGURE 11–2   The ADDIE Structure of Instructional Design Models

Analysis, the A in ADDIE, is the stage where one learns if any instructional problem needs an intervention. Conducting the analysis involves conducting needs assessments, determining learner characteristics, and conducting task and content analysis.

Design, the first D of ADDIE, involves decisions about how information should be presented or taught depending on your analysis. Considerations include type of learner, type of content, learning philosophy, instructional or performance goals and objectives, and instructional or performance context.

Development, the second D of ADDIE, is the stage where you take all your analysis and design and make it tangible/visible. You create storyboards, you design the message, you create prototypes. You write code, use an authoring package, write text, and create graphics or animation. If you are thinking that development is where instructional message design takes place, you are right (although some think it belongs in design.)

Implementation, the I of ADDIE, is the stage where you plan for the implementation and management of the instructional product in increasingly realistic contexts. Considerations such as delivery platforms, training, and resources take place during this stage.

Evaluation, the E of ADDIE, is the stage where you test your visual to see if you can make it better and to see how effective, efficient, and appealing it is.

What is interesting about ADDIE is that it can be interpreted on macro and micro levels. It can help you design entire curriculums, lessons, and the tiniest element of an instructional visual. As you cycle through ADDIE, you find yourself recycling through ADDIE. Sounds confusing? That is probably why design is called a "messy process."

Consider this example. Suppose you are creating management skills training. As you develop this training, you use the ADDIE model. While in the design stage of ADDIE, you come up with different strategies to teach managers how to set priorities. While creating these strategies you create visuals to go along with them. As you create the visuals, you find yourself *analyzing* what the visual should say, *designing* the visual on paper by sketching it out, *developing* it in PowerPoint, testing (*implementing*) it with a sample audience, and revising (*evaluating*) it. You've just cycled through ADDIE while you are technically using ADDIE to create the larger management training. I've simplified this description of the inner instructional design process for visuals to focus on **ACE: analyze, create** (which includes designing and developing), and **evaluate** (which includes implementation and evaluation.)

As you can see from this example, the ACE model is a micro process within the larger macro ADDIE process. Of all of the instructional design models, the Morrison, Ross, and Kemp model (1999) explains the nature of ACE most directly since this model uniquely addresses an **instructional message design** component (see the design section of Figure 11-2). Designing the instructional message is the phase where you decide the format of your instruction. Is it going to be visual? Auditory? Kinesthetic? A combination? What specific cues and signals will you include to focus and direct attention?

Although it is not a major component of many design models, you can assume that attention to message design principles typically takes place in both design and development phases of the ADDIE model (see Figure 11-3). During design you may sketch out your visual, and during development you use tools to refine and strengthen it. As Figure 11-3 shows, you cycle through steps of analyze (plan for design), create (sketch or develop using a tool), and evaluate (assess the visual's effectiveness). You continue through this process until the visual is satisfactory.

The ACE model is derived from Reigeluth and Nelson's (1997) ASEC model of instructional design (analysis, synthesis, evaluation, change). ASEC is similar to ADDIE. The key difference between the ASEC model and the ADDIE model is ASEC is considered an emerging paradigm of instructional systems design whereby design and development move through "iterative series of ASEC cycles for progressive sets of instructional decisions" (Reigeluth & Nelson, 1997, p. 31). Essentially the ASEC model works best for prototyping instruction. That is creating a quick representation, then revising it, and continuing that cycle until the prototype has reached its objective.

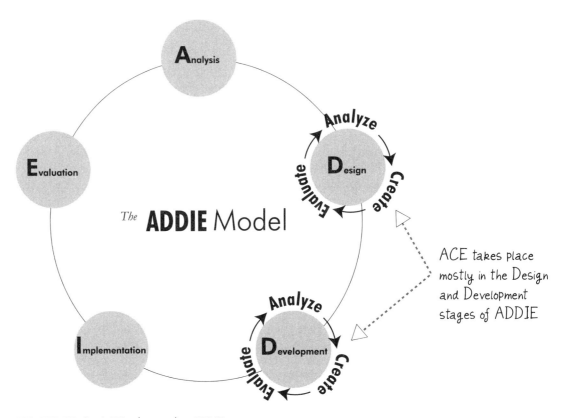

FIGURE 11-3   ACE's place within ADDIE

I've reduced the four phases of ASEC to three because based on my research (Lohr, 2000), these three phases (analyze, create, and evaluate) capture the core activities that take place, with the added benefit that they are easy to remember. Though each phase is described later in this chapter, the following overview is provided to give you a big-picture idea of what takes place. In order to do this, I'll share how ACE was used to create Figure 11-2, the table that shows ADDIE and its relationship to common instructional design models.

During the analysis phase I identified the purpose of the visual. My instructional objective was to teach the concept of instructional design models. My instructional strategy was to show the similarity between models and to also show the details of each model. I made quick notes during the analysis phase consisting of the words, "Show similarity of models to each other as well as some details of each model."

During the create phase I started by sketching the rows and columns I'd need to show *similar* steps of ADDIE and specific *details* of each model. After the sketch I focused on what I wanted you to see and perceive instantly (figure/ground). A table seemed right because it allows you to see data and its relationships. When creating the table, I worked mostly with text, shape, space, alignment, repetition, and proximity. I also wanted to establish an order of importance (hierarchy). Since I considered the underlying ADDIE structure to be important, I made the words Analysis, Design, Development, Implementation, and Evaluation larger and bolder than the rest of the text.

During the evaluate phase I made several changes to the table based on how effectively I thought the image was working. I asked myself if the image met its objectives. Did the image show the underlying similarity of the different design models? Did the image show the detail sufficiently? I evaluated the image as I was creating it and after it was considered first-draft complete. Then I showed the image to students who read and tested this textbook.

While this description may seem pretty linear, I wasn't really thinking or performing as clearly as I describe it here. In reality I was working on many of these decisions at once. I was constantly adjusting the space between columns and lines of data (proximity). I was making some lines bolder and thicker than others (contrast). Because of the simultaneous nature of these actions and decisions, Figure 11-1 at the start of this chapter best represents the process I used.

WHAT HAPPENS IN THE ANALYZE PHASE OF ACE?

In the analyze phase, you identify the purpose of the instructional visual. This analysis is greatly influenced by the purposes of the overall instructional or performance context, as identified in the ADDIE process. For example, based on what you've learned by conducting analysis for the overall instructional context, you'll already have an idea of the audience, their task, and the overall instructional objective for the visual.

During the analyze phase, you consider figure/ground, hierarchy, and gestalt—at a high level. You want to make the instructional objective clear (figure/ground), provide well-organized and comprehensive information (hierarchy), and create an environment or context where the overall message and organization are easy to understand (gestalt). You'll also want to consider the instructional functions of visuals identified by Levin (1981):

- Decoration (to improve aesthetic appeal)
- Representation (to make information more concrete)
- Organization (to make information easier to understand logically)
- Interpretation (to explain difficult information)
- Transformation (to change your visual representation of something in order to help you remember it)

WHAT HAPPENS IN THE CREATE PHASE OF ACE?

In the create phase, you translate analysis into physical form, something that might be visual, auditory, or kinesthetic. You essentially take your goals and objectives and make them into something you can see. The create phase involves moving design from a conceptual form to a physical one. This book, with its emphasis on tools, actions, and perception principles is all about this create phase.

The create phase is where you manipulate figure/ground, hierarchy, and gestalt to enhance the instructional quality of your visual. You decide how to emphasize the overall message (figure/ground), how you want to direct learners through layers of organized information (hierarchy), and how to convey the relationship of the visual to other parts of the instructional setting (gestalt). The previous chapters have covered these principles in detail.

Not covered yet are three other important tasks:

- Generating a good visual idea or approach to instruction (how you come up with something motivating to catch attention, convey relevance, inspire confidence, and result in learner satisfaction)
- Arranging the elements of the visual (some basic tips on putting it all together)
- Representing your visual instruction in a way that communicates effectively and facilitates the process of its development

1. Generating the Visual Idea

Everyone faces the daunting blank sheet of paper or the blank computer screen. You have knowledge of design, tools beyond the dreams of previous generations, and the opportunity to edit and revise easily. It is easier than ever to create, right? Maybe, maybe not. Regardless of relative ease, the task is still challenging. Where do you come up with an idea for an interface that is visual, or a suitable theme for instruction, or a clever advance organizer?

In the fictional example at the start of this chapter, the wise old author tells his young student to "just start typing." If the student couldn't think of anything to type, he was advised to copy someone else's work and type until the words became his own. This isn't bad advice, but be sure you don't use the original work unless you credit it (review the copyright section of Chapter 5; more on that subject in the next chapter). Even Picasso is credited with saying, "Good artists copy. Great artists steal." The idea for using inspiration has been around for a long time. Most artists work from inspiration, and you should, too. Use examples of other graphic artists' work! You'll see examples everywhere, from advertisements in magazines, on the Web, and on television to billboards on the highway and direct mail you receive at home. This next section helps you generate ideas.

Ideas for Developing a Visual Concept

Landa (1998) suggests becoming thoroughly familiar with the concept you are trying to communicate. Some suggestions for getting visually unstuck include:

- Thinking through your topic, to the point of looking words up in a dictionary in order to fully understand concepts
- Making a comprehensive list of *anything* related to your content (ironically, most visuals start with words, sentences, even paragraphs)
- Looking everywhere and at everything you can think of pertaining to your subject (paintings, book covers, websites, toys, posters)
- Giving your subconscious a chance by putting the idea away and allowing your mind to work on the problem without pressure
  - Trying lots of directions or approaches, including:
  - taking notes
  - analyzing great books, movies, and advertisements
  - fooling around
  - talking to people
  - taking your list and brainstorming with it

Synectics

The last step in the previous list, brainstorming, can be exceptionally effective when employing a synectics strategy. The word *synectics* is derived from the Greek roots *syn* (bring together) and *ectics* (diverse elements); it is the name for a set of strategies used to stimulate and enhance creative thought (Gordon, 1961). The primary tool of synectics is the analogy and metaphor, which are used to help you "break set" and explore new ideas. You use this approach to enter the world of "soft thinking" where the illogical and emotional aspects of a topic are emphasized (vonOech, 1983). The synectics model is based on the belief that creativity can be developed in most people but is often stifled by "hard thinking" norms of logic and rationality. By sparking new ideas and associations, we can sometimes solve problems. The route to this type of problem solving is through divergent, preferably generative, thinking, as Weaver and Prince (1990) suggest:

Divergent thinkers consider relevant material, but often discard it and look for widely different, even seemingly irrelevant connection-making material... [Generative thinkers] are open to divergent beginnings but eagerly search for connections that make things workable. (p. 380)

The synectic strategy encourages divergent and generative thinking through activities that encourage the development of metaphors. When brainstorming visual ideas, you might try one of two recommended metaphor-provoking exercises: (1) making the familiar strange (see Figure 11–4) and (2) making the strange familiar (see Figure 11–5). These exercises get you to think of metaphors that give you some distance from the topic and allow you think about it in a different way.

1 **Think through the situation or concept and define it as it is now.**

Describe in as few words as possible what you are trying to teach

2 **Think up analogies that relate to the concept.**

Ask yourself what the idea/concept is similar to. You try here to think about the idea/concept in a new way; thus, it doesn't matter how close your comparison is to the real thing.

3 **Select one of your analogies and become it.**

Think about the idea/concept as if it were yourself. Try to empathize with the ideas being compared.

4 **Create a compressed conflict.**

Think of a two-word description of the idea/concept where the words conflict with each other (friendly fire, beautifully repulsive).

5 **Create another direct analogy.**

Think of an analogy based upon your compressed conflict.

6 **Reexamine the task**

Think through your concept again and recycle through the steps if needed.

FIGURE 11–4 Making the familiar strange
Source: Clip art modified from Dover Images.

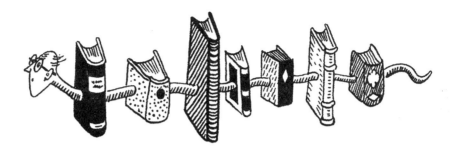

1 Review information about the topic.

Explore the idea or concept.

2 Think up analogies that relate to the concept.

Ask yourself what the idea/concept is similar to. You try here to think about the idea/concept in a new way; thus it doesn't matter how close your comparison is to the real thing.

3 Select one of your analogies and become it.

Think about the idea/concept as if it were yourself. Try to empathize with the ideas being compared.

4 Compare similarity of analogies

Identify how the personalized analogies match the idea or concept. Identify specific points that are similar.

5 Explain the differences.

Identify how the personalized analogies do not match the idea or concept. Identify specific points that are not similar.

6 Reexamine the task.

Think through your concept again and recycle through the steps if needed.

FIGURE 11–5 Making the strange familiar

Source: Clip art from Dover Images.

TABLE 11-1   *Making the Familiar Strange*

1. **Think through the situation/concept and define it as it is now.**	Viruses are keenly bent on multiplying themselves, and they are deadly.
2. **Think up analogies that relate to the concept.**	■ A virus is like a war.
	■ A virus is like the plague.
	■ A virus is initially unobservable—it is lurking unseen, like a thief.
	■ A virus is a greedy Scrooge counting its copies as Scrooge counted his money, not happy with what he had, always wanting more, regardless of who he hurt.
3. **Select one of your analogies and "become" it, personalize it.**	If I were a greedy virus, I'd want gold copies of my power, like Scrooge's gold coins.
4. **Create a compressed conflict.**	Golden destroyer, kingly sadist
5. **Create a direct analogy.**	A golden destroyer is like a king who killed many, like King Henry who wanted only sons (dedicated to his own duplication) and thereby had his wives beheaded if they bore him daughters.
6. **Reexamine the task.**	I like the King Henry analogy so I'll go with it.

The King Henry the VIII virus analogy was thought of using the "making the familiar strange" Synectic strategy.

Q

What is compact, hard, logical, & dedicated to making copies of itself?

A virus is made of membranes, proteins, and one or more DNA or RNA strands. These strands allow the virus to replicate. A virus is "compact, hard, logical, totally selfish, and **dedicated to making copies of itself**" (Preston, 1994).

Viruses are **parasites**; to replicate they must be attached to something else. When a cell comes along, the virus will attach itself to the cell, making the cell its host. When this happens, the cell wraps itself around the virus, drawing it into its system.

King Henry the VIII

FIGURE 11-6   The virus analogy

Making the familiar strange   When you use this strategy, you try to visualize familiar things in unfamiliar ways. The following steps (Joyce & Weil, 1986) take you through this process (see Table 11-1). I used this strategy when I designed the Figure 11-6 virus graphic.

Making the strange familiar   You often need to teach something that is a new idea, and to do this you need to think something the learner already knows. The following steps (Joyce & Weil, 1986) take you through this process (see Table 11–2). Bea Doyle used this strategy when she designed the graphic in Figure 11–7 to teach the concept of choice.

FIGURE 11–7 Conveying the concept of choice
Source: Created by Bea Doyle. Used with permission.

The "making the strange familiar" synectic strategy was used to come up with the Candy Shop analogy for the concept of "choice."

TABLE 11–2 *Making the Strange Familiar*

1. **Review information about the topic.**	People must make choices throughout their lives, choices about who they become, who they marry, what career they pursue, what values they uphold, what houses they buy, how they invest their money, and more. Though it seems simple, choice isn't always so easy. Choosing requires education about alternatives, and the education must be as free of bias as possible.
2. **Think up analogies that relate to the concept.**	Choice is like a fork in the road.
3. **Select one of your analogies and "become" it.**	■ I am standing in front of a fork in the road. ■ I have two ways to go. ■ The directions are marked.
4. **Compare similarity of analogies.**	There are alternative ways to go, directions to take, just like in real life.
5. **Explain the differences.**	There are only a few clearly marked options available and the decisions are thus fairly informed. In real life there are more options and they are more ambiguous.
6. **Reexamine the task.**	I'm standing in front of a decision, there are several alternative decisions that can be made. The alternatives are all attractive. I like the opportunity of each and don't know which to take. I'm like a child in a toy store. I am like a child in a candy store. I like this analogy.

Hopefully you can use some of the suggestions in this section to come up with visual ideas. Once you have those ideas, you need to arrange them for whatever media you plan to use: paper, the computer screen, electronic slides, perhaps even a flip chart.

2. Arranging the Elements

Figure/ground, hierarchy, and gestalt help you arrange instructional displays, but Elizabeth Boling (Heinich, Molenda, Russell, & Smaldino, 1999) makes additional suggestions to keep in mind. Though these suggestions are made specifically for a computer screen, they work for most displays.

1. **Assemble all elements.** This includes all the text elements and all the visual elements in your image. If you are working on computer-based training, consider navigation, windows, and panels as the elements of your work.

2. **Choose a background and underlying pattern.** This is a particularly helpful piece of advice because I've observed students with elements "floating" in a display space, but nothing really holding them together or connecting them to any concept or idea. Since the background or underlying pattern's purpose is to emphasize the important information, it does this through proximity. That is, it visually groups elements because they are close together in the designated space. Parts A and B of Figure 11-8 show before and after images employing this step.

The elements in Figure A seem to float around whereas the elements in Figure B seem more connected. The outside brackets in Figure B create an underlying rectangle shape.

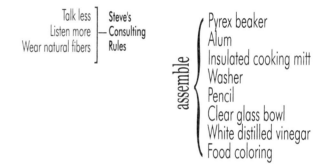

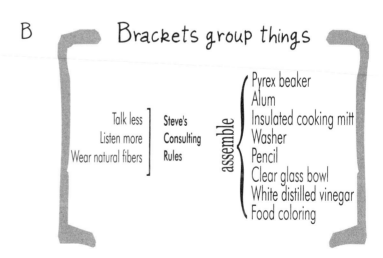

FIGURE 11–8   Adding a background

3. **Arrange the elements.** Arranging is an "action," and you know all about actions from reading Chapter 7. Pay attention to contrast, alignment, repetition, and proximity.

4. **Check and revise.** We'll actually cover this step in the evaluate step of the ACE model. Essentially you review your design and watch people using it. By doing this you can see what needs to be changed.

3. Representing the Visual Instruction

You've worked hard to generate and arrange a visual idea and don't want it to be misinterpreted if someone else is developing it or working with it. Visual ideas need to be communicated clearly to avoid confusion and misrepresentation. Doing this often involves sketching your idea on paper or the computer and sharing these sketches with the people involved. Storyboards are essentially visual and verbal outlines of your visual instruction. A good storyboard serves many purposes.

- It helps you *plan* because you draw out in detail all the elements of your instruction. You show what your screens/pages look like, what the text says, what graphics are used, and how you name your files (lesson1.htm), among other things.
- It helps you *manage* an instructional project as you identify all graphics, text, audio, and naming conventions used.
- It helps you *communicate* with others during development. You can show interested parties the entire instructional project or specific pages or screens.

What does a storyboard look like? They are all different. Storyboards aren't standardized. They are unique for each setting, reflecting the templates and standards of their development environments. Some storyboards are simple, showing only file names, sketches of visuals, and scripts. Other storyboards are complex and interact with databases and other files.

Storyboards might include the following (see Figure 11-9):

a. the filename associated with the storyboard page
b. a rectangle where a rough sketch of the page/screen can be displayed
c. a "you are here" map showing where a particular page falls within a larger context (a gestalt feature)
d. a description of the page/screen
e. other files involved with the page/screen, including animation files, graphic files, sound files, and text files
f. link information, including next, previous, begin, end, and branching links
g. revision dates and naming conventions
h. sign-offs for the lead programmer and instructional designer
i. feedback links, including any branching that takes place, such as distractors
j. glossary terms
k. notes

The rectangular sketching space (see "B" in Figure 11-9) should reflect the height and width for the type of media used. Figure 11-10 shows storyboards with specific height and width ratios for 33 mm slides, flip charts, overhead transparencies, and video, computer, and television screens.

What Happens in the Evaluate Phase of ACE?

You carefully edit your work and learn what you need to change in the Evaluate Phase. Notice the assumption that you'll change your visual? Rarely are visuals perfect the first time through. Since as a society we are not schooled in visual syntax, you can expect that people will interpret your visual in a variety of unexpected ways. You can count on it!

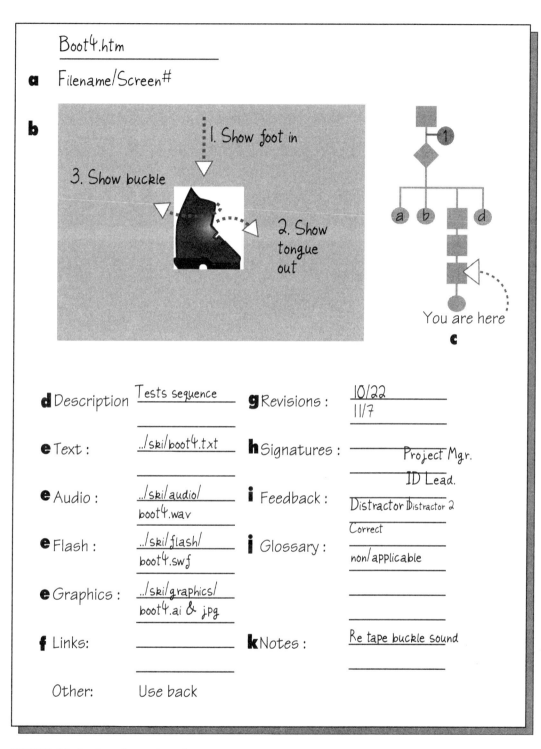

a Filename/Screen# <u>Boot4.htm</u>

b

1. Show foot in

3. Show buckle

2. Show tongue out

c You are here

d Description <u>Tests sequence</u>

e Text : <u>../ski/boot4.txt</u>

e Audio : <u>../ski/audio/</u> <u>boot4.wav</u>

e Flash : <u>../ski/flash/</u> <u>boot4.swf</u>

e Graphics : <u>../ski/graphics/</u> <u>boot4.ai & jpg</u>

f Links:

Other: Use back

g Revisions : <u>10/22</u> <u>11/7</u>

h Signatures : Project Mgr. ID Lead.

i Feedback : Distractor Distractor 2 Correct

j Glossary : non/applicable

k Notes : <u>Re tape buckle sound</u>

FIGURE 11-9 Sample storyboard

Use these dimensions for different media formats

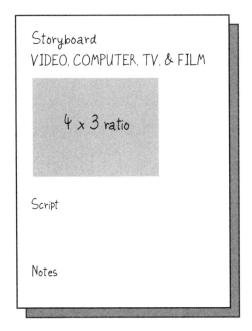

Storyboard
VIDEO, COMPUTER, TV, & FILM

4 x 3 ratio

Script

Notes

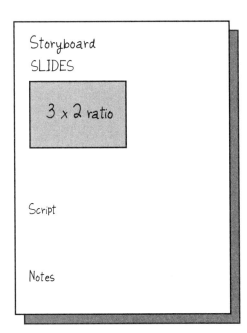

Storyboard
SLIDES

3 x 2 ratio

Script

Notes

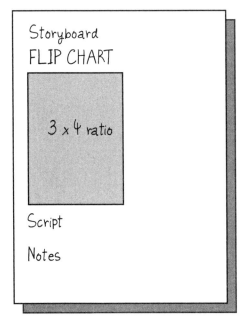

Storyboard
FLIP CHART

3 x 4 ratio

Script

Notes

Storyboard
OVERHEAD TRANSPARENCY

4 x 5 ratio

Script

Notes

FIGURE 11-10 Storyboard media formats

You can evaluate effectiveness of your instructional visuals (Lohr & Eikleberry, 2001) by asking three overall questions:

1. Do teacher and learner cues in the visual help perception of figure/ground, hierarchy, and gestalt?
2. Is the visual learner-friendly?
3. Have you weeded out the extraneous data?

Teacher and Learner Cues

Start by looking over your visual with your learners in mind. Would the visual make sense to them? Do you need to add or take away elements to increase understanding? Your essential elements are type, shape, color, depth, and space and their arrangement. Do these elements form cues that do things a good teacher would do, such as help direct attention to important information (figure/ground)? Let you know what to do next (hierarchy)? Provide an orientation and overview (gestalt)? Likewise, does the visual anticipate the types of questions learners typically have? Does the visual help the learner answer questions like these: What am I supposed to do with this visual? Am I interpreting this in a way that helps me understand instructional content?

Learner-Friendly Visuals

You'll use three usability criteria to determine the learner-friendliness of your instructional visuals: effectiveness, efficiency, and appeal. There are two approaches to evaluation, and both are important. First, you need to go through the visual yourself and self-edit its effectiveness. After you are satisfied, you should test the visual with the target audience.

Testing Out the Visual Yourself

Try answering the following set of questions as you assess your work.

Effectiveness   You determine effectiveness by asking questions such as:

- Does the visual work instructionally?
- Does the visual cover the correct content?
- Does the visual cover an optimal amount of information?

Efficiency   You determine efficiency by asking questions that deal with perception principles, such as:

- Does the visual make important information (figure/ground) easy to perceive?
- Does the visual help the learner relate (gestalt) the information to the overall learning or performance context?
- Is the visual organized (hierarchy) so that information is easy to access?

Appeal   You determine appeal by asking questions that deal with how motivating the image is, such as:

- Is the information in the visual relevant and important to the learner in the learning context?
- Is the visual attractive?
- Does the visual get the learner's attention?

Testing the Visual with Your Target Audience

Up until this point, the usability testing process has been directed or structured around specific criteria of interest and you have been the sole editor of your work. This final step—perhaps the most important step in the entire process—is unstructured and involves other people. If you do this step correctly, you'll get the chance to see problems or learner confusion you hadn't even envisioned, perhaps because you are too close to the design to see the problem, or you just don't have the unique perspective of the learner.

During this step you ask the learner to use the visual in a realistic context, if possible. For example, if the visual is to accompany a set of instructions, you'd want to provide the learner with the instructions and any materials that are mentioned in the instructions. If your situation isn't readily observable, you can ask learners to share what they are thinking when they look at the visual. Ask them what the visual communicates. Try not to tell learners what you were hoping the visual would do, because you'll bias their perspective. You want to get information about how they really are seeing your visual so you can change it and make it better.

How many people should you use? Try to get up to four people. The more eyes on your visual, the better. Nielsen (1993) suggests a minimum of three to five users for Web usability testing. While this falls short of sample size requirements learned in basic research methods and statistics courses, this rule of thumb is real-world and fits with the demands of most development environments, where time and money are always key drivers of design.

Weeding Out Extraneous Design Elements

Of all the advice in this book, this is the most important: **Take out visual elements that do not add anything.** It is hard to make yourself do, especially if you spent a long time creating something and find it isn't needed. Your ability to *remove* unneeded elements makes you an effective designer.

Peterson (1996) describes the design process as diamond shaped (see Figure 11-11). You begin with your idea and build it up to a certain point (using tools like type, shape, color, depth, and space) where it makes sense. Then, you eliminate all but the most essential elements. You stop when you have removed any of the elements that do not add anything to your design.

The best way to get good at removing (it's a hard step) is to start doing it. If you bitterly regret not being able to include an element you spent hours designing, try to think of that element as moving you toward your visual solution. All was not lost. You might even save the element to use for another situation.

Part A of Figure 11-12 is an image I spent at least two hours creating (while writing this book I didn't have that kind of time). I made the image for the Chapter 1 cover because I thought the architectural look of the typography would be a good way to communicate the thought and deliberation that go into designing instructional visuals. Many of the readers, however, where confused by the graphic. They weren't aware of what typography was, and the image was too abstract. The architectural analogy was lost on them. Ironically, the graphic was a bad example of the very thing it was trying to accomplish. Part B is the graphic eventually used in its place.

Even when I knew Part A was bad, I had a hard time cutting it. I rationalized by saving it and using it in the Type chapter and then it did not fit there either. Many images do not make it to the final stage. Just remember the ability to take away actually moves you toward the finished product (see Part B of Figure 11-11). In many ways it is like the writing process. You may struggle over a sentence for a long time only to find later that you need to delete every word.

HOW DO YOU PUT ACE ALL TOGETHER?

Figure 11-13 shows two cycles of the ACE process used to create a graphic describing the 80/20 rule. Keep in mind that not everything covered in the book and this chapter will be employed, just the points that were relevant to the 80/20 graphic. For example, you won't see a storyboard because this is a single visual and doesn't require extensive documentation.

The diamond shape represents quantity of design elements in a visual as it is being created. At the start you have few ideas or elements. You gradually add them until you reach the middle and wide part of the diamond where what you have developed has many elements. At this point you then begin to take away elements and ideas until you have only those that are critical for your message.

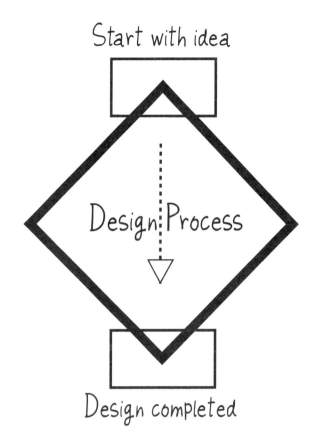

FIGURE 11–11 The diamond-shaped design process

Source: Courtesy of "Using Design Basics to Get Creative Results," by Brian Peterson, North Light Books, Cincinnati, OH. Used with permission.

Figure A was the original image for the Chapter I cover. Too many readers were confused with it so it was discarded for Figure B.

A

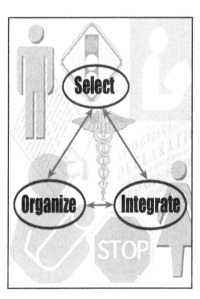

B

FIGURE 11–12 Learning to let go

ACE in action (depicting the 80/20 rule)

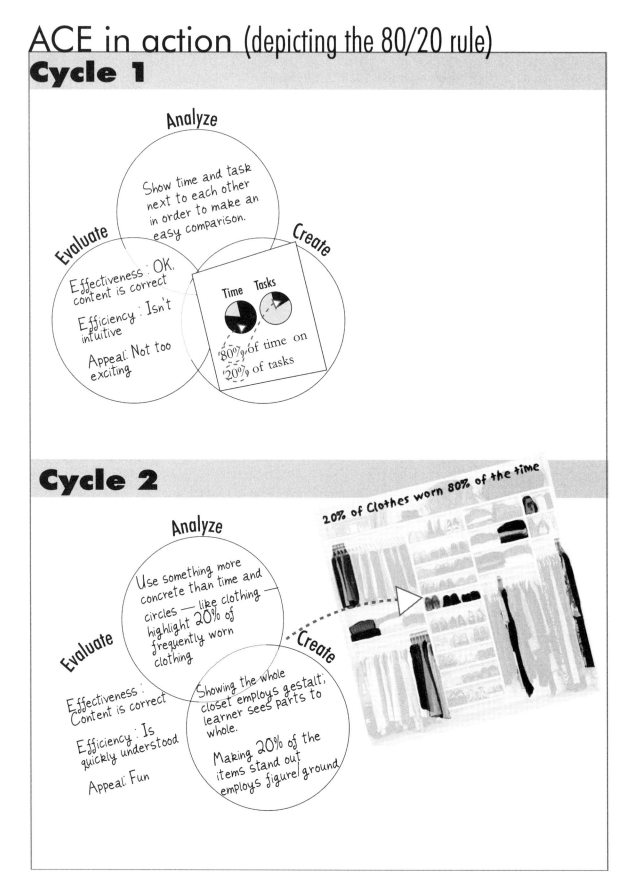

FIGURE 11–13   ACE in action (depicting the 80/20 rule)

Source: Closet image created by Erin Hunt. Used with permission.

SUMMARY

Throughout this book you learn tools and actions that can be manipulated to influence learner perceptions (TAP). This chapter describes *when* and *how* TAP is used. An ACE model is suggested as one approach to create visuals for learning and performance.

ACE stands for analyze, create, and evaluate. In the analyze phase you review the purpose of the visual. Here you consider the overall goals and objectives of the larger instructional context as well as the purpose of the visual. Is the visual for decoration, representation, organization, elaboration, or transformation (Levin, 1981)? Instructional visuals are usually part of a larger instructional design project; therefore, much of the analysis that takes place when designing for the larger training or performance context influences the analysis that goes into your visual.

In the create phase you transform your analysis into something visual. The create phase involves generating and representing ideas. Several strategies are suggested to help you open your mind, including brainstorming and using synectic strategies.

In the evaluate phase you critically edit your work using two approaches: (1) reviewing your design yourself and (2) having others review it. When you review your design, you attempt to see the visual as the learner would. When you have others review your visual, you observe representative users or learners as they interact with it. Of the two approaches, the second is a better way to get a true picture of how well your visual communicates.

Often you'll find that communication improves when you remove some of the elements you added. Though a difficult step to implement, it is a critically important one. The ability to take away, or subtract, often clarifies the message and increases its simplicity.

REFERENCES

Dick, W., & Carey, L. (1996). *The systematic design of instruction.* New York: Harper Collins.

Gordon, W. J. (1961). *Synectics.* New York: Harper & Row.

Grabowski, B. L. (1995). Message design: issues and trends. In G. J. Anglin (Ed.), *Instructional technology, past, present and future* (pp. 221–231.) Englewood, CO: Libraries Unlimited, Inc.

Heinich, R., Molenda, M., Russell, J., & Smaldino, S. (1999). *Instructional media and technologies for learning* (6th ed). Upper Saddle River, NJ: Prentice Hall.

Joyce, B. & Weil, M. (1986). *Models of teaching* (3rd ed.). Englewood Cliffs, NJ: Prentice Hall.

Landa, R. (1998). *Thinking creatively: New ways to unlock your visual imagination.* Cincinnati, OH: North Light Books.

Levin, J. R. (1981). On the functions of pictures in prose. In F. J. Pirozzolo & M. C. Wittrock (Eds.), *Neuropsychological and cognitive processes in reading* (pp. 203–228). San Diego: Academic Press.

Lohr, L. (2000). Designing the instructional interface. *Computers in Human Behavior (16)*12, pp. 61–82.

Lohr, L., & Eikleberry, C. (2001). Learner-centered usability: Tools for creating a learner-friendly instructional environment. *Performance Improvement (401)*4, pp. 24–28.

Morrison, G., Ross, S., & Kemp, J. (1999). *Designing effective instruction.* New York: John Wiley & Sons.

Nielsen, J. (1993). *Usability engineering.* Boston: Academic Press.

Peterson, B. L. (1996). *Using design basics to get creative results.* Cincinnati, OH: North Light Books.

Reigeluth, C. M., & Nelson, L. M. (1997). A new paradigm of ISD. In R. M. Branch & B. B. Minor (Eds.), *Educational media and technology yearbook* (Vol. 22, pp. 24–35). Englewood, CO: Libraries Unlimited.

Smith, P. L., & Ragan, T. J. (1993). *Instructional design.* Upper Saddle River, NJ: Merrill/Prentice Hall.

vonOech, R. (1983). *A whack on the side of the head: How to unlock your mind for innovation.* New York: Warner Books.

Weaver, W. T., & Prince, G. M. (1990). Synectics: Its potential for education. *Phi Delta Kappan, 46*(1), 378–388.

CHAPTER *12*

Resources

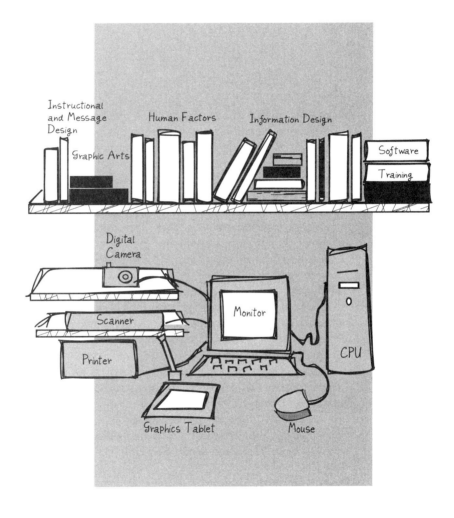

"I get by with a little help from my friends."

The Beatles

NOTES ABOUT THE OPENING VISUAL

The chapter cover shows a cartoon sketch of all the "things" you might want to have around as you create instructional visuals: reference books, computer, and peripherals. This sketch is essentially an overview of the topics covered in the chapter.

Did you notice how I broke out of the grid structure used for all the other chapter covers throughout the book? The previous opening visuals fall *inside* the gray rectangle, whereas this opening visual extends beyond the rectangle. As mentioned in an earlier chapter, grids are great, but you don't have to force everything into them. There are times when you can deviate from the grid. I used the same gray background rectangle, which I think provides enough contiguity (there's a gestalt principle!) with the rest of the book. I also wanted to make this chapter cover look different because the chapter is unique.

KEY TERMS

BROWSER   a type of software that can display information (graphics, text, animation) on the Internet; Explorer and Netscape are two popular browsers.

BYTE   unit of measure for the space in memory required for the images you create; each byte has eight bits, each representing a zero or a one. The byte is simply a hexadecimal number (a number system with a base of 16; each number is separated by eight digits of 0 or 1) that is created by the presence or absence of an electrical pulse. Each bit is either in an "electrical pulse off" status (a zero) or an "electrical pulse on" status (a one). The combination of "off" and "on" makes up the hexadecimal number, which, when combined with others, make up computer instructions. It's amazing that the complexity of computer systems boils down to "off" and "on."

HARDWARE   the physical equipment, such as the monitor, central processing unit, printer, and scanner, that makes up your computer system (see Figure 12–1).

INTERNET AND WWW   the information highway that is composed of a vast network of computers; WWW stands for the World Wide Web, the part of the Internet with which most people are familiar.

LISTSERV   a type of e-mail account used by a group of people with similar interests; all members of the listserv receive the same e-mail messages.

MEMORY   computer components for storing data; examples of types of memory include RAM (random access memory), which provides temporary memory to run programs like Microsoft Word and Adobe Illustrator, and ROM (read only memory), used to store prerecorded data on computer chips and compact discs (as in CD-ROM).

SEARCH ENGINE   program that finds information on the Internet based on words you type into a browser.

SOFTWARE   computer programs, like Microsoft Word or Adobe Illustrator, that provide the instructions to make the hardware work.

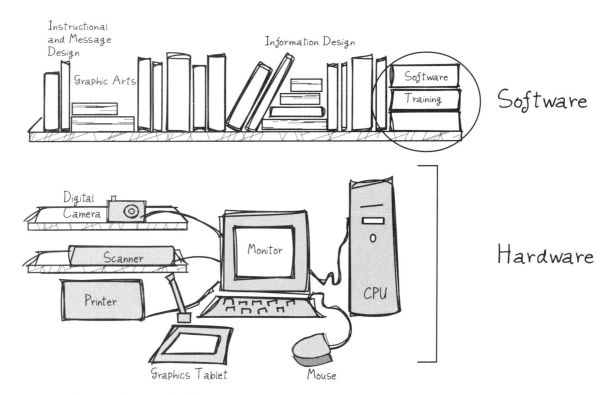

FIGURE 12-1 Hardware and software

Focus

The focus and format of this chapter is very different from previous chapters in the book. This chapter is basically a reference guide to basic information on hardware, software, and training resources you use when creating instructional visuals. For this reason, the chapter consists of seven charts to review as you see fit. These charts are divided into three categories: hardware, software, and training resources.

The hardware
  The central processing unit (CPU) (see Figure 12-2)
  Storage devices (see Figure 12-3)
  Input and output devices (see Figure 12-4)

The software
  Graphic design software (see Figure 12-5)
  Software features (see Figure 12-6)

Training resources
  Books, newsletters, professional organizations (see Figure 12-7)
  Internet resources (see Figure 12-8)

If you were buying a computer, would you know what this sales tag means?

Let's take it bullet by bullet ...

• 2.0 GHz Processor
This refers to the speed of the CPU. The CPU is the core of your computer system, often called the system's brain. Speed is measured in megahertz and gigahertz which refer to the number of bytes processed per cycle.

• 40 Gb Hard Drive
This tells you how much information you can save or store on your hard drive. Your computer programs will take up some of this space, along with the files you create. Here's a handy table to help you understand what a gigabyte is.

> **1 Byte** = 8 bits (8 "on" or "off" signals)
>
> **1 Kilobyte** (Kb) = 1,000 bytes
> *The text-only version of this chapter is approximately 45 Kb*
>
> **1 Megabyte** (Mb) = 1,000 Kb
> *The 300 dpi version of this page (an Adobe Illustrator file) is 4 Mb*
>
> **1 Gigabyte** (Gb)= 1,000 Mb
> *The combination of all of the black and white 300 dpi .tif extension graphic files in this book (approximately 500 images) take up approximately 1 Gb of memory.*

• 128 Mb RAM
This tells you that the computer has 128 Mb of random access memory (RAM). RAM is what makes your programs run effectively when you are working with them. When a program seems to be running slowly, it may be because there isn't enough RAM.

How much RAM and hard drive do you need? As much as you can afford. Both graphic programs and the images they create require plenty of RAM and storage space.

FIGURE 12–2 Information about the Central Processing Unit

Do you understand and need all of the items in the last bullet on the sales tag?

SALE TODAY!
- 2 GHz (1200 MHz) Processor
- 40 Gb Hard Drive
- 256 Mb RAM
- CD-ROM, Zip, & Floppy Drives

The last line of the ad (**CD-ROM, Zip, & Floppy Drives**) tells you that you have three ways to save/store information on removable devices.

CD-ROM, Zip, and Floppy drives are critical for saving files, but do you really need all three? Most people find they do, based on how much work they want to save at a given time. CD-ROMs are great for storing and accessing big files (professional photographs). Zip disks are useful when your files aren't big enough to justify saving on a CD-ROM, but they are still large (which is often the case with most graphic files). The floppy disk is useful when your file sizes are small.

This chart shows you each type of removable memory device, its size, and how much information it stores.

Type	Size	Memory
CD-ROM	4 ¾"	650+ Mb
Zip disk	3 ¾"	100 Mb – 4.6 Gb
Floppy disk	3 ½"	700 Kb – 1.6 Mb

How big are graphic files?

The size of graphic files depends on several things: the resolution of the color, the resolution of the image, the width and height measurements of the image, and the format in which the image is stored. Black, white, and gray images that are small (about 1" x 1") and saved in a .gif or .jpeg format are about 1 or 2 Kb. Color images that are the same size, saved as 300 dpi, and stored in a .tif format are about 160Kb. When you increase color resolution, image size, and use a .tif or .eps format, your files can be several megabytes.

FYI

You'll want to save your graphic files two ways: (1) as an original layered image and (2) as the final image. You'll want to save a copy of the original image because you can edit it when you need to make changes. The original image is still in layers that allow you to go back and edit words and other things without disturbing other parts of the image. The final image is the version of the graphic that is flattened, takes up less memory, and is used in the layout or multimedia program.

FIGURE 12–3 Storage devices

What are the most common devices to help capture, create, and display your visuals?

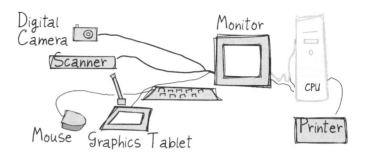

Input

Digital cameras are good for keeping up-to-date, last-minute, realistic, emotion-provoking images. They operate like any camera, but store the photograph as a digital file that you upload to your computer. Since the technology for digital cameras has advanced and prices have dropped, they have become a "must have."

Scanners allow you to copy all kinds of images into a digital format including documents, sketches, objects, and fabrics.

Graphics tablets are useful if you like to draw or trace images, but find the mouse limits your ability to do so. Though a tablet works like a mouse, it feels like a pen, capturing different pressures and creating lines of different widths, making drawings look more realistic and less mechanical.

Output

Laser printers produce high quality black-and-white or color documents at 300, 600, and 1,200 dpi (dots per inch) and are reasonably affordable.

Professional printing companies produce top-quality print jobs that may require color separations. You work with a service bureau (the printer usually recommends one) to prepare your files for this type of printing.

Dot matrix printers produce a lower quality document and, given the dropping prices of laser printers, may be used on a less frequent basis. Color dot matrix printers, however, are quite affordable and can produce quality overheads and documents that for many are still too expensive to produce using a laser printer.

Monitors display images in relatively low resolutions thus lose some of the crispness found in print publications. Because of the lower resolution requirements, however, image file sizes for monitor viewing can be much smaller, making them easier to manage.

FIGURE 12–4 Input and output devices

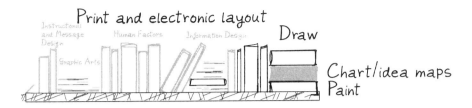

Draw See Chapter 5 for review

Draw programs create **vector/object oriented** graphics, **good for typography, shapes, and line artwork, especially when printing and resizing is needed.**

Paint See Chapter 5 for review

Paint programs create **bitmap/raster** graphics, good for showing lots of detail (as in photographs) and for having very small file sizes when saved in .jpeg and .gif formats. Bitmap **images are not as good as vector images for printing,** and they do not resize well when increased.

Software *a partial list*

Adobe Illustrator, CorelDraw, Freehand, Macromedia Flash art tools, **Microsoft Word** art tools, as well as the flowchart/idea mapping programs, such as **Inspiration, Mind Mapping, Chart Draw,** and **VISIO.** These programs allow you to create and easily adjust logical and conceptual visualizations.

Corel Painter, Fractal Painter, Adobe Photoshop, MacPaint, Microsoft Paint

File types

file.**eps**, file.**wmf**, file.**pict**, file.**cdr**

file.**bmp**, file.**tiff**, file.**pcx**, file.**pict**, file.**pnt**

Print & electronic layout

Print (**PageMaker, Quark, Framemaker, Microsoft Publisher**) and electronic (**FrontPage, Dreamweaver, Authorware**) layout programs allow you to create, publish, and manage multimedia documents. You import text and images into these programs and are given many tools to adjust their layout and order of presentation.

FIGURE 12–5 Graphics design software

How do you customize images?

You can easily change clip art to match your instructional purpose. In addition to the images you see on the right, you can try different fills and filter effects (making strokes look like they are paint, crayon, pastels, for example).

recolor, duplicate, resize

add a drop shadow

frame and rotate

add emotions

distort

FIGURE 12–6 Software features

How do you stay up-to-date?

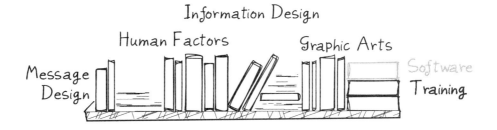

Listed in alphabetical order by category

Message Design Books

Instructional Message Design, 1993
> *Fleming, M., & Levie, H.*
> Englewood Cliffs, NJ
> Educational Technology Publications
> **Overview:** The classic

Visual Design for Instructional Multimedia, CD-ROM, 2000.
> *Misanchuk, E, Schwier, R., & Boling, E.*
> www.extension.usak.ca/vdim.htm
> **Overview:** A treasure of references and examples
> of research-based design principles

Human Factors Books

Designing Web Usability, 2000
> *Nielsen, J.*
> Indianapolis, IN: New Riders Publishing
> **Overview:** Teaches the importance of simplicity;
> though written for the Web, applies to most design

The Design of Everyday Things, 1988
> *Norman, D. A.*
> New York: Doubleday
> **Overview:** You'll see the world (especially doors)
> differently after reading this book.

Information Design Books

The Visual Display of Quantitative
> **Information,** 1983
> *Tufte, E. R.*
> Cheshire, CT: Graphics Press.
> **Overview:** The book on data integrity

Envisioning Information, 1990
> *Tufte, E. R.*
> Cheshire, CT: Graphics Press.
> **Overview:** Timeless information design advice;
> beautiful book design

Visual Explanations: Images & Quantities, Evidence & Narrative, 1997
> *Tufte, E. R.*
> Cheshire, CT: Graphics Press
> **Overview:** Gripping information design examples
> and analysis

Professional Organizations*

International Visual Literacy Association (IVLA) www.ivla.org
> *A not-for-profit association of educators, artists, and
> researchers dedicated to the principles of visual literacy*

American Institute of Graphic Arts (AIGA) www.aiga.org
> *A place professionals turn to first to exchange ideas
> and information, participate in critical analysis and
> research, and advance education and ethical practice*

Graphic Artists Guild (GAG) www.gag.org
> *A union of designers and other creative professionals
> who pursue common goals, share experiences, raise
> industry standards, and improve the ability of visual
> creators to achieve satisfying and rewarding careers.*

* Join organization listservs to learn more and meet other
professionals that share your interests.

FIGURE 12–7 Books, newsletters, and professional organizations

How do you stay up-to-date?

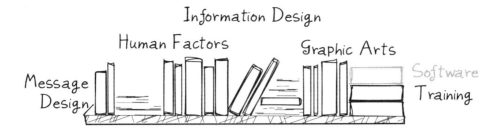

Graphic Arts Books

Color Harmony for the Web, 2001.
Boyle, C.
Gloucester, MA: Rockport Publishers, Inc.
Overview: You'll keep this book by your computer! Great color combinations for the Web!

The Designer's Guide to Color Combinations, 1999.
Cabarga, L.
Cincinnati, OH: North Light Books
Overview: Helps you find color combinations based upon different themes (historic, current, rave, and even "bad" color themes).

Legal Guide for the Visual Artist, 1999
Crawford, T.
New York: Allworth Press
Overview: Nice to have around.

Stock Photo Smart, 1998
Farace, J.
Cincinnati, OH: North Light Books
Overview: Helpful information on working with stock photos.

Clip Art Smart, 1998
Joss, M.
Cincinnati, OH: North Light Books
Overview: Lots of useful information on working with clip art.

Looking Good in Presentations, 3rd ed., 1999
Joss, M.
Scottsdale, AZ: The Coriolis Group
Overview: Helps you choose the best presentation medium for your message.

Designing Visual Interfaces: Communication Oriented Techniques, 1995
Mullet, K., & Sano, D.
Englewood Cliffs, NJ: Sunsoft Press.
Overview: Comprehensive resource of design principles applied to the interface.

Looking Good in Print, 4th edition, 1998
Parker, R.
Scottsdale, AZ: The Coriolis Group
Overview: The primer for better looking printed materials with good before and after images.

Type Rules!, 2001
Strizver, I.
Cincinnati, OH: North Light Books
Overview: Covers the do's and don'ts of typography.

The Non-Designer's Design Book: Design & Typographic Principles for the Visual Novice, 1994
Williams, R.
Berkeley, CA: Addison-Wesley Publishing Company.
Overview: See the simple power of contrast, alignment, repetition and proximity.

FIGURE 12–7 Books, newsletters, and professional organizations *(continued)*

How do you stay up-to-date?

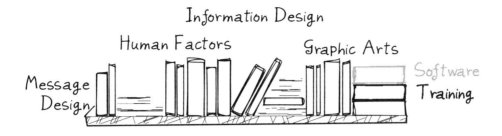

Magazines

HOW: Design Ideas at Work

Published bimonthly by F & W Publications, Inc.,
1507 Dana Ave., Cincinnati, OH 45207;
(513) 531 – 2690

Step-by-Step Graphics

Published six times a year by Step-by-Step
Publishing, a division of Dynamic Graphics, Inc.,
6000 N. Forest Park Drive, Peoria, IL. 61614-3592
sbspub@dgusa.com

Training

If you need to learn a graphics program, check first with
the tutorials and documentation that come with your
software. Don't be shy about using the Help files either.
Many people learn entirely by experimenting and then
looking up information in the Help file when needed.

You'll also find many how to books in bookstores. If you'd
rather have face-to-face instruction, consider community
colleges, public school systems, and companies that offer
hands-on training. In this section are some excellent
resources for learning more about computer programs and
basic design.

Adobe Classroom in a Book: Illustrator and Photoshop

Adobe Press
Overview: Self-paced instruction covering basic,
intermediate, and advanced skills

Element K Journals

Element K Press
2165 Bri-Hen TL Rd. Ste. 3
Rochester, NY 14623
www.elementkjournals.com

Overview: Online training for Photoshop and
Illustrator, monthly newsletter with step-by-step
instructions on program features

Online training

Lynda Weinman Graphics
www.Lynda.com
Overview: Excellent step-by-step CD-ROM
training on a variety of graphic programs

World Wide Learn
www.worldwidelearn.com
Overview: Accreditied degree program in graphics;
good Web page for other online learning links

Software sites with tutorials:
www.adobe.com
www.macromedia.com
www.corel.com

FIGURE 12–7 Books, newsletters, and professional organizations *(continued)*

Where do you find images on the Internet?

A. Find images using search engines:
www.altavista.com
> *This search engine lets you click on the "image" tab to bypass text and search for picture/images only*

www.askjeeves.com
www.goto.com
www.excite.com
www.infoseek.com
www.webcrawler.com
www.yahoo.com

Good search terms*:
"free clip art" "free fonts"

B. Try these sites:
Adobe Systems
www.adobe.com

Artville
www.artville.com

Corbis
www.corbis.com

Corel Corporation
http://www.corel.com
Web site full of designer resources and how-tos for special effects and more.

Image Club Graphics
www.imageclub.com
Images from a variety of publishers

Microsoft Design Gallery Live
(free for licensed users)
dgl.microsoft.com
Extensive Web site of images for Microsoft users

PhotoDisc
www.photodisc.com

C. Check out these "free" images:

Clip art and other images
www.onlinebusiness.com
www.barryclipart.com
www.free-graphics.com
www.mediabuddy.com
www.boulder.earth.net/~jlinhoff
www.zdnet.com

Fonts
www.softseek.com
www.mediabuilder.com
www.loadlink.com/mrw/freefonts.html

For the Julesart font used in this book:
www.urgentartwork.co.nz/freefonts.htm
Download the juleswriting font if you'd like a copy of the handwriting you see in this sentence and throughout this book.

*Be wary of anything called "free" on the Internet. See the copyright section of Chapter 5 for more information, or go to http://lcweb.loc.gov/copyright/

FIGURE 12–8 Internet resources

316

SUMMARY

While the previous chapters describe *how* to design instructional visuals, this chapter identifies the resources you need to actually create something. Knowing the requirements and types of hardware and software is important; therefore, some of the basic jargon and software products useful for visual design are introduced. Since most designers tend to be inspired by others, a list of exceptional reference books from instructional message design, graphic arts, human factors, and information design are listed for your reference and inspiration.

This also marks the end of the book. I hope you have experienced developing instructional visuals as not only challenging, but fun, and something you will continue to learn and explore. By helping your learners select, organize, and integrate information, you will undoubtedly improve their learning experience. Good design will influence the future, so be part of it!

INDEX

Page numbers followed by *f* indicate figures, by *t* tables